WILLIAM COBBETT

WILLIAM COBBETT,

by an unknown artist. Reproduced by courtesy of the National Portrait Gallery, London.

William Cobbett:

his thought
and his times by
John W. Osborne

RUTGERS UNIVERSITY PRESS

NEW BRUNSWICK   NEW JERSEY

To the memory of my Father

Contents

Preface

For almost a hundred years after his death in 1835 no worthwhile book-length study of William Cobbett was written. Most attempts to evaluate his career were highly biased and superficial. It was not until 1924, with the appearance of *The Life of William Cobbett* by G. D. H. Cole, that a first-rate appreciation of Cobbett's life and thought became available. However, in the last forty years many assumptions about early nineteenth-century England, which Cole shared, have been challenged. It therefore seemed useful to attempt a re-examination of Cobbett based upon the latest knowledge of this period, as well as a thorough study of all of his writings.

The purpose of this book is to analyze Cobbett's ideas and their relation to the England of his time. It is not intended to describe Cobbett's role as a practical farmer or as a writer on the cultivation of the soil, but to concentrate upon his career as a political journalist during the first thirty-five years of the nineteenth century. Despite his apparent changes of mind and confusion of ideas, Cobbett was often more consistent than has been realized. Yet, although committed to a point of view, he was not an orderly thinker. Perhaps the combination of mental rigidity, disorganized thought and very flexible tactics accounts in part for the many varying (and usually inaccurate) interpretations of his life's work. The nature of the latter becomes clearer when Cobbett's ideas are examined topically rather than chronologically.

I wish to thank Professor Henry R. Winkler of Rutgers University for his considerable assistance. Thanks are also due to Professor David L. Cowen of University College, Rutgers, for advice and encouragement for more than a decade. It is a pleasure to acknowledge the fine cooperation of the Special Collections and Reference Departments of the Rutgers University Library. This is also true of the staff of the library of Nuffield College, Oxford University, for permission to read private papers pertaining to Cobbett and for providing a friendly atmosphere in which to do research. The receipt of a Louis Bevier Fellowship for two consecutive years permitted me to devote full time to research and writing, and I am grateful to the committee at Rutgers which was responsible for this award. Without the support and cheerful cooperation of my wife in typing and checking manuscript, this book could not have been completed. Of course, all responsibility for error is my own.

WILLIAM COBBETT

I
The making of a writer

The town of Farnham is set in the valley of the River Wey, near the Hampshire border, on the westernmost fringe of the county of Surrey. Even today it has little in common with the more populous part of the county, which is indistinguishable from the boroughs of south London at the point where suburb blends into city. For Farnham is a market town for the farmers of the area. It is a place whose slender streets seem inadequate to bear the burden of modern traffic and whose antique buildings are rather out of place in this century. Even the most insensitive stranger cannot remain aloof to the fact that Farnham is ancient, for it imposes its own pace and the hasty traveller, who is hurrying on to Winchester and Salisbury, would do well to remain on the by-pass road.

Modern transportation has ensured that Farnham can be neither remote nor placid, as it was two hundred years ago.

Times have changed the sounds of the town. Residents no longer expect to hear the gentle noises of the river and must listen for the sound of the church bell that once rang out in magisterial tones over the silent streets. It is the church itself, which was old when Henry VIII was young, and the castle, which still dominates the town from a height, that remind the visitor of the antiquity of the place. Old houses, built for the centuries from indigenous stone, convey a suggestion of the time when London was the tale of a traveller and France was a legend. So much has changed there that it is best to remain apart from it a bit, on one of the low hills surrounding the town, in order to sense more fully how it must have looked in Cobbett's time. Hilly, narrow, blending gracefully into the lovely, adjoining farming country, it was a thriving place in which to live and work.

Born in Farnham of peasant stock in the year which saw the end of the Seven Years' War, Cobbett, like most eighteenth-century men, spent his early life on the land. Far from the febrile excitement of unhealthy cities, he was further still from the ferment of ideas which is connoted by the term "eighteenth century." At that time life was measured by the rhythm of the seasons rather than by the clock, and still less by the rapidly shifting styles of intellectual fashion. The countryman, a simple person with limited needs, who had absorbed a religious faith of a fundamental kind and an honest, impulsive patriotism, was quick to take offense at any slight to either. As a youth, Cobbett toiled on the grounds of what was once a house of the Cistercians and also worked for the Bishop of Winchester in that castle which overlooks Farnham. Originally built in the twelfth century, it was destroyed by Henry II during his campaign to stamp out anarchy. Later rebuilt, the castle served as the home of the Bishops of Winchester. Queen Elizabeth was entertained there and Charles I garrisoned it. This ancient structure seemed to young William an eloquent reminder of England's past.

Free as a youngster from the complexities of modern society, the attitudes which he imbibed in childhood were to remain with Cobbett in spite of considerable travel and contact with radically different environments. For he was a plain man, lacking in introspection, a person for whom life was hard but not complicated.[1]

As a boy growing to manhood during the last years of unquestioned agricultural supremacy, William Cobbett was fortunate in at least three ways. To begin with, his father's circumstance as the proprietor of a tavern made the elder Cobbett better off financially than most other residents of the town. George Cobbett was also definitely superior to members of his class in learning and could impart to his sons an unusual degree of education and example. Although as a youngster William had no true formal education and worked very hard for wages before he was even in his teens, he escaped the hopeless labor of so many of his contemporaries. Finally, he was endowed with a healthy body at a time when physical stamina for a poor man was necessary for survival. A husky youth, he became a robust, powerful man who retained an unusual physical vitality until almost the end of his life. When past sixty he rode forty miles in a rainstorm to cure a chest cough,[2] and many commented upon his ruddy complexion and rude good health.

Set to work although scarcely more than an infant, he quickly developed the habit of incessant industry which was

Cobbett's Political Register is abbreviated as P.R.;
Cobbett's Annual Register is abbreviated as A.R.;
Cobbett's American Political Register is abbreviated as Amer. P.R.
Dates, e.g. (12/24/19), refer to the 1800's.

---

[1] Cobbett's early life is best described in G. D. H. Cole, *The Life of William Cobbett*, London, W. Collins Sons and Co., Ltd., 1924, Chs. I and II. William Reitzel has edited an "autobiography" of Cobbett from the latter's published writings. *The Autobiography of William Cobbett, The Progress of a Plough-Boy to a Seat in Parliament*, London, Faber and Faber, Ltd., 1947.

[2] Cole, *op. cit.*, p. 320.

to distinguish him all of his life. One may go further and state that the four characteristics which Asa Briggs enumerates as being the major elements of Victorianism—the gospel of work, seriousness of character, respectability, self-help—could all apply to Cobbett. Frugality, perseverance, exertion, qualities which he admired in others, he possessed in abundance. And he knew this well. What is his famous book, *Advice to Young Men*, but the story of a personal triumph over adversity? Issue after issue of the *Political Register* contains expressions of the pride which a once lowly farm boy felt at being raised entirely by his own exertions to a position of influence. He once advised a reform group:

> I cannot but feel great pride upon receiving from you, the commendations contained in your addresses; and I will not pay so bad a compliment to your judgment and sincerity as to appear to suppose that I am not worthy of these commendations, great as they are. To pretend to believe in one's own unworthiness, upon occasions like this, is not modesty, it is affectation at best, and, perhaps, it is more worthy of the name of hypocrisy. . . . It is very certain that I have been the great enlightener of the people of England. Had I not written it is hardly possible to conceive the base and dejected state in which the nation would have been at this time.[3]

We will meet again and again Cobbett's conviction that he was the sole prop of virtue in the kingdom.

Like so many people who have risen entirely because of their own efforts, Cobbett despised anything that smacked of affectation. All his life he detested the meretricious and the hypocritical. Perhaps the person he hated most was neither Pitt nor Castlereagh, both of whom he considered as little better than devils in human guise, but William Wilberforce, the great Evangelical. Wilberforce was the very personification of hypocrisy in Cobbett's eyes, entirely without virtue because

[3] P.R. (12/24/19), cols. 485–86.

of his great, overwhelming vice. Unfortunately, this forthright trait of character tended to betray Cobbett's sense of proportion, which was at best not too secure. For he had great difficulty distinguishing between frivolity or idle vice and that genuine elegance and refinement of taste which we call culture. His repeated castigations of drunkenness and gambling, for example, were commendable, especially in consideration of the fact that these vices symbolized dissolute elements in the society of his time. Yet he extended his strictures to tea and coffee drinking and innocent card playing as well.[4] He did not forget either that the government which he hated collected most of its revenue from excise taxes on such items as spirits, tea, coffee and tobacco. Many of his writings (the *Grammar* in particular) were double-edged.

Somewhat more to the point was the case of the theater. This institution was certainly in a decline, but, led by Irving and Sheridan, it was spasmodically showing signs of maturity and intelligence. Cobbett, whose literal mind forbade him the enjoyment of Shakespeare because of the liberties which the Bard took with nature, bemoaned the changing taste of the public. Bring back the mountebanks and the jack puddings, he cried, regretting the disappearance of these traditional buffoons.[5]

Like Addison a hundred years earlier, he complained about the invasion of the English stage by foreigners. Cobbett was not ill-read; his taste in the theater demonstrates a simple man's preference for the old and tried as well as an identification of the intellectual with artificiality. Even Bentham's alleged lack of sensitivity toward the arts was eclipsed by

---

4 *Thirteen Sermons*, London, C. Clement, 1822, No. 8. Also, P.R. (1/22/20). cols. 649 ff.; P.R. (6/8/14), cols. 773–74.
5 P.R. (4/28/21), cols. 244–46; P.R. (11/22/06), cols. 812–13. He later admitted that he attended plays up until the birth of his third son (his third son to survive childhood was born in 1803). *Rural Rides*, G. D. H. and Margaret Cole (eds.), 3 vols., London, Peter Davies, 1930. Vol. II (4/19/30), p. 653.

Cobbett who revealed in his own cultural attitudes a lack of moderation.[6] In politics this failing was to hurt him, not only because he was much too violent for the taste of those brought up in the tranquil traditions of eighteenth-century political life, but in his inability to form accurate judgments. His famous diatribes against tea drinking and simple amusement should be seen as reflections of a consistent failure to place more weighty affairs in their proper perspective.

In addition to absorbing the political and religious atmosphere of rural England, another way in which Cobbett demonstrated the effect of his early environment was his lifelong affection for the land and dislike and suspicion of cities. The growth of great towns was a new phenomenon in English life, for as late as 1800 no city in the British Isles outside of London and Dublin had a population of 100,000. Together with their satellite suburbs they represented the coming to power of a new entrepreneurial class which Cobbett, with his peasant prejudices, hated. In his opinion, the greatest city, London (that "monstrous WEN") existed simply to devour the wealth of the countryside and impoverish the agricultural laborer, upon whose misery its inhabitants fattened.[7] He never liked the ways of towns or of their inhabitants. Hence his strictures against places like Cheltenham ". . . to which East India plunderers, West India floggers, English tax-gorgers, together with gluttons, drunkards, and debauchees of all descriptions—*female* as well as male, resort, at the suggestion of silently laughing quacks, in the hope of getting rid of the bodily consequences of their manifold sins, and iniquities." [8] The manners of the bourgeoisie being detestable to him, Cobbett never tried to understand this increasingly important group—or indeed anyone or anything which he disliked.

6 A similarly absurd position was taken toward music, which he blamed for the "Italian-like effeminacy" that he considered to plague the yeomen. P.R. (10/27/04), cols. 617–18.

7 P.R. (2/22/23), cols. 480–84.

8 *Rural Rides*, Vol. II (9/30/26), p. 446.

He could never grasp, for example, that conflict involving commercial capitalism and agrarianism was not a life or death struggle. The social and economic relations between the dominant agricultural interest, the landlords, and the world of capital moderated tension. Also, the lack of firm party lines meant that representatives of each group were to be found among both Whigs and Tories. It was in more democratic America that a true confrontation of interests existed. There, the exponents of agrarianism had a first class fighter in a man whom Cobbett greatly admired, Andrew Jackson, and also a philosopher in John Taylor of Caroline. Between the antipaper money views of the latter and those of Cobbett there is a strong similarity. It is quite possible that Cobbett was familiar with Taylor's writings, for he kept in close touch with events in America. But accurate or not, his views, the product of early influences, help explain why Cobbett's basic opposition to change has nothing in common with the rationale of laissez-faire capitalism which masquerades as conservative thought in our own time. It was based on faith in the land, England, family life and the validity of ancient institutions. The individualistic, dynamic, business-oriented world of twentieth-century capitalism would have been as repulsive to him as its nineteenth-century genesis was.

Although the growth of industry tended to act as a solvent, the concept of class was still an important factor in almost all phases of English civilization during Cobbett's lifetime. It is true that the lines between the classes were not rigid, nor were they an absolute impediment to a talented (and fortunate) youth.[9] Yet they were there just the same, although for the most part seemingly accepted by the less fortunate members of the social hierarchy. In a country which was ruled by law, the common people were free from the casual

---

[9] See R. J. White, *Waterloo to Peterloo*, London, William Heinemann, Ltd., 1957, pp. 25–26, for the subtle conventions which governed marriage at the time.

violence and intimidation inflicted upon the masses of the aristocrat-dominated countries of the Continent. Besides the personal interest taken by the English upper classes in the management of their estates and perhaps even their delight in sports and games brought them closer to the lower classes than the aloof nobles of the courts of other nations would care to come. Naturally this must not be overstated, for the interests of the powerless masses were sacrificed by their betters without hesitation at times. After the war, the agricultural laborers bore the brunt of the hardship on the land and might have had more burdens thrust upon them had their endurance been greater. But the country's social structure was not ossified and even the humble could travel the road to success. Any nation which could produce contemporaries of obscure origin as talented and distinct in their abilities as Lord Eldon, John Dalton, Richard Porson and William Cobbett was vital. Class distinctions dominated but did not smother the life of the country.

In principle, these differentiations of rank were never odious to Cobbett. When he was nearly seventy, he wrote in *The Emigrant's Guide,* that it was "perfectly proper, that people in the lower walks of life should carry themselves respectfully towards those, whom birth, or superior talent, or industry, have placed above themselves. . . ." Equality of wealth, he later declared, was contrary to "the order of the world and the decrees of God. . . ." The happy lot of the healthy laborer, whose constant toil freed him from temptation was compared with the careworn squire. (How like his enemy Wilberforce's *Practical View of the System of Christianity!*) Time after time we see examples of Cobbett's essential Toryism manifest themselves late in his life, often in the midst of a violent denunciation of the Church, royal family or aristocracy.[10] Plainly, class was necessary, for if there was equality there would also be

10 *The Emigrant's Guide,* London, William Cobbett, 1829, p. 30; P.R. (4/2/31), cols. 9–10.

no store of food since no one would work except to provide sustenance for the day. Nor would there be security of person or property, as there would be no statesmen, judges, or laws. It was the increasing dominance of bankers, stock-jobbers, merchants, commercial men of all descriptions that Cobbett loathed. Many of them had achieved knighthood; some were even members of the nobility; all were symptomatic of the malignancy afflicting England.[11] Although in his later career he might occasionally be provoked into irritable outbursts,[12] he had no basic objection to the institution of aristocracy. Indeed, part of his dislike of the theater was undoubtedly due to distaste for the newly enhanced social position of the actor.[13] The fact that George Canning's mother was an actress irritated Cobbett as much as it did any aristocrat. Like most of his countrymen, he considered that character and talent were connected with birth and his references to this happy relationship were almost as frequent as those of Dickens. It was the "paper-aristocracy," the monied interest, whose purchase of homes in the country was clear evidence of a change in rural England, which drew his bitter hostility. Cobbett seemed unaware that this situation had been developing for centuries.

Although he overcame early influences enough to learn the French language and to live abroad for years, Cobbett was almost always preoccupied with the condition of England. Strongly nationalistic, he jibed at foreigners, yet opposed the

[11] At the time, peers who engaged in commerce had feudal origins or were the descendants of those who had invested wealth won by commerce in land and had intermarried with the gentry. The heyday of the "beerage" was a long way off. See Ralph E. Pumphrey, "The Introduction of Industrialists into the British Peerage: A Study in Adaptation of a Social Institution," *The American Historical Review*, Vol. LXV (October, 1959), pp. 1–16.

[12] P.R. (11/4/20), col. 1061.

[13] Harold V. Routh; "The Georgian Drama," A. W. Ward and A. R. Waller (eds.), *The Cambridge History of English Literature*, Vol. XI, New York, G. P. Putnam's Sons, 1914, pp. 283–314, sees the period as a time when the actor was advancing and the theater decaying.

War of 1812, had a defeatist attitude toward the Napoleonic wars, cared nothing for overseas expansion, and could admire the French for their patriotic virtue. Usually his position on specific questions of foreign policy was determined by the way he felt about events in England. His dithyrambs on the old regime in France were at one time as ardent and fanciful as those of Burke but as his opinions of domestic matters changed, so did those expressed about the French Revolution and the character of Napoleon.[14] It would be possible to form a reasonably accurate picture of what Cobbett thought about life in England at a given time from his observations on France. Read apart from the context of English affairs, these observations contrast favorably with the fatuous optimism and downright lies to be found in the ministerial journals. It would be wise, however, not to consider them too seriously as revelations of Cobbett's opinions about the events themselves. He was fond of using foreign news to provide moral lessons for his readers. His observations about the virtues of Napoleonic France (and simultaneous observations about the virtues of the Spanish patriots' revolt against Napoleon in 1808) were too clearly written with conditions in England in mind to be taken at face value.[15]

The same must be said of his numerous writings concerning the United States. For several years after his career as a publicist in America had ended unhappily, he pointed out faults which he found in almost all areas of American society.[16] But when he was imprisoned at Newgate in 1810 after having been convicted of sedition, Cobbett began to look at America and the Americans in a new light. Enthusiastic descriptions of the workings of American democracy provided counterpoint

14 Compare almost any issue of *The Porcupine* (1800–1801) with P.R. (8/1/07), col. 177; P.R. (2/10/10), cols. 199–200; P.R. (11/13/13), cols. 613–14.
15 On the Spanish revolt, see P.R. (6/25/08), col. 1001; P.R. (7/9/08), col. 36.
16 P.R. (2/5 to 2/12/03), col. 192.

to denunciations of the English government.[17] From then on, praise for American political and religious liberty and press freedom appeared regularly in the *Political Register.* Cobbett had begun to create a well of sympathy for himself across the Atlantic and when conditions became difficult for him in 1817, he chose to exile himself to America in order to escape government prosecution.

His best work during this stay was a book called *A Year's Residence in the United States of America,* a potpourri in three small volumes, containing advice to farmers, travel descriptions, political observations, and asides about almost everything under the sun. The once hostile critic could now see almost nothing wrong with America and his reports furnish a refreshing contrast to those of other English travellers during this period. Cobbett compared the English and American political systems. The honesty, economy and tolerance of the latter commended it to him. Indeed, apart from excessive drinking, he could see nothing but good in the whole American "way of life." [18] He had come to feel that America was the only hope of freedom in the world and it was imperative that she remain strong in order to continue to set an example. The part which English institutions had played in creating this new American society afforded Cobbett considerable pride. "Here is the language of England; here are the laws of England; sheriffs, judges, juries; all has its origin from England." Free from the incubus of established political and ecclesiastical interests, a wholesome community based firmly on English traditions had evolved. For a while, he seemed to lose his taste for a hierarchical order in society.[19]

Cobbett's writings on America were empirical and knowledgeable. He had experienced at first hand both good and bad

[17] P.R. (12/15/10), cols. 1189–96; P.R. (9/14/11), cols. 324–34.
[18] *A Year's Residence in the United States of America,* 3 vols., London, Chapman and Dodd, n.d., passim.
[19] Amer. P.R. (1/6/16), cols. 9–15; P.R. (4/11/18), col. 413.

in the practice of American democracy and knew well the settled area around New York and Philadelphia. A trip to Harrisburg in 1818 took him across the Alleghenies and allowed him to see another side of American life. Conversations with those who had been further west had furnished him with accounts of conditions on the frontier and, coupled with the rawness which was present even in comparatively genteel Long Island or Philadelphia, allowed him to arrive at the conclusion that the frontier was no place for the emigrant.[20] The utopians who visualized settlements in wild and unexplored hinterland drew his sarcastic ire. Many of his own beliefs were reflected in the practices of the Americans: an instrumental approach to education, no established church, a society in which almost everyone earned his own living. But the occasional references to unsettled conditions, drunkenness, and the squalor existing outside the limited area of cultivation around each farmhouse or settlement, show that Cobbett was too much attached to the neat, precise English countryside and its inhabitants to consider changing his allegiance. Above all, it should be remembered that Cobbett was dedicated to reform in England and that he used America as an approximation of the prosperous, well-fed society which he wanted in England.

Thus, the foreign policy of the government, liberal and national revolts in Europe and South America and even developments in America and Ireland, were little more to Cobbett than raw material from which he could fashion an attack upon or defense of some institution, idea or person in England. Of Ireland he wisely said, "It is a great misfortune to this Kingdom in general, that Ireland is separated from England by water; because, besides many other evils, it is productive of this, that the people of England are not only, generally speaking, ignorant of what is passing in Ireland, but

20 *The Emigrant's Guide* was written by Cobbett with America in mind.

they, as best seem to *care* but little about the matter, too many of them looking upon the Irish as scarcely being countrymen, not a few considering them as an inferior race of beings, and almost the whole regarding the interests of Ireland and those of England as being perfectly distinct." [21] Cobbett thus noted the lack of understanding by Englishmen of Irish problems, which has been the tragedy of Ireland's history. For years he pleaded for conciliation in dealing with Irish unrest and consistently supported measures for reform. Cobbett was, with justice, regarded as a friend of the oppressed majority of the Irish population. But in the final analysis he opposed the 1828 legislation which emancipated Catholics who could otherwise qualify to sit in parliament and ridiculed the Irish people themselves.[22] The type of change which Cobbett thought necessary for both Ireland and England could only be accomplished by a reformed parliament. The satisfying of Irish demands would lessen the agitation for such a reform ("it would naturally quiet the most noisy of them for a little; and I want these noisy ones to continue to be noisy. . . ."). [23] Therefore, Catholic Emancipation must be postponed until it could be incorporated into the sweeping changes to be made by an English legislature reconstituted on a popular basis. This last point provides a clue to understanding his entire career.

Erratic as Cobbett was, full of ingrained prejudices and subject at times to sudden emotion and even simple caprice, it is still possible to discern a germ of consistency in his attitude toward most subjects. This cannot be found in a zeal for reform because Cobbett was not a true reformer; he was too fond of radical means of solving problems. Thus, his remedy for fiscal difficulties was the elimination of paper money and for abuses in the Church he could only visualize

[21] P.R. (12/9/09), cols. 865–66.
[22] P.R. (3/21/29), col. 354; P.R. (8/29/29), cols. 257–74.
[23] P.R. (2/7/29), cols. 176–77.

complete disestablishment. Moreover, he was highly selective about what should be reformed and was certainly not at all times the champion of the common man that many have claimed him to be. Although usually sympathetic toward the poor, Cobbett's major concern lay elsewhere and he was by no means a simple pragmatist who spontaneously struck out at abuses. His famous comment, "What is a pauper . . ." only "A very poor man," widely accepted as characteristic of simple generosity, is shortly followed by a statement which claimed that poverty is not only inevitable but useful. For poverty serves a social need since it provides a spur to the virtues of abstinence, sobriety, care, frugality and industry.[24] Cobbett's career is not noteworthy either for devotion to change or compassion for those who suffered. Change is an ambiguous word when applied to Cobbett, and he could be sympathetic and humane only when personally touched.

The key to Cobbett's thought—that consistency which makes his mature career intelligible—emerges around 1805. For it was then that he gradually became convinced that England was governed by an interlocking tyranny of government creditors ("fund holders") and owners of seats in the House of Commons ("boroughmongers"). The "System," as he called this cluster of privilege, dominated the royal family and the Church of England and ran the country for its own selfish benefit. Thereafter his approach to society was characterized by hatred of the "System," plus a fixation with an ideal way of life which, in his imagination, had already existed. This personal vision separated him from others who desired change; that is, those who were radical in both means and ends. It also contributed to his tendency to oversimplify situations so that he only extracted those elements which he desired to

---

24 *Advice to Young Men and (incidentally) to Young Women*, London, William Cobbett, 1829, paragraphs 340, 342, 343. Both Cole and G. K. Chesterton have tried, not very successfully, to exonerate Cobbett from any taint of Samuel Smiles. See Cole, *op. cit.*, p. 267; G. K. Chesterton, *William Cobbett*, London, Hodder and Stoughton, Ltd., n.d., p. 49.

notice. Such a private conception of society meant that, with reference to his life's work, Cobbett was a lonely man. Although his advice on farming problems was widely respected, the central part of his career, which was devoted to major changes in English society, was not. Cobbett's proclamation that the criterion of national prosperity is the condition of the laboring classes and that if an ordinary worker could not secure sufficient food and clothing with hard work and sober living, then the society in which he lives ought not to exist is unexceptional radical doctrine.[25] Yet the crucial point is that he did not contemplate reform as emancipating the worker from his age-old shackles so that he might march forward into a brighter tomorrow. His purpose was not forward-looking but reactionary. Reform was to be the means by which the common laborer might regain the plenty which had been stolen from him. This tendency to be radical in technique and the opposite in objective perhaps explains why there have been conflicting interpretations of his career. It is noteworthy that the editors of volumes dealing with the English radical and conservative traditions in the *British Political Tradition* series both saw fit to include excerpts from Cobbett's writings in their respective anthologies.[26] Cobbett's writings have been a fund of ammunition for a variety of interested parties. Like most prophets, he would be amazed at the uses to which his thoughts have been put.

Cobbett's persistence in looking back into the past for answers to contemporary problems put him into the company of the Tory ministry, which formed part of the hated "System." These men generally shared Cobbett's agricultural background (but, of course, were from a higher social stratum) and also his tendency to respond to new stimuli in terms of social

[25] P.R. (9/11/19), col. 115.
[26] S. Maccoby (ed.), *The English Radical Tradition, 1763–1914*, London, Nicholas Kaye, 1952; R. J. White, *The Conservative Tradition*, London, Nicholas Kaye, 1950.

attitudes which had existed in the romanticized past of their childhood. Liverpool and Castlereagh, too, were the products of a simpler age. Although no longer considered the monsters which reform-minded historians such as the Hammonds have made of them and much more adaptable to changing conditions than is often believed, like Cobbett they had been born and raised before 1789 and before the industrial changes of their century became of major significance. Both Cobbett and the Ministers believed in the values of a hierarchal society, the basis of which was land. They were out of touch with the new England which was rapidly forming. On balance, however, the latter showed a greater ability to accommodate to it than did Cobbett.

The land of England, rich and generous, bestowing ample sustenance and warm satisfaction to the skilled cultivator was Cobbett's lifelong love. On no other subject was he as thoroughly at ease as when writing about agriculture. According to his own testimony, he was happiest working on his farm. It was Cobbett's restless nature and ambition which led him into journalism and politics and kept him bound to office or study during most of his life. These traits manifested themselves early. Despite later glowing accounts of early life in the country and the deep impression which it made upon him, young William ran away from home three times. The last (at age twenty) brought him to London. A few months' stint as a clerk in an attorney's office made him ready to try anything else—even the army. Acceptance of the King's shilling made Cobbett a private soldier and opened to him a career of danger and discomfort. For many men life in the army during the eighteenth century must have resembled a Hobbesian state of nature. If it was not solitary, it was at least poor, nasty, brutish and short. Not so with Cobbett. Overcoming all difficulties he used his time wisely; above all, he learned English grammar but also read as widely as possible and even attempted to write. Only an unusual man could have progressed so far after such an unpromising beginning.

Between the ages of twenty-one and twenty-eight Cobbett was a soldier. He rose from private to sergeant-major and spent most of his service in Canada. Soon after his discharge in December, 1791, he married a simple girl whom he had met in the New World. Almost immediately he had to flee to France when charges of corruption, which he placed against certain officers of his regiment, threatened to boomerang. The charges were probably accurate but given the relative positions of the accuser and the accused and the spirit of the times, Cobbett was in more danger than the group at which they were directed. Even today one wonders at Cobbett's naïveté. In any event, the episode does not seem to have affected his generally favorable opinions of English society. As the French Revolution progressed in violence, he realized that France was no place for an Englishman and with his wife took ship for America, landing in October, 1792 and setting up residence in Philadelphia.

It has been said that "Anglo-American relations were fairer in the last years of the eighteenth century than they were again to be until the last years of the nineteenth." [27] With a Federalist administration in office and a growing distaste for recent developments in France, the United States government (if not the American people) had reasons for seeking friendship with Great Britain. However, the results of Cobbett's seven years' residence in America were to widen, however imperceptibly, the gulf between the two countries. He was drawn into his career as a writer by the friendly reception given to Joseph Priestley, the radical scientist, who had left England to find a more congenial atmosphere in which to express his political views. Welcoming addresses by American

[27] H. C. Allen, *Great Britain and the United States, A History of Anglo-American Relations (1783–1952)*, London, Odhams Press, Limited, 1954, p. 347.

societies and Priestley's replies angered Cobbett and provoked him to a defense of the British Crown and Constitution. A pamphlet which was written in a white heat of anger launched Cobbett on his literary career. His vigorous polemics won him recognition in Philadelphia and more than once his windows were in danger from an aroused populace which had been goaded by his anti-democratic thrusts.[28]

Although the substance of Cobbett's writings in America differed greatly from the majority of the opinions expressed during his later career in England, his direct style was evident at once. So, too, was his partisanship and concern for events and personalities rather than ideas. His subsequent *volte-face* after returning to England was occasioned by disillusionment with the cause which he had so vigorously championed. The bluff patriotism which supported his attacks upon Democrats, Jacobins, critics of monarchy and traducers of England was the result of childhood impressions which experience had not yet shaken. It is significant that from the time he joined the army at age twenty-one until he returned to England from America in 1800 at the age of thirty-seven, Cobbett had resided in England for a total of only one and a half years. Even his encounters in the army did not convince the self-educated Cobbett that corruption was part of the way of life in England. Much later he admitted his error in defending something of which he had no real knowledge. Still, one must not ignore entirely Cobbett's American career. It was at this time that his literary style was formed and, most importantly, he realized that his true vocation was writing and publishing.

28 For Cobbett's American career see Mary Clark, *Peter Porcupine in America*, Gettysburg, Times and News Publishing Co., 1939, passim. Also, Cole, *op. cit.*, pp. 48–63.

II
The young Tory

In June 1800, Cobbett, thirty-seven years old and of strong Tory convictions, delivered a philippic against Americans in general, boarded ship in New York and returned to the land of his birth. He left behind considerable rancor and enough writings against the spirit and practice of American democracy to fill twelve volumes. Upon arriving in England, Cobbett was at once the recipient of friendly attention from the government. Prime Minister William Pitt was pleased to dine with him and William Windham, secretary for war, took the journalist under his wing. This is not surprising, for in America Cobbett had been known as Peter Porcupine, a prickly defender of all things British, and a powerful opponent of any form of radicalism. Prospects of a rewarding career as a government-sponsored publisher were so enticing that any man with a wife, two children, and no means of support, save his own abilities, might well be tempted.

The time was ripe for anti-Jacobin magazines and newspapers, and a bright young man of humble surroundings might, like George Canning, find the key to advancement in position and wealth in a literary defense of the existing order of things. Certainly Cobbett had an ideal opportunity. Courted by the ministry and offered his own newspaper in addition to tempting financial rewards for writing what he actually believed, Cobbett was in an enviable position. Yet the man's stubborn streak of independence (one of his most endearing qualities) made him refuse all importunities and become instead a supporter of the government while remaining separate from its influence. For several years he was to be closer to its general position than he acknowledged. But, as a buttress of society and not as a pillar, he was free to reprove the ministers over such matters as their conduct of the war.

Indeed, after the Treaty of Amiens, that "mark of infamy," which was arranged between Pitt's protégé and successor, Addington, and Napoleon, Cobbett devoted most of the *Political Register* to denouncing the "peddling politicians" and "grovelling statesmen" responsible for the peace.[1] A breach had been opened in his relations with the ministers. Almost every *Political Register* for the next several years carried an attack upon the motives and deeds of those in charge of the country. Hating the French Revolution with all his heart, Cobbett poured unmeasured abuse upon the ministry for treating with Napoleon. These attacks soon came to signify more than a denunciation of Addington's weak and incompetent ministry by an hysterical patriot. In his free-wheeling, uninhibited style of writing, developed in America, the journalist began to deal with matters other than personalities and touched upon certain themes that would recur in his career. Cobbett showed this tendency in appealing to Pitt shortly before the latter replaced Addington as head of the cabinet in 1804.

1 P.R. (6/30/02), col. 798; A.R. (11/27 to 12/4/02), col. 730.

We must again be great, or we must be nothing; and, great-ness is not to be re-acquired by implicitly yielding to the councils of merchants, manufacturers, and bankers. The gen-erous spirit of the people must once more be appealed to: men must be called upon to fight, not for their property . . . but for the *honour* and *glory* of their country; for the preservation of the *name* and *fame* bequeathed them by their fathers, and which is their duty to hand down untarnished to their children. If this motive be insufficient, all others will be unavailing: our enemy is triumphant, and we are enslaved.[2]

The trumpet call of patriotism was still sounded, but a new note had crept in. Aware now of the government's sen-sitivity toward financial interests, he became concerned and then outraged at its lack of enthusiasm for the destruction of Jacobin France. "Men of reflexion and elevated minds, will, indeed, prefer the bearing of taxation, and will even support poverty and misery, rather than see the safety of their country endangered, or its honour tarnished. . . ." However, this feeling did not prevail among the commercial groups, he said.[3] The next few Registers contain examinations of the system of national finance and show his suspicion of these commercial interests. In this way Cobbett took his first steps down the path which was to lead him eventually to complete opposition while at the same time he was to retain his most cherished views of society.

Except *national valour,* nothing else is excluded from some share of wisdom: money and manufactures; the nasal twang of a methodistical nose; the extermination of bulldogs; the con-verting of negroes into saints; Sunday schools for making scholars of those whose business it is to delve; soup-shops for feeding those who are too idle to work and too proud to beg; the abolition of the tithes; thick handkerchiefs for ladies bosoms: each of these, as being *the means of national salvation,* has its numerous partizans, while, in resistance of France and her half a million of soldiers, to use powder and steel, to call on the

2 A.R. (2/11 to 2/18/04), col. 254.
3 P.R. (4/2 to 4/9/03), col. 513.

people to buckle on their armour, is almost universally regarded as madness.[4]

It was well that a man of such zeal for war against revolution had chosen to remain apart from the government. Although Cobbett still was respectful toward Pitt, he had
developed a contempt for Addington and most of those who
composed the latter's ministry. Criticism of Addington for
his soft policy on France was broadened to include an attack
upon "the doctor" for awarding a sinecure to his twelve-year-
old son. What concerned Cobbett was not so much dishonesty
or extravagance in government, but the donor's lack of
family background and proved incompetence in his position.[5]
"What will now be said to this cowardly crowing of pompous
chanticleer upon his own dunghill?" asked Cobbett, referring
to a speech by Addington. The country needed a new ministry
"composed of talents, and of great public influence . . ." to
rouse the people from lethargy.[6] Here again, in Cobbett's
references to the lack of patriotism of the monied interests
and in the critical look at England's rulers, are evidences of
his later attitudes, thoroughly mixed with traditional Toryism.

Tory, too, was his position upon questions of politics.
Republican institutions were inimical to liberty and the
American and French Revolutions meant the exchange in
each country of "the mild sway of a lawful prince, for the
odious and capricious tyranny of a democratic rabble." [7] His
feelings toward monarchy were sentimental and reverential.
Veneration was expressed for the spirit of monarchy and for
the occupant of the throne sincerely and artlessly.

[4] P.R. (5/7 to 5/14/03), col. 729.
[5] A.R. (7/31 to 8/7/02), cols. 153–54; A.R. (8/7 to 8/14/02), cols.
182–83; P.R. (2/12 to 2/19/03), col. 252. "The doctor" was a popular
term for Addington, who was the son of a physician to George III. Created
Viscount Sidmouth in 1805, he was Home Secretary during the trying post-
war years.
[6] P.R. (4/2 to 4/9/03), col. 536; P.R. (4/23 to 4/30/03), cols. 639–40.
[7] P.R. (6/23/04), cols. 979–80; P.R. (12/3/03), col. 787.

The crown is the guardian of the people, but more especially is its guardianship necessary to those who are destitute of rank and of wealth. The King gives the weakest and poorest of us some degree of consequence: as his subjects, we are upon a level with the noble and the rich; in yielding him obedience, veneration, and love, neither obscurity nor penury can repress our desires, or lessen the pleasure that we feel in return; he is the fountain of national honour, which, like the sun, is no respecter of persons, but smiles with equal warmth on the palace and the cottage; in his justice, his magnanimity, his piety, in the wisdom of his councils, in the splendour of his throne, in the glory of his arms, in all his virtues, and in all his honours, we share, not according to rank or to riches, but in proportion to the attachment that we bear to the land which gave us birth, and to the sovereign, whom God has commanded us to honour and obey.[8]

This attitude did not require examination of government in detail. Strongly swayed by circumstance, Cobbett in later years adumbrated but never consistently followed a political philosophy. At this time his determination "to cherish an adherence to long-tried principles, an affection for ancient families and ancient establishments; to inculcate unshaken attachment to the person and office of the King, an obedience to the laws, a respect for the magistracy, a profound veneration for the church, and a devotion of fortune and of life to the liberties and glory of the country"[9] could rest upon "the true touchstone of politics," the writings of Edmund Burke.[10] Regardless of his shifting points of view, politics, for Cobbett, was always a simple struggle of good versus evil.

Devoted to the principle and practice of monarchy, a

8 P.R. (6/30/02), col. 796.
9 P.R. (10/6/04), cols. 529–30.
10 A.R. (12/4 to 12/11/02), col. 763. Later, Cobbett affected to regard disputes over Burke's ideas as amusing. "He had no notions, no principles, no opinions of his own when he wrote his famous work. . . . He was a poor, needy dependant of a Boroughmonger, to serve whom, and please whom, he wrote; and for no other purpose whatever." P.R. (3/28/18), col. 362.

proponent of a vigorous war policy, Cobbett was also the possessor of an outstanding collection of prejudices. A lusty, strong man with an appreciation of outdoor sports, he called boxing, wrestling and quarter-staff pastimes "which string the nerves and strengthen the frame, which excite an emulation in deeds of hardihood and valour, and which imperceptibly instill honour, generosity, and a love of glory, into the mind of the clown." These sports brought together nobles and peasants and made the poor man "proud of his inferiority." Eliminate boxing, Cobbett warned darkly, and there would be a growth of "foreign methods," knifings and duels, to settle disputes.[11] Of course, this was an age when the high-born mixed with the mob in cheerful juxtaposition at sporting events. When the most subtle lines between the classes were often preserved with exquisite care, a man like Thomas Assheton Smith fought a common labourer with his fists on even terms and the Prince of Wales himself might lead a coterie of riffraff in his search for common pleasures. In these early years of his return to England, Cobbett gloried in the way of life of a country which in his eyes had been blessed by Providence with an absolutely unique history and traditions.

At this time he could always find space in the *Register* for criticisms of the latest novelty. Compulsory inoculations to prevent smallpox, the Society for the Suppression of Vice and "wild and dangerous" proposals to abolish the slave trade were unwelcome innovations.[12] The later Cobbett, with his mind upon more weighty matters, did not always give vent to his prejudices spontaneously. He did, however, retain most of them and even added to his stock from time to time. His opposition to the abolition of the slave trade was stated over and over, in part because of a sympathy with the interests of

11 P.R. (2/27/02), col. 176; P.R. (8/10/05), cols. 195–201.
12 P.R. (1/22 to 1/29/03), cols. 97–100; A.R. (1/7 to 1/14/04), cols. 54–55; A.R. (8/21 to 8/28/02), col. 230.

the West Indian planters, also because of a belief in the basic inferiority of the Negro. The latter was fit only for "servitude and subjection." "No monarchs were ever more mild than those of the House of Bourbon, and no masters were ever more merciful and mild than the planters of St. Domingo," wrote Cobbett in the face of available evidence. Finally (and certainly of more consequence to Cobbett than the Negroes themselves), was his resentment at the charitable efforts of religious groups, which were devoted to the Negro instead of to accomplishing the domestic changes which he favored.[13]

In this persistence of prejudice there is a permanent mental peculiarity. The statement, ". . . I never shall proceed upon the principle that *numbers* only are to be attended to; that an Italian, a Negro, or a Jew, is as good as an Englishman; that stock-jobbers are as *good* as farmers; and that the squalid inhabitants of commercial and manufacturing towns are worth as much to the state as an equal number of the inhabitants of villages and the skirts of commons," [14] could have been made in 1834 as well as in 1804. In the same vein, he never lost his love for England despite the persecution which he had to endure. He repeatedly compared a man's country to his parents, claiming that it had protected him when he was young and deserved his loyalty. "The maxim of Dr. Franklin, 'where *liberty* is, there is *my* country,' does in my opinion, contain as immoral and vile a sentiment as ever disgraced the mind of man," wrote Cobbett in 1822, after he had suffered imprisonment, bankruptcy and exile at the hands of the English government.[15] The object of his later life was to institute major reforms so that people would once again have a stake in their country. But in times of oppression the people should remain at home to free their country and not emigrate

13 P.R. (7/28/04), cols. 125–26.
14 P.R. (10/20/04), col. 596.
15 P.R. (11/9/22), col. 324.

to an easier environment. Although he wrote a great deal on
the subject of emigration for those thinking of leaving England, his heart was never in it.[16]

For the first few years, then, after returning from America,
Cobbett, while sharing with the government many basic
assumptions about society and public policy, felt compelled
to lash out at certain tendencies. Certainly, his independent
quality made him unsuitable as a safe journalistic hireling.
Yet, his general feelings, despite the exuberance of his caveats,
kept him closer to the ministry than to any outside group. It
was the important army question which demonstrates best
his earliest disillusionment, not merely with the unfortunate
Addington and his band of followers, but with the entire range
of government policy. In examining the role of the army, this
unorthodox champion of orthodoxy begins to turn into the
more familiar figure of the singular radical.

After the resumption of hostilities which ended the flimsy
truce established by the Peace of Amiens, the prospect of an
invasion from the Continent presented itself to Englishmen.
Efforts had been made to rebuild the army squandered in
campaigns from Egypt to the West Indies by Pitt's ministry,
which was prodigal in distributing British gold to keep continental sovereigns in the field against France, but parsimo-
nious when equipping the British army for the manifold
tasks demanded of it. Nevertheless, despite these efforts, the
army was inferior in size, equipment and training to Napoleon's Grand Army massed on the French coast. At this time,
when the Third Coalition had not yet been formed and
Trafalgar lay in the future, there were numerous suggestions
from various quarters concerning both the policy which should
be adopted for increasing the size of the army, and the form
which this army should take. Cobbett was not behindhand

---

[16] See *The Emigrant's Guide,* passim.

in this movement and his interest continued even after the immediate danger of invasion had ceased.[17]

At first Cobbett proposed to the ministers a permanent, well-equipped standing army of 200,000 men raised by voluntary enlistment, of which 40,000 to 50,000 would be ready to sail anywhere. He wanted this professional force in preference to the government's policy of increasing the size of the militia and using temporary volunteers. He also opposed conscription and the use of convicted felons and Negroes as soldiers. Cobbett thought that nothing less than a well-trained, professional army could meet Napoleon's veterans on equal terms, for the militiaman was physically soft and conscription brought in an unwilling rabble. The traditional argument that a large standing army was a menace to English liberty was regarded as once valid but now obsolete. He was to alter his opinion drastically a few years later. Now, however, he said that England needed such an army to give weight to her foreign policy. Cobbett concluded that the English must become a military people or lose their freedom, arguing that England could not be saved by trade and money, but by men and arms.[18]

He was particularly opposed to the government's attempts to form a volunteer corps for home defense. His numerous objections to the scheme tried to show it as leading to the undermining of the country. The volunteers' lack of discipline and particularly their open discussions regarding the terms of service they would accept were a source of ridicule and concern.[19] Citing the example of France, where revolutionary clubs purged the Assembly, the Cobbett of 1803 felt that putting arms into the hands of 400,000 men was an invitation to the Republicans to attempt to overthrow the govern-

[17] See J. W. Fortescue, *A History of the British Army*, vols. V *through* XI, London, Macmillan and Co., Ltd., 1921–1923 for details of army organization.

[18] P.R. (6/5/02), col. 688; P.R. (6/12/02), col. 701; P.R. (8/16/03), cols. 94–95; P.R. (11/17/04), cols. 787–89; P.R. (2/15/06), cols. 201–05.

[19] P.R. (9/10/03), cols. 382–84; P.R. (11/5/03), cols. 623–40.

ment.[20] He was also deeply concerned that the lower classes had received commissions and thus had lowered the social status of regular army officers, who were now on a par with "hair-dressers, shoe-makers, and taylors." Formerly army officers could console themselves by reflecting that while militia officers lacked military experience, they did possess rank and fortune. Now even this consolation was extinguished.[21] Another indication of how deeply Cobbett reflected the prevailing anti-Jacobinism of the period was his expressed fear that the Volunteer system would disturb the harmony of society if apprentices could join. In order that the relations between masters and men would not be adversely affected, the masters should have the liberty of refusing permission for their apprentices to join, otherwise their servants would cease to be obedient.[22] Perhaps the most eloquent comment upon these crabbed Tory observations is Cobbett's change of attitude as revealed by his own remarks on the army only a few years later.[23]

The type of army which Cobbett visualized was set forth in a long article in the *Register* in March, 1806, intended to influence his friend, William Windham, who had been appointed Secretary of State for War and the Colonies in the newly-formed Ministry of All the Talents. Confident of "the industry, the honesty, the bodily and mental capacities, the hardihood and the bravery" of Englishmen, Cobbett desired to raise the profession of arms to a level of respectability equal with trade or agriculture. Opposing a hired or conscript army,

20 P.R. (12/31/03), cols. 950–53.
21 P.R. (6/16/04), col. 950.
22 P.R. (5/26/04), col. 799.
23 An interesting exception to the above is a proposal for an unpaid army of youths to drill on Sundays. Particularly significant is his observation that Sunday was the only day on which the children were released from schools "and pestiferous prisons ycleped [sic] manufactories, may stretch their little cramped up limbs in following their seniors to the drill." Cobbett realized the existence of factories, and their unhealthy nature, long before he is generally credited. See P.R. (7/23/03), cols. 120–27.

he placed his confidence in a permanent standing army of volunteers. This force, which was to include only white Christians, was designed to provide a reserve of comparatively young men at the end of fifteen years of service. There was no provision made for an increase in pay, for Cobbett did not trust the soldier with money in his hand. Instead, there were to be opportunities for the ex-soldier to settle in any parish in the United Kingdom and to pursue any trade or calling. More significantly, he should be allowed to vote and kill game.[24] This farrago of sound common sense, practical experience and stubborn prejudice had a good deal of merit but did not have the slightest chance of being accepted. English society in the early nineteenth century simply was not constructed in a fashion to permit such concessions to its most humble members. Comfortable classes in England traditionally had an unfavorable attitude toward the regular army, and the army in turn was largely composed of the most depressed groups in the kingdom. These two circumstances reinforced each other and secured that no major change in the soldiers' status would be forthcoming. Windham himself, Cobbett's best friend among the political leaders, was a vigorous advocate of a strong army and an anti-French policy. But he was too conservative in his general social attitudes to allow the adoption of Cobbett's suggestions.[25] He and Cobbett had actually terminated their friendship before the publication of the plan. After this, Cobbett's writings concerning the army were almost exclusively devoted to attacks on the government for using it against the people.

In the course of his argument justifying the use of a professional army instead of a militia, Cobbett observed that property did not give people something to fight for, but rather something to live for. This made them incline toward pacifism. Cobbett's initial loathing of the businessman re-

24 P.R. (3/22/06), cols. 385–406.
25 For Windham's views, see Fortescue, *op. cit.*, vol. V, pp. 303–05.

sulted from his perception that the person who made his living through trade was unlikely to be moved by any appeals, either patriotic or humane, that might interfere with profits. This had been demonstrated by business backing for the Treaty of Amiens. He had also heartily opposed a fund formed by London bankers to provide for gifts of stock to outstanding soldiers and sailors and the dependents of those who lost their lives in service. Suspicious of this class, Cobbett regarded the scheme as a device for manipulating securities to the benefit of commercial interests. Since Cobbett had come to believe that these interests were too wealthy when compared to the agricultural groups of the country, his clash with the government could not long be delayed.[26] This antipathy toward the "stock-jobbers" and "omnium eaters" helped disillusion him first with the Tories' method of handling the war effort, then with the war itself.

It is evident that Cobbett had a misconception about the purposes of the government ministers. He was under the impression that they were concerned with the same goals that he was, but simply lacked the necessary knowledge to achieve them. Hence, he offered constant advice. Soon, however, he came to wonder why he was estranged from the ministry and why the ministers were not vigorously supporting English ways. His attitude in these years was one of growing impatience with Pitt and his followers. His suggestions to them became more blunt as his tone increased in stridency. Before Cobbett realized that the faults of the government did not simply rest with a few men but, instead, were reflections of an entire design for ruling the country, he developed an intense, life-long hatred of Pitt.[27] Because of differences with the government over foreign policy, public finance and the military establishment, he began to feel, little by little, that evil in the country was not confined to a few politicians working with

26 P.R. (8/27/03), cols. 281-85.
27 P.R. (2/1/06), cols. 133-38.

selfish interest groups. Cobbett's misconceptions, based on a failure to understand the power structure in the kingdom, explain his frequent shifts of attitude toward the country's leaders during the years 1800–1806. Finally, he was able to grasp unwelcome reality. In 1805 he announced that there existed in England a *system* and that it was this system and not any one person with which he was at war.

> The system of upstarts; of low-bred, low-minded sycophants usurping the stations designed by nature, by reason, by the Constitution, and by the interests of the people, to men of high birth, eminent talents, or great national services; the system by which the ancient Aristocracy and the Church have been under-mined; by which the ancient gentry of the kingdom have been almost extinguished, their means of support having been trans-ferred, by the hand of the tax gatherer, to contractors, jobbers and Jews; the system by which but too many of the higher orders have been rendered the servile dependents of the minister of the day, and by which the lower, their generous spirit first broken down, have been moulded into a mass of parish fed paupers. Unless it be the intention, the solemn resolution, to change this *system,* let no one talk to me of a *change of min-istry;* for, until this system be destroyed; until this race of up-starts shall be supplanted by men of birth and talents; until this abject servility, this willing pauperism, shall give place to that independence of spirit which was once the characteristic of Englishmen; until the filthy tribe of jobbers, brokers and peculators shall be swept from the councils of the nation and the society of her statesmen; until this corruption shall not have put on incorruption, and this principle of ruling by the base passions shall be changed for a principle exactly the reverse; until this shall be, there is no change of *men,* that can, for a single hour, retard the mighty mischief that we dread.[28]

Thus, when Pitt died in January, 1806 and a broad-based government was formed which included Cobbett's old friend, Windham, and new friend, Charles James Fox, his tolerance was short-lived. Even before the army proposals were ad-

[28] P.R. (4/20/05), cols. 597–98.

dressed to Windham, Cobbett had begun to criticize the
new "Ministry of All the Talents." [29] All the old abuses—in
short, the "system"—were to be retained. There had been in
Cobbett's estimation no change of parties, simply a shifting
around of personalities. From this time Cobbett was to state
repeatedly that there were no political parties in the kingdom,
just alliances of powerful men interested only in achieving
power. With this Namierlike view of politics went a belief
that what the country needed was wholesale change. He began
to draw close to the small Radical group in parliament,
especially Sir Francis Burdett, whom he had once hated for
expressing irreverent views toward monarchy and traditional
government.[30] The stage was set for Cobbett's experience at
the Honiton election, which broadened his outlook considerably and made him realize that corruption extended far
beyond Westminster. The portion of his career which had
been considered radical was about to begin. But time was to
prove that his personal prescription for what the country
needed would always prevent a real meeting of minds with
those demanding fundamental and rapid change.

These years from 1800 to early 1806 witness Cobbett reacting to situations which he detested. It was essentially a period
of disillusionment in others. However, his belief in himself
and his own ideas remained constant. He did not flinch in his
determination to fight for what he thought was right: Old
England, simple, rural, unchanging; unencumbered by stock-
jobbers and self-seeking politicians—a heritage of freedom at
home and greatness abroad. This was what Cobbett was to
struggle for in the years to come, sacrificing for himself and
for his family the wealth and comfort which could have been
his had he devoted himself to safe journalism or to that other
area in which he showed genius—farming. Often inaccurate,

29 P.R. (2/15/06), cols. 195–98.
30 Compare A.R. (7/31 to 8/7/02), col. 151 with P.R. (11/15/06), cols.
749–51.

sometimes wrongheaded, always exaggerating, occasionally lying, frequently prudent, and even (surprisingly) a trimmer, Cobbett pursued his narrow way for the rest of his life.

A married man with two children upon his return to England, he was the father of five by 1806. But having turned down an easy living, he never reneged. Instead, he dogged "the vermin-breeding system" for thirty years. Never fully understanding what he was struggling against, he heaped invective upon this "System," which he sometimes referred to by different names but always hated. Of course, there was no single "System" at all. Cobbett was a perennial over-simplifier and looked instinctively for unqualified explanations. In reality, he was confronted by an extraordinarily complex series of events and almost imperceptible alterations in society which might have baffled even a cool, knowledgeable observer. Also, although a seeker after the uncomplex when dealing with issues, Cobbett himself was a bundle of contradictions. Certainly he was not concerned, in his later years, with the condition of the laboring people to the extent that this became the sole test of any doctrine.[31] At best, Cobbett was a spasmodic humanitarian. It would be well to consider certain aspects of Cobbett's character, his prejudice and his involved, sometimes personal, motivation in addition to his basic courage and real love of England.

[31] As G. D. H. Cole suggests, *op. cit.,* p. 145.

III
The "System" and reform

Having identified England's enemy as the "System," in 1806 Cobbett commenced in earnest his career as a radical pamphleteer. Many former opinions were quickly left behind (to the delight of his enemies who created a whole literature, known as "anti-Cobbett," composed of Cobbett's erstwhile observations contrasted with his newer ones) as Cobbett shifted his attacks to the targets which occupied his attention regularly thereafter. He developed into an astringent critic of both institutions and men and produced the writings against the "System" upon which his present reputation lies. For the rest of his life Cobbett devoted himself to attacking this interlocking tyranny of politicians and government creditors which, as he saw it, ran the country for the benefit of a favored few. "All my plans in private life; all my pursuits; all my designs, wishes, and thoughts, have this one great object in view: *the*

overthrow of the ruffian Boroughmongers. If I write grammars;
if I write on agriculture; if I sow, plant, or deal in seeds;
whatever I do has first in view the destruction of those in-
famous tyrants." [1]

He became a perpetual critic of government policy. Since
the Tories were the group which dominated the country's
politics during most of Cobbett's career, they naturally became major targets for his abuse. But he did not care for
the Whigs either. Traditionally, he said, there had been a
court party and a country party and the latter defended the
rights of the people from the encroachments of the ministry.
However, in the reign of George III the opposition party
attached itself to the Prince of Wales, with the result that
there were two court parties and no country party. "The
Crown had one party in *possession* and another party in
expectancy, while the people had no party at all," because the
only opposition was "as one *courtier* makes to another."
Cobbett's great complaint about the Whigs was simply that
they were a sham party; that in reality there was only one
party in political life. He abused those calling themselves
Whigs for their lack of partisanship and constantly tried to
persuade the Whig aristocrats to take the position of leadership to which they were entitled by rank and tradition.[2]
Nevertheless, after the dissolution in 1807 of the broad-based
but short-lived Ministry of All the Talents Cobbett seemed
to lose much of his faith that appeals would be of use. By
this time, although still favoring the prosecution of the war,
he had developed to the point where he urged the rooting
out of electoral abuses and a reduction of pensions and sinecures. His efforts were useless because for many years reform
was for all practical purposes almost a dead issue, supported
in parliament by only a few individuals such as Romilly and
Whitbread. His belief in the Whigs had been based upon an

1 P.R. (8/14/19), col. 8.
2 P.R. (2/22/12), cols. 242 ff.

optimistic estimation of the power and intentions of Charles James Fox. The failure of Fox to accomplish anything in the direction of the reform Cobbett desired convinced him that the strength of the conservative wing, the Grenvillites, was too strong and that actually there was no real Whig party.[3] The acid test of a party was its willingness to reduce expenditures and make proposals for reform. When Cobbett assured himself that those calling themselves Whigs were going to do little about either, he took pains to ridicule their pretensions and their sham opposition.[4]

Cobbett was caustic in his denunciation of political parties, regarding them as motivated by nothing more than a desire on the part of their members for power and plunder. After the fashion of extremists, he imputed unworthy motives to the Whig leaders for their failure to introduce an effective opposition. His judgment of political conditions influenced his concept of government, which did not include provision for party politics. Cobbett was ignorant of the benefits which a healthy, vigorous two-party system could bring to the country. Though we must not rebuke him for failing to realize the value of such a system decades before this innovation became a part of the British constitution, it would be inaccurate to judge from his remarks that he had faith in the principle of an Opposition, or that he even thought it desirable. Still after being persuaded that radical reform was needed Cobbett concentrated upon achieving it and would work with any group or person which he felt would be useful. There was not a major political faction in the country which he did not court on one occasion or other in his search for support.[5]

3 P.R. (10/18/06), col. 588 ff. Cobbett was not impervious to the charm of Fox. However, it was his considered opinion that Fox was a talented but weak man who allowed himself to be led by the wing of his party headed by Lord Grenville. P.R. (9/20/23), col. 707.

4 P.R. (1/30/08), cols. 161–67.

5 P.R. (10/12/22), cols. 92 ff., for praise of one of Cobbett's old hates, Canning, after the latter had become Foreign Secretary and leader of the House of Commons. Also, P.R. (12/13/34), cols. 648–50, for a favorable

Although he did not make a distinction between the two parties, Cobbett at one time applauded the actions of a few advanced Whigs, notably the wealthy Baronet, Sir Francis Burdett. Burdett and Cobbett were quite close during Cobbett's early career as a reformer. But when hunger caused the working classes to enter the political arena in 1816, Burdett found their proximity too much for his delicate sensibilities and gracefully moved away in a rightward direction. While fear and revulsion were causing the dominant Whig and Tory groups to come closer together than ever, Cobbett rated his once warm but rapidly cooling friend for this betrayal of the cause of reform.[6] Actually, by 1816 Cobbett had changed more than Burdett, particularly in regard to suffrage. Still an adherent to the principle of moderate reform, Burdett eventually found himself cast as a conservative. Like a once iconoclastic American Progressive who lived until the 1930's, he was bewildered and alarmed at a world which had passed him by. Burdett's squeamishness about accepting support from the masses irritated Cobbett, who asked, "Is not a plough-man or a journeyman artizan as *respectable* as a farmer or shop-keeper of the same morals and manners? Is not a coal-heaver as reputable as a Lord, if their minds and morals are upon a level?" He went on to inquire of the radical reformer Henry Hunt, why Burdett could recommend physical force and not he [Hunt]. "Why is that violence and coarseness in you, which is moderation and politeness in him? Is it because you have not immense landed estates and a father-in-law with a million in the funds?"[7] This anger testifies to Cobbett's identifica-

---

comparison of the Wellington ministry with that of the existing Whig government. These are extreme but not isolated examples. For all his thrusts at the nobility, he could fawn upon them when he wanted something. See his praise of Grey for calling for an examination of the government's finances. P.R. (5/6/26), col. 357.

6 P.R. (12/20/17), cols. 1155–66. The effect of the working class agitation upon the Whigs is noted in Arthur Aspinall, *Lord Brougham and the Whig Party*, Manchester, Manchester University Press, 1927, p. 72.

7 P.R. (10/3/18), cols. 205–07.

tion of himself with the workers and the radical leaders, Hunt and Cartwright. Distinctions of class were always important to him and the above quotation reads strangely when put alongside later testimonials to a stratified social system. But he did oppose weighing similar remarks in different scales.[8] Judged by his attacks upon the political and financial structure of the country (combined, in his eyes, into the "System"), Cobbett was a true radical—far more extreme than the advanced wing of the Whig party with which he could no longer work comfortably.

After the Honiton election of 1806, as he began to emerge as a radical, Cobbett placed under his hostile scrutiny most of the actions of the government. The *Register* delved into finance, foreign policy, labor unrest, the army and navy, agriculture: all were handled with vigor and decision. Based on his hatred of the "ruffian Boroughmongers" and shaped by his conviction that radical reform was imperative, these judgments vary in quality from shrewd perception to utter nonsense. They are the product of a mind which was often acute but also thoroughly prejudiced. Cobbett had a tendency to see only what he wanted to see. For example, after becoming an enemy of the government, he began to notice the suffering of the workers in the factories as well as on the land. The real privation of these people furnished Cobbett with excellent ammunition, which he used with great propaganda effect upon the "System." The doings of the ministers were now attacked all along the line from a point of view which was radical in its desire to remake society but also intensely personal concerning what should be re-created. It is noteworthy that this attack sheds more light upon Cobbett than do his numerous proposals for reform.

Despairing of the existing structure of politics, Cobbett

[8] See J. L. and Barbara Hammond, *The Town Labourer, 1760–1832*, London, Longmans, Green, and Co., 1919, pp. 60 ff., which shows the great latitude of expression allowed to a fortunate few

turned on the royal family as well. It was inevitable that in view of the policies of King George III and the character of the royal family, Cobbett would be led to include them in his widening net of suspicion. He went on record as opposing increased pensions for younger members of the royal house. Printing a list of its income, he indicated that pensions were already too large and that any increase should be made from money in the privy purse.[9] A number of other irritations had developed by then. The exemption of the King's property in the funds from the income tax, the tenderness of parliament toward the King's Hanoverian property (to which Cobbett, like many Englishmen, was totally indifferent), the presence of German troops on English soil, the refusal of the King to allow Fox to serve in the government and the sorry record in the field of the Duke of York all provoked Cobbett.[10] No amount of self-deception could persuade him by this time that it was entirely Pitt's prejudice which had excluded Fox from his ministry. Nor could he overlook the inferior characters and accomplishments of most of the King's sons. The awe which he once felt as he paid homage to the monarch was replaced by a matter-of-fact analysis of the King's great power. He then went on to say, "These are not the marks of impotence, I take it; and, therefore, I once more beg my friend the true Englishman to keep his vows of devotion to himself, lest he expose himself to ridicule and contempt, as being, not the supporter of the weak, but one who shouts '*huzza for the strongest.*' " [11]

This statement suggests Cobbett had lost that feeling of personal attachment to the Crown, which is essential in the relation between monarch and subject. The non-rational tendency to overlook or excuse human frailties, to invest the occupant of the throne with qualities which the King did not

[9] P.R. (7/12/06), cols. 33–44; P.R. (7/19/06), cols. 65–75.
[10] P.R. (5/23/07), col. 921; P.R. (6/13/07), col. 1033.
[11] P.R. (3/21/07), cols. 433–34.

possess, to believe that there is an intrinsic bond between them and that the well-being of the people is bound up with the health of their ruler had been destroyed in Cobbett. The fragile nature of this sentiment is always susceptible to shock. In this case the fabric, once torn, could never be repaired. Prejudice, in the form of an unreasoning commitment, no longer existed for him. From this time he was to look coldly at the royal family as a force which might hinder or aid the type of reform he desired.

In general, Cobbett was progressively hostile and he identified George III and his family with the "System." As he said in 1816, "Why then am I to look upon the family of Guelph, a band of Boroughmongers, a half Hanoverian army . . . as constituting England?" [12] The fecklessness of most of the King's sons, their selfishness and extravagance, disturbed many people, including members of parliament. Cobbett stated bluntly what others felt to be true (the Duke of Wellington's famous remark about the royal dukes being "the damnedest millstone about the necks of any Government that can be imagined" sounds like that of a restrained Cobbett). The second son of George III, the Duke of York, that "notorious stinking coward," who earned old-soldier Cobbett's early hatred by an inept performance as Commander-in-Chief of the army and retained it all his life, was a favorite target for abuse. Veiled references to the Duke's military incapacity appeared as early as 1803 but the affair of Mrs. Clarke gave Cobbett an opportunity for a more overt attack.[13] The affair gave an impetus to his discontent with current society.

Despite his growing dislike of the royal family, in two instances, his attitude toward the King's eldest son and the

[12] Amer. P.R. (1/6/16), col. 8.

[13] Mrs. Clarke, the Duke of York's mistress, had systematically used her influence at court to conduct a trade in army commissions. A parliamentary investigation enabled Cobbett to fill his columns with moral indignation and ridicule. P.R. (8/6/03), cols. 191–92; P.R. (2/11/09), cols. 223–24 and *Political Register* for the next two months, passim.

part that he himself played in the cause of Queen Caroline, Cobbett demonstrated a certain subtlety. Both are worth examining briefly.

In 1810, while Napoleon was at the peak of his power, George III lost his reason completely and a regency headed by the Prince of Wales had to be formed. Up to this time, Cobbett had often spoken well of the Prince and, despite the scandal of the younger George's private life, had never singled him out for attack as he had done the Duke of York. Perhaps the Prince's adherence to the hallowed Hanoverian tradition of being on bad terms with his father caused him to have merit in Cobbett's eyes. It was a tendency of Cobbett to credit others with good qualities when he was angry with their opponents. He was also well aware that the Prince would one day sit on the throne. Little fragments of praise appeared from time to time in the *Register* and during an earlier illness of the King, Cobbett had earnestly hoped that, in the event a regency was formed, nothing would be done to circumscribe the power of the Prince Regent.[14] But in 1810 and 1811, he opposed limitations on the Regent's power as a denial of the Prince's inheritance.[15]

Much of what Cobbett wrote about the heir to the throne at the time is humbug. For he knew as well as most people that the Prince had flagrant weaknesses in his character. Cobbett believed, however, that the Prince might be more favorable than his father toward a reform of parliament, and, therefore, took a stand in favor of allowing him to exercise regal powers during the regency. Here he was in opposition to the Tory ministry which feared it would be replaced by the Prince's Whig friends and took the novel position (for that party) that the powers of the throne should be regulated by

14 A.R. (2/11 to 2/18/04), cols. 255–56. He also favored the side of the Prince concerning the issue of whether the education of the Princess Charlotte should be left to him or the King. P.R. (12/22/04), cols. 1205–06.

15 P.R. (1/28/10), cols. 1036–37.

parliament. The Whigs, scenting office, threw tradition to the winds as well and declared for the exercise of royal authority in its fullness. When the Prince decided to keep the Tory group and thus surprised everyone, including the ministers themselves, Cobbett claimed that he had foreseen this. He contented himself with laughing at the discomfiture of the Whigs but said nothing which might offend the Prince.[16]

It was not long before this era of tolerance and restraint ended. Cobbett, realizing the unyielding nature of the Prince's reactionary views, began to jab at him by championing the character of the Princess of Wales and reviewing the history of their marriage. George had detested his wife since he first sighted her and put her out of his way as soon as he could. In 1806, a parliamentary commission conducted what was inaccurately termed the "delicate investigation" into her morals and conduct. Acquitted of the most serious charges against her, Princess Caroline faded once more into her forced obscurity. In 1812, while still in Newgate, Cobbett took up her cause and in the following year continued his defense of her by demanding that she be allowed to visit her daughter and condemning the ostracism to which she was subjected by the royal family. He also maintained that if the Regent died before Princess Charlotte reached her eighteenth birthday, the Princess of Wales should be made Regent for her daughter.[17] At this time he wanted the future heir to the throne to be guided by someone who would be likely to support the popular cause. That is why nine years previously he called upon the Prince (and not George III) to supervise the education of Princess Charlotte. There is no doubt that he was also personally disgusted at the callous

---

16 He did not say, for example, as he did twenty years later, that the Tories were kept in office because the Prince feared they would blackmail him about his treatment of his wife if he let them go. *History of the Regency and Reign of King George The Fourth*, London, William Cobbett, 1830. Ch. III. (Hereafter cited as *History of George IV.*)

17 P.R. (2/13/12), col. 198.

treatment meted out to the Princess Caroline by her husband since their marriage. Feelings of antipathy toward George grew, and early in 1816 Cobbett advised the people of the United States of certain shortcomings in the character of the Regent. "His enjoyments are merely of an animal kind. Voluptuousness has made him effeminate and timid . . . His amusements are those of a great overgrown baby, his conversation such as is not to be repeated *anywhere*." [18] These remarks, typical of the manner in which he now paid his respects to the royal family, mark a complete break in his attachment to any male members of the royal house.

In 1820 the "old, mad, blind, despised" George III finally died and the Prince Regent now assumed the throne in his own right. The new King had no desire to reconcile himself to his wife and allow her to reign at his side. Divorce proceedings were begun soon after the now Queen Caroline had refused a ministerial bribe and had made a triumphal landing in England.[19] Cobbett played his usual solitary role during the crisis. He had become a personal adviser of the Queen and used his influence to urge her to maintain to the full her right to the Crown. He subjected to continual criticism the Whigs, Brougham and Denman, who were skillfully conducting her defense in the House of Lords. This was not only because he felt that their moderation was intended to make Caroline part with some of her prerogatives but (very important) a compromise settlement would not advance radical reform. He wanted her to make common cause with the people, whose resentment at the King and his ministers was demonstrated by their fanatical identification with her position. This emotion Cobbett exploited in the *Register,* and many of his defenses of her read like his usual articles on reform. The

[18] Amer. P.R. (3/23/16), col. 374.

[19] For the story of this episode and interpretations of Cobbett's part in it, see Elie, Halévy, *The Liberal Awakening, 1815–1830*, New York, Peter Smith, 1949, pp. 84–104 and Cole, *op. cit.*, pp. 247 ff.

Queen's struggle often appears as nothing more than a peg for him to hang an essay on. Cobbett's role in the affair may easily be exaggerated and he acted more as a supporter of the popular mood than as a causative agent. Yet he did strengthen the resolve of the Queen during his period of influence.

Regardless of the validity of the evidence which was used against the Queen in the trial, it is now agreed that she had a rather unsavory character. Hedonistic, frivolous and insubstantial, she would seem to have been the type of person whom Cobbett, with his self-publicized moral principles, would have hated and shunned. In many ways Caroline was a proper mate for her husband, whose coarse behavior Cobbett referred to more than once.[20] Of course, her appearance on the scene at a time when his own influence was very weak suited Cobbett's purposes. His opportunism would certainly allow him to overlook her soiled reputation if by working with her he could further the cause of reform and regain the influence among the workers which he had lost after his flight to America in 1817. Yet while these elements undoubtedly comprised part of his motivation, he also appeared to have a genuine fondness for the Queen. This was not due simply to a chivalrous approach toward women, for he could be quite unreserved in his attacks upon them singly or collectively, whether the occasion demanded stringent measures or not. The answer to his apparently wholehearted defense of Caroline's character probably lies in three elements of Cobbett's thinking. The first was his sincere and lifelong devotion to the principle of monarchy. Another was his tendency to see intricate questions in polarized terms and to identify himself completely with one side. The last was his inability to judge character. These factors and a hitherto unrevealed side to his vanity put Cobbett into the queer role

20 See Sermon number 2 in *Thirteen Sermons,* which was certainly written with George in mind.

of the simpering courtier. He could, therefore, endure being in juxtaposition with, and "kissing the pretty little hand" of, a person whose way of life might reasonably have been expected to excite his disgust.

All of Cobbett's attacks upon the personalities and actions of the royal family, "this unfortunate, stupid, and really ill-treated family of foreigners," [21] were rooted in his hatred of the "System." They were personal, for he supported the principle of monarchy and did not consider the Crown beyond redemption. The problem began with that "most villainous rebellion," the Glorious Revolution of 1688. At this time, the aristocracy, using William of Orange as their tool, overthrew the mild rule of the Stuarts, fastened a despotism upon England and introduced the national debt and paper money and the corruption of parliament by wealthy borough-mongers.[22] The source of evil was not the royal family but the boroughmongers. George III and his selfish successor were to blame only for being willing tools of the boroughmonger system and forming an indifferent background to the suffering of the people.[23]

Since Cobbett believed that the true cause of misery in the kingdom was not the insane George III or his profligate son, George IV, but the boroughmongers and their corrupt financial System, he did not want to destroy the Crown. Radical reform would refurbish the institution of monarchy, which had become decrepit through abuse and neglect. By the sweeping away of the System, the throne would regain its rightful place in the life of the nation.[24] His complaint

[21] P.R. (2/24/16), col. 255.

[22] P.R. (6/20/18), cols. 721–24.

[23] Cobbett once noted twelve events which occurred during the reign of George III which acted to the detriment of the people. None of them was the result of an action by the King. P.R. (1/24/24), cols. 214–37.

[24] Archibald S. Foord has described the reduction of royal powers as making for more honest government—an opinion which most would share today. See "The Waning of the Influence of the Crown," *The English Historical Review*, Vol. LXII (1947), pp. 484–507.

against the occupants of the throne was that they were not properly playing their roles of protecting and fostering the welfare of the people. If the Hanoverians had shown any disposition to resume this traditional role, Cobbett's qualms about their foreign origin and doubtful legitimacy would have been forgotten and he would not have urged that the Crown lands be used to diminish the debt.[25] Both George III and George IV had ignored the active interest which a king of England was supposed to take in his subjects. Extravagance and licentious conduct could be forgiven, but not neglect. Their responsibility for the condition of the monarchy was great, but it was upon the shoulders of the boroughmonger aristocracy that Cobbett placed most of the blame.

What was wrong with England, as Cobbett frequently pointed out, was that a conspiracy of politicians, clergymen, aristocrats, fundholders and boroughmongers had overthrown established usages and waxed wealthy at the expense of the people. The symptoms of this condition were unearned sine-cures, harsh game laws, absentee clergymen, hungry workers and cruel repression. During his lifetime a revolution had taken place which overshadowed that of 1688. The funda-mental laws of the land had been abrogated, a standing army introduced, elections corrupted and the people afflicted by taxes and paper money. With sorrow he related that the "happy climate, the industry of its inhabitants, their punc-tuality and their perseverance . . . the farms which are so many gardens on the top of the land, and the inexhaustible mines which are beneath. . . ." could not bring happiness to England because of this alteration.

> In the whole world there was not so happy a country as England was. In the reading of our books and in the hearing of verbal descriptions of cottages in England; of the industry, the neatness, the order and the regularity of those dwellings of our labourers, the people of other countries think they are

25 See P.R. (2/28/35), cols. 513–17 for details of this proposal.

listening to romances. . . . Brass and pewter were seen every-where. It was a disgrace not to have window curtains, bed-curtains, and feather beds.

The labourers were happy. Each had his little home. He had things about him worth possessing and worth preserving. . . . Men lived in the same cottage from the day of their marriage 'till the day of their death [like Cobbett's grandfather]. They worked for the same masters for many years . . . without any legal engagement and without any other dependence than that occasioned by respect, and good will. In numerous instances, son succeeded father, generation after generation, as the work-man or the servant of son after father. The liberality and kind-ness of the employer were repaid by the respect and fidelity of the servant.[26]

All this had been swept away and could be restored only through radical reform.

So Cobbett became an ardent champion of the principle of parliamentary reform. For him the reform of parliament was always connected with the ending of the System and all its attendant abuses. From the time when he scoffed at the idea of universal suffrage and said that when the existing system of public finance ceased to operate there would be no need for projects of parliamentary reform until he became an advocate of radical change, he always had this uppermost in his mind. As a supporter of reform, he at first held that one of its benefits would be the complete destruction of the System, but later swung to the position that reform of parlia-ment could not come about until this scheme had blown itself up.[27] Cobbett always viewed the destruction of the System as imminent. Yet until that happened, the enemy was in its grip. Any reform that was made before the end of the System was bound to be minor in scope and would be harmful rather than beneficial. That is why he eventually scoffed at Burdett, Lord John Russell and other Whigs who wanted a limited

[26] P.R. (7/26/17), cols. 513 ff.; P.R. (11/22/17), cols. 1029 and 1043–44.
[27] P.R. (3/15/06), cols. 366–68; P.R. (1/26/11), col. 193; P.R. (6/13/29), col. 738.

reform.[28] Cobbett was so confident of an apocalyptic end to the System that he ignored or ridiculed all attempts at piecemeal reform. This is one of his most salient yet frequently overlooked characteristics. Of course, in the final analysis, he supported the Whig reform bill of 1832 but this represented a reversal of his former stand. By 1830 all of his prophecies about an imminent ending of his aversion had proved false. He had also never achieved his ambition to sit in parliament and at nearly age seventy he was still pulled in this direction.

Only when parliament was free from domination by vested interests could it once again act on behalf of the people. A reformed parliament would end bribery and corruption at elections; put a stop to favoritism in promotions in the army, navy and church; eliminate unearned sinecures, military academies, spies and informers; cut exorbitant salaries, the civil list and the national debt; and free the press.[29] Cobbett was not interested in the structure of government; his proposals concerning elections and procedures were concrete but not developed. What he was really concerned with was *"the effect produced by his* [the Prime Minister's] *measures upon the state of the nation at large . . ."* [30] He thought that a House of Commons constructed along the lines he suggested—honestly and openly elected by universal male suffrage, with zeal for the public welfare—would act for the benefit of the country as a whole. In short, he desired a reign of public virtue, pure and unselfish. No wonder he was so ferocious in dealing with the existing government!

Beginning in 1812 with the economic disturbances of that year and reaching a peak after Waterloo, the *Political Register* carried Cobbett's castigations of the government's policy of meeting the complaints of starving workers with repression.

---

28 *A Grammar of the English Language,* New York, William Cobbett, 1818, p. 115.
29 P.R. (10/12/16), cols. 339 ff.
30 P.R. (1/9/11), col. 37.

The disturbances, Cobbett said, were caused by want and misery ("It is *want;* it is *sheer* hunger . . .") arising out of the war.[31] The government blamed agitators who urged reform or revolution. Protests of the hungry workers and their families were answered with troops, the suspension of habeas corpus and terrible new laws. Cobbett described the suffering of the workers and denounced the use of troops, *agents provocateurs,* and the whole battery of legal weapons used against them.[32]

Here were two contrasting points of view. Neither Cobbett nor the government had a sophisticated understanding of what was causing the workers to riot, but Cobbett was far nearer the truth. Economic difficulties had been building up for Britain, and the end of the war was followed by a terrible depression. Markets for manufactured goods diminished sharply and employers had to retrench. The situation was aggravated by the discharge of thousands of service men. Wages fell for those fortunate enough to be employed, yet because of the new corn law, the price of food was high. The result was terrible hardship among the people, which led to riots in both industrial and agricultural regions.[33] Although Cobbett shared the general ignorance of the times with reference to the basic causes of unrest, he was at least on the right track in regarding them as economic. The ministry, haunted by the spectre of the French Revolution, saw only organized sedition.[34]

[31] P.R. (6/1/16), col. 691.

[32] P.R. (6/1/16), cols. 685 ff.; P.R. (5/6/16), cols. 548 ff.; P.R. (8/16/17), cols. 611 ff. This last, very interesting and sympathetic article, was published separately in *A History of the Last Hundred Days of English Freedom* as Letter no. III.

[33] W. W. Rostow has identified three major economic forces that contributed to unrest from 1790–1850. They were: cyclical unemployment, fluctuations in domestic harvests, and technological unemployment. England suffered from all three in an aggravated form after Waterloo. See *British Economy of the Nineteenth Century,* Oxford, Oxford University Press, 1948, p. 109.

[34] This situation is more fully discussed in Chapter X.

"They sigh for a PLOT. Oh, how they sigh! They are working and slaving and fretting and stewing; they are sweating all over; they are absolutely pining and dying for a Plot!" [35] This was Cobbett's way of noting that the outcry against Jacobins was very convenient in deflecting the public mind away from other questions of the day. He was convinced that the government deliberately chose to interpret spontaneous riots as evidence of a revolutionary plot in order to prevent an examination of the financial system. While attacking the government policy, he used his influence with the workers to direct them away from violence. Nevertheless, frightened by the agitation for an improvement of the workers' living conditions and baffled by the complexity of the problems facing it, the Liverpool government passed a series of acts in 1817 which suspended habeas corpus and placed drastic curbs on the press. To the disgust of many of his fellow radicals, Cobbett secretly boarded ship for America and landed there early in May, 1817. He spent two and a half years in the United States, living inconspicuously on a farm on Long Island and busying himself by writing several books in addition to the usual *Register* articles.

In 1816 and 1817, aided by the publication of a special edition of the *Register* priced at 2d., Cobbett was able to present his message to more people than ever before or ever again. For a short time he became an important figure, a leader of a small group of radicals and a larger body of hungry, frustrated, but inarticulate workers. There was no organization; it was simply a case of Cobbett's being read and admired by people with grievances who were outside the power structure of the kingdom. The 1817 legislation put an

---

35 P.R. (12/14/16). col. 627. The highly questionable main thesis of a recent book holds that there was much more conscious radicalism among the working classes than most historians have recognized. If this is true, the actions of the government would have been more rational. See E. P. Thompson, *The Making of the English Working Class,* London, Victor Gollancz, 1964, passim.

end to this situation rather abruptly and Cobbett never regained his position. Of course, he was not a real menace to the government. What made him attractive to many of the poor was his vigorous attacks upon their oppressors; as an organizer he would have been a failure. If it is true that Cobbett won greatest acclaim during the years immediately following Waterloo, it is only because his violent opposition to the government placed him on the side of the oppressed. His articles and books denounced spies and *agents provocateurs,* the suppression of the press and suspension of habeas corpus. This was done in a simple style and was directly related to the situation which the people faced.

> Elegant dresses, superb furniture, stately buildings, fine roads and canals, fleet horses and carriages, numerous and stout ships, warehouses teeming with goods; all these, and many other objects that fall under our view, are so many marks of national wealth and resources. But all these spring from *labour.* Without the Journeyman and the labourers none of them could exist; without the assistance of their hands, the country would be a wilderness, hardly worth the notice of an invader.[36]

His sympathy for the predicament of the poor and bewildered was sincere. Adversity in those for whom he felt a degree of comradeship brought out the best in him.

In November, 1819, expecting the death of George III, Cobbett landed at Liverpool after his exile in America. His reason for returning, as he admitted soon afterward, was to run for parliament in the election which was then mandatory after the passing of a sovereign. To further the end of reform, Cobbett proposed that a sum of £5,000 be raised and placed in his hands for him to do with as he saw fit. Naturally, to specify what the money would be used for would be bad tactics: contributors were expected to accept Cobbett's judgments on faith.[37] The fund was a failure. The expenses of

---

[36] P.R. (11/2/16), col. 433.
[37] P.R. (3/25/20), cols. 82–83; P.R. (1/6/20), cols. 568–70.

the Coventry election, which Cobbett lost in 1820 and the quick demise of *Cobbett's Evening Post,* a daily paper started in order to circumvent the government's restrictions on the *Register,* brought on bankruptcy.

Bankrupt, deprived of his beloved estate at Botley and reduced to living as a rent payer in London, the circulation of the *Register* crippled by government duties, Cobbett reached a crisis in his life. One of his creditors, Sir Francis Burdett, whom Cobbett had recently attacked bitterly, generously waived his rights during the bankruptcy proceedings. Cobbett was further embarrassed in a libel trial a few months later (which he lost despite an unsavory attempt to shift the blame for a *Register* article to his son) by having to rely upon a friend to pay the damages. The record of his writings from 1820 onwards does not reveal that these years "were probably the happiest of his life" [38] but just the opposite. He generally stuck to the familiar themes, but while his tone was more strident, the criticism was less incisive. Still, although he had lost his influence among the workers, he did not relinquish all interest in them. He preferred to concentrate, however, upon such topics as parliamentary reform and Catholic emancipation.[39]

During these years he tried frantically to gain the support of the middle and upper classes for reform. Naturally, the inherently conservative nature of reform was stressed ("There is no need of *new schemes.*").[40] The landed magnates were warned that commercial interests would replace them, and the manufacturers were advised that in order to save themselves from the rapacious agricultural interests, they must join the reformers.[41] Obstinacy became a theme. "It was this same sort of obstinacy, that lost America; it was this same

[38] Quoted from Cole, *op. cit.,* p. 244.
[39] Cobbett's position regarding the industrial workers and the Catholics is explained in later chapters.
[40] P.R. (11/13/19), col. 384.
[41] P.R. (1/12/22), cols. 67 ff.; P.R. (7/22/26), cols. 229–30.

sort of obstinacy that finally cost Louis the 16th his life; it was the same sort of obstinacy that cost one Stuart his life and another his throne; it was the same sort of obstinacy that caused the South American Insurrection. It is *a refusal to yield in time;* and, in the meanwhile, a system of stern persecution of those who ask for reform." [42] But with increasing prosperity and the gradual emergence of a less reactionary Tory ministry in the 1820's, reform was at a low ebb.

England began to change rapidly in the 1820's. Peel's reforms at the Home Office contributed to a more humane penal code. William Huskisson at the Board of Trade lowered the tariff duties and started England on her free trade policy; one effect was lower prices to pay for necessities. Emancipation of the Dissenters and Catholics was carried, probably in the case of the latter, against the wishes of the majority of people in the country. In 1824 trade unions were made legal. Altogether, it was a momentous decade, particularly when combined with the British role in terminating the Quadruple Alliance and freeing South America.

But Cobbett was still plugging away at his old themes. Many of the important events of the time received little comment from him and only in the case of the Catholic Emancipation movement could he have been said to play a relatively important role. Here he gave bad advice to the Catholics, who wisely refused his pleas to identify their cause with radical reform. His own schemes: an attempt to unify all the agricultural classes against the boroughmongers, to take advantage of discontent among the urban workers, and to win election to parliament at Preston—all failed. Time had passed him by and we may agree with Halévy when he said that Cobbett had lost every shred of his influence over the masses by 1829.[43] Had it not been for the mighty events of the early 1830's,

[42] P.R. (4/15/20), cols. 334-35.
[43] Halévy, *The Liberal Awakening,* p. 281.

which contributed to his partial vindication, his life from 1820 would have been an anticlimax.

The last two chapters, in sketching an outline of Cobbett's development as a reformer, also permit us to see him as a person of shifting tactics but one who was also a prisoner of his idea of the System. For thirty years this doctrine shaped his writing. Major problems affecting the country—the political, economic and legal structure of the kingdom, church and state, social change—were all seen in its light. It is therefore possible to sift Cobbett's writing between 1806 and 1835 and discern this idea which so strongly influenced his career. Yet consideration should properly begin with the one area in which Cobbett is nearly universally acknowledged to have displayed remarkable ability: his journalistic efforts. Principally through the *Political Register,* but also in his other writings, Cobbett made his attacks on the System and discussed his ideal society. Also, it was the limitations upon the press imposed by the government which compelled him to tack frequently, alter course at times, to leave England on one occasion and even to serve time in jail. A journalist with unconventional opinions worked under a constant threat of persecution. It would therefore be futile to examine Cobbett's ideas on weighty issues without observing his role as a newspaper proprietor, editor and writer. Cobbett himself knew what the issue affecting the press was when he said ". . . the truth really is, that corruption must destroy the press, or the press will destroy corruption." [44]

[44] P.R. (2/27/10), col. 237.

IV
The press

In the beginning of the nineteenth century the independent press of Great Britain was subject to rigid restrictions, backed by laws of such severity and comprehensiveness, that it might seem surprising that political dissent could find a means of expression. To say conditions in England were mild by comparison with the practices of Continental despotisms, including that of Napoleon, is true but does not signify very much in terms of actual freedom. Englishmen took great pride in the fact that their press was "free" since it was not subject to censorship. Yet the laws on libel were stringent enough to give pause to the boldest. As Blackstone said, "The Liberty of the Press is, indeed, essential to the nature of a free State; but this consists in laying no previous restraints upon publication, and not in freedom from censure for criminal matters when published." [1] The law of seditious libel, for example, made it an offense to tend to bring into hatred or contempt or create dissatisfaction with the King, his heirs, the government and the administration of justice, or to excite the King's subjects to attempt by non-lawful means the alteration of church or state.[2] This law had been enforced more rigidly since the outbreak of war against France in 1793. There were many other weapons which the government could use against the printed page but none so awesome as this sword which hung over the heads of every writer and his publisher.

Independent publishing in that day of high costs and a small reading public required a man of courage. A publisher in opposition to the government could rely upon being harassed and possibly prosecuted. In the event of the latter, he could only hope that the jury would refuse to convict him. It is true that in our cruel century the punishment for dissent in William Cobbett's time seems light and the judicial procedure for determining guilt biased but still in accordance with existing legal forms. The totalitarianism of the mid-twentieth century has deprived us of the comfortable satisfaction indulged in by former historians when they wrote with horror of the repression which, in their opinion, characterized the early nineteenth century in England. On the other hand, the fate of Cobbett, the Hunts and especially Richard Carlile, was evidence of the intensity with which the law was enforced.[3] Those who guided the country were generally satisfied with conditions as they already existed and were prepared to resist to the limits of their considerable power those who were not. Cobbett's famous flight to America after the passage of the 1817 repressive legislation may appear cowardly when

[1] Quoted from W. H. Wickham, *The Struggle for the Freedom of the Press, 1819–1832*, London, George Allen and Unwin, Ltd., 1928, p. 15.

[2] *Ibid.*, p. 27.

[3] Leigh Hunt, the radical poet, and his brother served jail sentences for libel. Carlile was a persistent and courageous fighter for a free press and spent much of his adult life in jail.

it is contrasted with the behavior of those who stayed to fight it out with the government. Yet any poor man who turned down offers which would establish his fortune (as Cobbett did in 1800) in a day when the penalty for failure in business was terrible, indeed, was not lacking in spirit or fortitude. When the consequences of this refusal to become a lackey resulted in antagonizing a group of powerful politicians, who were firmly in control of the country's destiny, the deed becomes even more noteworthy.

In his attitude toward the two-headed evil inhibiting the publishing of political comment at the time—government intimidation by bribery and repression—Cobbett was uncompromising. His forthright attacks upon influence in either form sometimes rose above polemics and became an eloquent advocacy of a free press. At such moments Cobbett displayed a deeply-rooted concern for the cause of liberty, as well as an unexpected ability to conduct an argument on a somewhat impersonal and even a philosophic level. Basic to Cobbett's ardent championing of a free press was his insistence upon the ability of the people to choose correctly between truth and error if an argument was presented clearly and without favor. "Vice and folly, of whatever description, hate the light. Publicity is their natural enemy." This remark introduces a vigorous discussion which urges the free dissemination of news and proclaims the inutility of prosecutions unsupported by proof to sway public opinion.[4] Cobbett was trying to make truth the only criterion for libel as he felt that truth possessed sufficient rigor for this purpose, for where it was free, it always triumphed over falsehood. He was elated by the decision of Lord Ellenborough in the case of Carr, Hood and Sharpe, which insisted that free discussion of an author's work must be allowed so that liberty of the press might be a reality.

[4] P.R. (9/10/08), cols. 400–02. It was a similar spirit which moved him to compile *Cobbett's Parliamentary History of England* and *Cobbett's Parliamentary Debates*.

Cobbett wanted the principle of free discussion extended to political as well as literary comment, plus the right to criticize the author as well as the book. Hurt feelings were not regarded as evidence of a libel, for if a critic was unfair, the public would perceive it.[5] Even before his trial, Cobbett believed that the true function of the press was to expose weak and wicked government officials for he considered that to safeguard any person's talents from ridicule by legal means was dangerous to the public interest. Since he believed that *every* person in the country was deeply interested in the ability and honesty of men in office (a "radical" notion at that time!), they ought to be regularly informed upon this subject by a press which must of necessity remain free and unshackled. The extension of the libel laws to include "scandalous" and "malicious" statements as well as falsehood would create new problems, for the former are open to interpretation, whereas "all the world are agreed with respect to falsehood and truth."[6]

This belief in the capacity (and willingness) of men to make dispassionate judgments based on facts seems naïve today. It is indeed an understatement to note that Cobbett failed to comprehend the paradoxes of the human personality. Nor did he make much effort to do so, usually reacting negatively to new ideas. Although he lived at a time when increasing attention was being paid by romantic writers and the Benthamites to problems of the individual, Cobbett had little sympathy for social or intellectual trends although he did exhibit "romantic" characteristics at times. He generally thought in terms of society, not of its individual members. His mind was instinctual and prejudiced rather than rational and dispassionate. Fortunately, some of the prejudices of this complex

---

[5] P.R. (9/17/08), cols. 417–31. This principle is underlined by his remark that "from a free press discussion will flow; and, where discussion is free, *truth* will always prevail. . . ." P.R. (2/1/12), col. 129.

[6] P.R. (7/30/08), cols. 171–73.

man were healthy and led in the direction of freedom. His writings on the subject of the role of a periodical press in society form a case in point. Throughout almost all of his career, by precept and by example, Cobbett proclaimed and advanced in a significant manner the principle of freedom of discussion of all public issues.

The shield and the sword of the government was how Cobbett once referred to corruption and persecution respectively.[7] It was against the latter that he directed his strongest and most accurate fire. Early in his career and before he began to appear as a political radical and a regular opponent of the government on almost every issue, Cobbett spoke in opposition to any suggestion of exempting men in public office from newspaper censure. This was to become a consistent practice in a career which is often noted for its inconsistency. Living at a time when government was regarded as the prerogative of a small class of men whose lofty enactments were not to be criticized by anyone outside their select circle, Cobbett insisted that all people were concerned with the workings of government and had the right to be informed. In 1804 Cobbett saw fit to justify this right of criticism of public men by observing that to refuse it would not only make a mockery of the principle of the liberty of the press, but would also weaken the state as the people would no longer trust the newspapers.[8] However, he soon dropped this latter justification, saying that the liberty of the press had no definite meaning "unless it means the liberty of *freely publishing our opinions of the talents and character of all men in a public capacity. . . ."* [9] To have meaning, he asserted, freedom of the press included examining and exposing the actions of men entrusted with national affairs, and this necessarily included men of high rank. Freedom of the press, according to

---

[7] Amer. P.R. (1/27/16), col. 98.
[8] P.R. (12/2/04), cols. 1023–24.
[9] P.R. (8/20/08), col. 272.

Cobbett, did not consist of "publishing books upon planting, farriery, or fox-hunting. There is not a despot upon earth, who attempts to prevent such publications. In short, it is farcial to talk about freedom of the press, unless by it we mean the *right,* the acknowledged *legal right,* of freely expressing our opinions, be they what they may, *respecting the character and conduct of men in power;* and of stating anything, no matter what, if we can prove the *truth* of the statement.

"It is in the character and conduct of *men in power* that the public are interested . . . The babble of the day is of no public utility." [10]

Probably as a result of Windham's influence, he initially opposed publication of parliamentary debates as a violation of the spirit of the English government and even suggested halting newspaper publication in the event of a French invasion due to the confusion and alarm which might result from the printing of rumors and falsehood.[11] Less than two years later, the emerging radical was arguing that comments upon what was printed and published under the names of members of parliament should be judged by the standards of sedition and libel as the law was interpreted in other cases. If they were judged seditious or libelous, then the writer should be punished by the house of parliament which was concerned. As long as standing orders forbidding comment on speeches were not enforced and while admission to the gallery of the House of Commons was sold at a high price, Cobbett felt that there should not be a restriction upon the right to comment upon publications thus produced.[12] Ultimately, while acknowledging the privilege of immunity for words spoken in parliament, Cobbett reiterated his opposition to allowing this immunity to be extended to written reports,

10 P.R. (2/4/09), cols. 183–84.
11 P.R. (3/12 to 3/19/03), col. 385; P.R. (10/15/03), col. 544.
12 P.R. (5/18/05), cols. 707–08.

since a person being attacked could not publish a reply. Hence, a member of parliament might ruin anyone against whom he had a grudge.[13]

Fines and imprisonment were not the only means which the government possessed to break the spirit of an independent publisher. The Post Office might delay forwarding an unfriendly newspaper or periodical or substitute another publication before it reached its destination. Extortion by individuals inside the Post Office and the publication of a competing newspaper were routine methods of harassment. Even those publishers who were generally favorable to the government were victimized in this way. Cobbett felt compelled to protest against these practices very early in his career.[14] This protest concerning what was taken for granted by many was not unique, but it did serve to make Cobbett a marked man. The next few years witnessed an intensifying attack upon almost all aspects of the government's activity and the issue of a free press became a chord which was frequently struck.

Clearly Cobbett was becoming too dangerous to endure for a ministry headed in 1809 by the lackluster Spencer Perceval. The ultra-Tories of this government, few of whom were marked by any real ability, did not need the goading of a hostile journalist to emphasize their difficulties at home and abroad. With Napoleon shattering England's allies in the field and widespread domestic distress, they were not in the mood to accept the increasingly pointed criticism which Cobbett directed at them. Taking advantage of his most violent pronouncement to date, the condemnation of the flogging of five English militiamen by German mercenary troops after the former had complained about a stoppage in their pay, the

13 P.R. (5/18/13), cols. 676–79.
14 A.R. (11/20 to 11/27/02), cols. 673–85. See also *The History of the Times, "The Thunderer" in the Making, 1785–1841,* Vol. I, New York, The Macmillan Company, 1935, pp. 96–105.

ministry charged him with seditious libel.[15] Cobbett was brought to trial by the procedure of ex-officio informations in which a special jury chosen out of forty-eight men appointed by the Master of the Crown was substituted for the grand jury. This technique allowed the Attorney General to delay indefinitely or abandon altogether the proceedings of the trial and the judgment as well. Also, the accused had to pay the costs, even if adjudged innocent. It was a splendid technique for intimidating a journalist.

Cobbett was not cast in the role of a martyr. When there seemed to be a possibility before his trial that he might make his peace with the government, he appealed for a unified country "without considering who is minister . . . Those, therefore, who, at Ely, and elsewhere, have quelled the spirit of mutiny among the Local-Militia, are certainly entitled to the thanks of the country. None can be pleased to see his countrymen flogged; but, when, as in this case, they have *voluntarily* entered, and that, too, for the sake of *a bounty*, I say, as I said before, 'flog them', if they do not abide by their bargain and strictly obey their officers." [16] Cobbett's equivocation failed and he was sentenced on July 9, 1810 to two years' imprisonment and a fine of a thousand pounds.

The lot of the prisoner in Newgate at this time was similar

15 The offending remarks ran as follows: "Well done, Lord Castlereagh! This is just what it was thought your plan would produce. Well said, Mr. Huskisson! It really was not without reason that you dwelt, with so much earnestness, upon the great utility of the *foreign* troops, whom Mr. Wardle appeared to think of no utility at all . . . He little imagined, that they might be made the means of compelling Englishmen to submit to that sort of *discipline*, which is so conducive to the producing in them a disposition to defend the country, at the risk of their lives . . . *Five hundred lashes* each! Aye, that is right! Flog them; flog them; flog them! They deserve it, and a great deal more. They deserve a flogging at every meal-time. 'Lash them daily, lash them daily.' What, shall the rascals dare to *mutiny*, and that, too, when the German Legion is so near at hand! Lash them, lash them, lash them! They deserve it. O, Yes; they merit a double-tailed cat. Base dogs! What, mutiny for the sake of the price of a knapsack! Lash them! Flog them!" P.R. (7/1/09), col. 993.

16 P.R. (7/29/09), col. 124.

to circumstances which surrounded those undergoing exile in Siberia during the reigns of the last Tsars of Russia. Persons who could afford to pay lived relatively comfortable lives with few restrictions save the constantly irksome captivity. Cobbett himself enjoyed private quarters with food, books and personal items sent in from outside. Friends and family constantly were allowed to visit him, and his youngest son was conceived during his incarceration. This was all due to Cobbett's being on personally friendly terms with the Sheriff of London, plus the fact that he was able to continue his publishing activities from jail while his wife and sons managed the farm into which the family had moved several years earlier. Still, it is understandable that Cobbett's restive spirit would be cramped. The disruption of his formerly happy family life had a traumatic effect upon Cobbett's sense of humor and intensified his proclivity for adopting an immoderate technique in argument. He said later that without his imprisonment and fine he might not have exerted himself so strenuously on behalf of freedom.[17] Characteristically, upon being released from Newgate, he promised to publish the facts relating to his prosecution on the last page of every issue of the *Political Register* for as long as he lived and suggested that this page be cut out and pasted on walls or other convenient locations. Also, characteristically, this scheme lasted only a few months.

Although Cobbett railed at government efforts to bribe the newspaper proprietors just as he did at attempts to intimidate them, he reserved some of his harshest invective for the "base" publishers who allowed their columns to be purchased by the government or by wealthy individuals anxious to present their side of an argument.[18] Incorruptible himself, Cobbett

[17] See his comments in *Advice to Young Men,* paragraph 301 and P.R. (4/25/18), col. 482.
[18] For example, see P.R. (5/7 to 5/14/03), cols. 730–31, and P.R. (4/11/07), cols. 546–47.

constantly referred to a "kept press" and on occasion indicated the rewards accruing to those proprietors, not only of newspapers but of magazines and reviews as well, who followed a line favorable to the ministry or allowed the government to insert its notices into their columns. Cobbett was adamant about this position ever since he began publishing, but his castigation of venal publishers in 1807, two years before the soldier flogging incident, reflects his increasing radical position. "If therefore there ever was in the world a thing completely perverted from its original design and tendency, it is the press of England; which, instead of enlightening, does, as far as it has any power, keep the people in ignorance; which, instead of cherishing notions of liberty, tends to the making of the people slaves; and which, instead of being their guardian, is the most efficient instrument in the hands of all those who oppress, or who wish to oppress them." Without such a press the people would be better off—not being misled by falsehoods and left to their own natural conclusions, the public would make judgments on the basis of events, with every man forming his opinion according to what he saw and felt. "It is by the semblance of freedom that men are most effectually enslaved." [19] It is not surprising that, for a man of such uncompromising standards, the corrupt press of the country stimulated his hatred.

> Have you ever seen . . . a parcel of *toads*, assembled very thickly, on the surface of muddy, stagnant and stinking pool; communing with one another, and reciprocating their filthy breathings and spawning. You have also seen a large stone, or a brick-bat, flung, suddenly, souse into the midst of such a Collective Wisdom. You have seen how the loathsome devils, some diving, others attempting to leap away, others turned on their backs and showing their nasty white bellies, and all croaking out their alarm, and emitting their poisonous matter . . .

[19] P.R. (4/11/07), col. 549.

imagine the scene now before your eyes, and you have a true picture of the state of the reptiles of the London Press. . . .[20]

Specifically, Cobbett loathed the venality of the press, its subservience to authority and frequent gross distortions of news. Especially in its early days, Cobbett's *Political Register,* with its abundance of factual data, its aggressive, manly style, and above all, its incorruptibility, provided a striking contrast to the average political journal of the time. It has been truly said that "The implications of the word 'journalist' in the eighteenth century were not pleasant. A journalist, by common conception, was a writer of paragraphs written in, or against, the interest of a political party or personage." [21] Cobbett's egocentrism and enormous self-confidence helped to prevent him from being the tool of anyone. These qualities, which, especially in later life, were to provoke in others amusement or disgust, were the very ones which enabled him to overcome all obstacles and to raise the level of periodical journalism. Only a person absolutely convinced not merely of the righteousness of his views but also of his ability to discuss a wide variety of subjects with greater accuracy than anyone, living or dead, could have surmounted the temptations and the threats which were the lot of such a maverick journalist.

Cobbett's contempt for the vast majority of his press contemporaries was displayed, therefore, in terms which scarcely knew bounds. He could be quite specific. Among other sins, he accused them of helping to cause the War of 1812,[22] of printing misleading information relating to the king's health,[23] of ignoring the sensational case of the Bishop of Clogher,[24] of printing falsely optimistic accounts of the Peninsula War,[25]

20 P.R. (1/11/23), col. 87. The words "Collective Wisdom" were also frequently applied sarcastically by Cobbett to the House of Commons.
21 *History of the Times,* p. 16.
22 *Norfolk Yeoman's Gazette* (2/8/23), pp. 3–4.
23 P.R. (11/21/10), col. 970.
24 P.R. (7/27/22), cols. 218 ff.
25 P.R. (8/10/11), cols. 144–46.

and of supporting for purely commercial reasons the South American countries struggling to free themselves from Spain.[26] Conforming to his conviction that on all important issues there was no real difference between Whigs and Tories, Cobbett referred to the *Morning Chronicle* and the *Courier* as "those sparrers in double–padded gloves; those hirelings, who appear to be so desperately angry with one another, and yet who, at bottom, have the same object in view, namely to support a tyrannical Borough–faction, who are able to make the nation pay the expence of Mr. Stewart and Mr. Perry's riding through the streets in chariots, instead of being, as nature intended them to be, employed in the sweeping of those streets. . . ."[27] His attacks on the *Edinburgh Review,* which he regarded as having been established by place seekers and its rival, the *Quarterly Review,* whose contributors did not sign their names to articles and who used the hated editorial plural pronoun, showed the impartiality of his antagonisms as well as his immoderation and frequent lack of proportion. Cobbett was too great an individualist and a partisan to shelter behind this device:

> The mysterious WE that they make use of, give men an idea that what they are reading, proceeds from a little circle of wise men, who have been sitting and deliberating upon what they shall put forth. Each paragraph appears to be a sort of little order in council; a solemn decision of a species of literary conclave. If the public could know how the thing is managed; if they could but know what wretches those are from whom these paragraphs proceed; if they could but know how a newspaper concern is in general conducted; if they could but once *see* all the rabble-rout of proprietors, and hear their bickerings and quarrellings about the profits; if they could once see and hear these, the delusion would vanish.[28]

26 P.R. (12/20/23), col. 709.
27 P.R. (1/3/18), col. 2.
28 P.R. (2/8/33), cols. 370–71.

The *Gentleman's Magazine*, controlled by the church and "as stupid as it is slavish . . . ," seemed to Cobbett to have been written in the time of Laud or Jeffries. His attacks upon the *Times* and its proprietors lasted through all of his career and are liable to be discovered in his writings on almost any subject. They were largely unreciprocated, but were no less virulent for that. The important contributions of the *Times* to the development of a free press was unnoticed by Cobbett and he scarcely mentions its great editor, Barnes, who started with the paper in 1817.[29] Only after 1830, when his energies were monopolized by the struggle for parliamentary reform did he declare a truce with many of his rivals and sink all private considerations for the sake of passage of the Reform Bill.

This overwhelming disdain for the weakness of others reflects more than Cobbett's usual self-righteousness. Here was a situation in which he was clearly and demonstrably superior to the majority of his contemporaries. He was right, he knew it, and he was therefore anxious to press his advantage and constantly remind everyone of his virtue. While his perception of the necessity of a free press accounts for some of the violence which Cobbett manifested in attacking corruption and persecution, he had a need to be justified in this area. Scorned or ignored concerning other matters, on the subject of a free press Cobbett had to be listened to. He was helping to fight the battle for those less courageous than himself. Although others may have ultimately done more to achieve a free press, Cobbett was the most vocal of this small disparate band. For once, the future was on his side.

Accurate as Cobbett may have been about the over-all conception of a free press, details of his argument betrayed him. For example, writing from Newgate he asked a correspondent why he referred to Greece and Rome for proofs that would

29 See P.R. (6/13/18), cols. 682 ff., for further examples of how Cobbett paid his respects to his fellow publishers and their papers.

support an argument in favor of this cause when the whole history of the liberty of the press belonged to England. "What did the Greeks and Romans know about printing? Pisistratus and Socrates and Demosthenes and Cicero are fine sounding names; they are very well calculated to make a noise in a sentence; but all these men put together did not know so much about the Liberty of the Press as my Printers boy does." Similarly, he asks why his correspondent did not turn to Lilburne or Tooke, or to Lord Erskine or Sir Francis Burdett (the two were still friends) for his mottoes, instead of to Virgil.[30] As usual, Cobbett, when seeking sanction from the past, saw no reason to consult foreigners.

Although this controversial figure was involved in several newspaper and periodical ventures, his major vehicle of expression was the *Political Register*. Cobbett's intensely personal journalism was best suited to a weekly paper where he could be free of the type of pressure involved in the operation of a daily. Publication once a week also allowed him to express himself forcibly about current news yet did not require the systematic thought involved in writing a book. In fact, several of his best known books, including *Rural Rides* and *Paper Against Gold,* appeared originally as articles in the *Register.*[31] In the very first issue of the *Register* he stated that the object of the paper was to support the king, "whom God has commanded me to honour and obey . . . ," and listed the following ten headings under which the contents of the paper were to be arranged. None of the headings were consistently adhered to, and items numbered 1, 6, 7 and 8 were eventually discarded altogether.

[30] P.R. (2/23/11), cols. 450–51.

[31] Cobbett's essays into daily journalism were futile, as witness the short-lived *Cobbett's Evening Post* of 1820. This paper, intended to compete with dailies supporting the two political parties, does not display Cobbett at his best and resulted in little save the hastening of his bankruptcy.

1. Abridged proceedings of parliament.
2. Short accounts of the actions of the French government, particularly if they affected England.
3. All State papers (translated, if necessary).
4. Discussions of government policy on a "fair and free" basis.
5. Selected news from foreign countries.
6. No advertisements.
7. News of major promotions of the peerage, statesmen and officers in the armed forces, taken from the *London Gazette*.
8. News of births, deaths and marriages concerning members of the nobility and of parliament.
9. Daily prices of 3% stocks, plus occasional reports of other financial news.
10. Prices of corn and bread in London.[32]

It was not long before the birth and death announcements and the weather news disappeared from its columns and the *Register* became almost exclusively a journal of political opinion. The practice of reprinting public papers was stopped in 1814 as Cobbett, now a confirmed adherent of radical reform, wanted to devote more space in the *Register* to his own writings in order to combat that part of the press which he deemed hostile to liberty.[33] Yet in 1806, Cobbett boasted that the *Register* was the only paper to contain all the important documents relating to international affairs. Stating that the major source of error concerning the past is the lack of available documentation, by providing all the authentic documents he was doing his best to prevent errors concerning the present.[34] Here we see the essentially plain man with his concern for facts as well as his persistent faith in the self-evidence of truth and the ability of people to recognize it.

The change from a newspaper to a journal of opinion

[32] P.R. (1/16/02), cols. 2–4. "The four last-mentioned heads are admitted, not as subjects of tittle-tattle, but as facts connected with history and political economy." It is amusing to speculate upon how the radical Cobbett would have treated information under items 7 and 8 had he remained faithful to his original plan.

[33] P.R. (1/22/14), cols. 97–102.

[34] P.R. (1/4/06), col. 21.

reflects Cobbett's growing belief that the liberties of England were menaced by a boroughmonger-fundholder conspiracy which controlled parliament, the church, the royal family and almost all of the press. The duty of combating it seemed to fall almost entirely upon himself, and this brings out one of Cobbett's less attractive qualities: his lack of generosity toward others engaged in the same task. His tendency to view himself as the only honest man in his field made Cobbett unappreciative of the struggle which other publishers were waging on behalf of individual freedom (including freedom of the press). He was for this reason an inaccurate reporter on the state of the press. Not only did he see conditions in simple black and white terms, which did not do justice to some of the major publishers such as Perry of the *Morning Chronicle,* but he nearly ignored his fellow radicals, especially Leigh Hunt and his *Examiner.*

A casual perusal of the table of contents of each bound volume of the *Register* indicates that Cobbett used the journal as the most important weapon in his attacks upon the government of the time. Yet he did not treat exclusively of great political and economic problems. The *Register* was a consistent source of irritation to the government in many petty ways. In February, 1809, in place of the usual motto at the head of the paper, he began printing the names of those individuals who had been granted pensions by the government, together with the amounts of the pensions. In the same year he furnished considerable space to French accounts of the battle of Talavera, in a manner which clearly showed his disbelief in official government reports. Despite this continual needling of authority, Cobbett seldom came to grief as a result of his sometimes violent, often humorous, thrusts.

He described the *Political Register* as a work "from the pages of which every thing calculated to amuse the frivolous or to entertain the indolent is sedulously excluded; which are occupied entirely with dry political matter, requiring seriousness and reflection in the perusal to render it at all valuable, and, not aided by the sprightliness of wit or the embellishments of style, but, in its unenticing garb, addressed directly to the understanding and the reason . . . ," [35] but the actual contents reveal a vigorous, forceful manner of expression, abounding with homey, pithy phrases. This is true despite Cobbett's well known habit of digression which often obscured his main point. Like Dickens, Cobbett had the gift of creating reality at the stroke of a pen, and some of the characters who people his writings, Sir Giles Jolterhead, Lord Tyger (the hanging judge), and Mr. Humbug, really live during the few occasions when Cobbett allows us to meet them. But by the year 1828 Cobbett displayed increasing irritability and egocentrism and the quality of his writings declined. Age, political disappointment and, perhaps, personal problems had taken their toll. During the final years of his life, his own contributions to the *Register* seem to grow more shrill and less interesting and his last books do not measure up to the literary standards which he achieved in *Advice to Young Men* or *Cottage Economy.*

The passage of the Six Acts in 1819 effectively curbed the famous *Twopenny Trash,* the cheap edition of the *Register,* which had won a favorable reception among the working class and raised Cobbett's prestige among the urban laborers to its highest point. These Draconian laws also forced Cobbett to increase the price of the *Register* to sixpence in order to circumvent the terms of the specific act which applied to newspapers. This naturally cut circulation and never again was Cobbett to enjoy much influence among the industrial working class. The *Register* underwent other changes. In 1821 gardening information began to appear and in the following year Cobbett resumed publication of market prices. In 1825 the columns of the *Register* were opened to advertising. These changes in format were evidently designed to extend the

[35] P.R. (1/5/05), col. 1.

appeal of the paper beyond those interested in "dry political matter."

The question of Cobbett's personal courage in fighting for a free press has been touched upon earlier in this chapter. In 1817 at the height of his influence he did not wait for the government to clap him into jail but fled to America following the passage of the repressive legislation which was promulgated after a stone or bullet broke the window of the coach in which the Prince Regent was riding. Despite his comparison of this flight to similar hurried journeys by Sidney, Paine and Voltaire [36] he was heavily criticized, particularly by the radical publisher, Thomas Wooler.[37] Cobbett's reasoning here was identical with his attitude a few years later when he conformed to the newspaper tax while Richard Carlile and other publishers were going to prison—that he could do more good in publishing even under restricted circumstances than in jail as a martyr. There is no need to doubt his courage; it is simply that Cobbett's belief in action did not allow him to seek martyrdom himself or truly to appreciate it as a virtue in others. The passage of the Six Acts made Cobbett proceed circumspectly for a time, but the replacement of ex-Prime Minister Addington (Lord Sidmouth) as Home Secretary by Sir Robert Peel in January, 1822 and the consequent relaxation of the press laws resulted in a style which gradually became more explicit.

Despite the unmeasured abuse frequently portioned out to those who were prominent in society, Cobbett was contemptuous of anyone who was provoked into a legal action by satire and ridicule. His belief in the ability of people to judge wisely when confronted with the facts of a situation, coupled with his self-confidence, allowed Cobbett to feel that the courts should not be used to decide such disputes. From bitter personal experience he cited the case of Dr. Benjamin

36 P.R. (10/4/17), cols. 804–05.
37 See the *Black Dwarf* (3/12/17), p. 112 and (2/29/17), p. 7.

Rush, the Philadelphia physician, accusing him of being unable to defend himself in print and therefore having recourse to lawyers. "Of all the acts of which a man can be guilty, none is so mean, none is so base, none is so truly detestable, as that of seeking, through the law, vengeance for a literary defeat." [38] He was especially critical of those writers who went to court in order to avenge themselves against the sallies of their rivals. "He who uses the press ought to defend himself solely with the press," remarked Cobbett, who himself set a good example by making light of the savage attacks upon him by the cartoonist Gillray.[39] His confidence in the correctness of his own position allowed him to adopt an attitude of forbearance toward most attacks by competitors. During these years he delighted in a fierce give-and-take and regarded the use of law by writers as an indication that a cause was weak.

As for those who claimed that the licentiousness of the press exceeded former times and therefore should be regulated, Cobbett replied sharply in a manner which indicated his own extensive reading. Suggesting that his opponents examine the writings of Swift, Pope and Gay, Cobbett cited specific works in support of his argument. He called licentiousness a very convenient word which allowed multiple interpretation, and then said, in a revealing passage, that the natural boundary is truth, for "We all know how to distinguish between *truth* and falsehood; but as to where liberty ends and licentiousness begins, who is able to determine that?" [40] Elsewhere, to counteract charges of libelousness against the press, Cobbett quoted Pope, whom he admired tremendously, and cited Swift and Milton.[41] In the early days of the *Register*, Cobbett was fond

---

[38] P.R. (7/30/08), col. 170. On his first trip to America, Cobbett not only condemned Rush's belief in blood-letting and mercurial purges as treatments for yellow fever but attacked him personally. The resulting trial for libel hastened his departure for England in 1800.

[39] P.R. (8/20/08), cols. 269–71. See also references to Gillray, P.R. (9/10/08), col. 402 and (2/17/10), col. 235.

[40] P.R. (3/6/11), col. 548.

[41] P.R. (2/4/09), cols. 185–92.

of illustrating his lead article with a quotation from Rousseau, Dryden, Cowper, or Pope on the masthead. His reading was wide, yet critical, and he demonstrated his strong preferences. Unfortunately, this practice gradually ceased after his imprisonment, which embittered Cobbett and changed the character of the *Register*.

The three categories into which the majority of Cobbett's writings about the newspaper and periodical press fall are the function of journalism in society, the attitude which the government assumed toward it and his own impressions of his fellow publishers. There seems to have been little change in his opinions on any of these matters for the last thirty years of his career. There are not the fluctuations, real or simply apparent, that make Cobbett the butt of innumerable jokes over other issues. The *Political Register* was as consistent in its opposition to exempting men in public office from criticism or in its firm support of liberty of the press as it was in its personal, partisan approach or in its incorruptibility. By example alone its service to the cause of a free press was considerable. It helps compensate for Cobbett's insistence upon his own solitary virtue in a field dominated by venality; a point of view which ignored the efforts of Carlile, Hetherington and many others who strived for a free press. The wide range of readers must also be remembered. As Hazlitt said: "The Reformers read him when he was a Tory, and the Tories read him now that he is a Reformer." [42] A born farmer, Cobbett made himself into a first-class journalist as well, demonstrating that integrity and success in this field were not incompatible. Unfortunately, skill in publishing and domestic agriculture did not ensure competence when dealing with other matters of importance.

[42] Quoted from A. M. D. Hughes (ed.), *Cobbett Selections, with Hazlitt's Essay and Other Critical Estimates*, Oxford, Oxford University Press, 1923, p. 4.

V
Political theory and practical politics

English political thought is noted for its empirical quality and for its tendency to eschew abstractions. Although exceptions exist, academic discussions about concepts unrelated to specific situations have never played the role in Great Britain that they have elsewhere. In contradistinction to economic theory, which has been a field in which Englishmen from Adam Smith to John Maynard Keynes have instructed the world, the English have been content to solve political problems pragmatically. Most of the classics of English political philosophy have been produced in response to conditions arising from actual events and bear this stamp throughout. The "great debate" of the late eighteenth century between Burke and Paine was couched in the language of political theory and displayed, in an exceptionally searching manner, the basic attitudes of the opponents to the large questions which this type of philosophy seeks to answer. Yet, of course, this dialogue about the nature of man and the state was provoked by the reality of the French Revolution, and the immediate reaction between stimulus and response may account for the lucid expression of these men.

Just as an interest in political economy was a characteristic of Cobbett's time, this period witnessed an increase in purely political writings as well. Some were lofty disquisitions in the manner, although not the spirit, of Hobbes. William Godwin's *Political Justice* is an example. Most did not deal with first principles but instead were concerned with matters which lent themselves to a ready application. Cobbett's own writings indicate that theory was not his line. One is more apt to encounter the dogmatic assertion than the cautious hypothesis. For example, "Good government is known from bad government by this infallible test: that, under the former the labouring people are well fed and well clothed, and, under the latter, they are badly fed and badly clothed." [1] Yet in *Advice to Young Men,* one of his most significant works, Cobbett sketched a basic "theoretical" viewpoint—one which was definitely "ad hoc" and supported an already determined point of view. He held that at one time men possessed the earth's treasures in proportion to the skill and strength of each person. Civil society arose when, in order to secure mutual protection, the land was divided with each man's being allotted a share of his own and a legal code established in order to safeguard this right of private property. If the people become worse off than they were in the state of nature, then the compact must be dissolved and the rights they enjoyed in the former state returned, for society was formed in order to benefit everyone. To insure that the privileges for which they gave up the state of nature would be respected, it was necessary for the people to take part in making the laws by which they were governed. The right to vote and to sit in

[1] P.R. (5/31/23), col. 514.

parliament was to extend to all except women, minors, criminals and the insane.[2] This is, of course, a statement of his mature views on suffrage, after he had been converted to the idea of one man, one vote by Cartwright in 1816. Yet even in justifying a predetermined point of view, Cobbett was not at home with political theory. Uncomfortable in the role of theoretician, he more frequently chose to support his views by tracing the course of English history. In this also he was not successful, partly because of his own lack of knowledge of the subject (although he seems to have read Hume and Robertson, then considered the two great authorities) but mainly owing to his violent prejudices, which rendered his judgments grotesque. Almost all that seemed necessary to say about the constitution and the liberties of the people had been said, in his opinion, in the Middle Ages. Magna Carta, for example, was a confirmation of the existing law of the land.[3]

While Cobbett believed that it was necessary to introduce new legislation from time to time, the basic problem of Englishmen over the centuries was to preserve their liberty against encroachment. This particularly applied after the Glorious Revolution, which resulted in the corruption of political life (along with the advent of The Bank of England and The National Debt). It is impossible to say how much Cobbett might have been influenced by the elderly Major Cartwright, who believed that annual parliaments and a universal franchise were characteristic of Anglo-Saxon times. Cartwright was evidently a lovable old man and one of the few reformers with whom Cobbett could get along for any considerable period. It was Cartwright who, in 1816, persuaded a radically inclined Cobbett to support universal male suffrage, a circumstance which contributed strongly to his popularity among the workers at the time. Like Cartwright, Cobbett

[2] *Advice to Young Men,* paragraphs 336 through 340.
[3] P.R. (5/27/09), col. 804.

claimed to venerate what he believed to be the ancient heritage of English liberty. This is what enabled him to insist at all times that he did not desire innovation but simply a return to what he imagined to be ancient practices that had been discarded by dishonest politicians: manhood suffrage, representative assemblies, taxation only after universal consent.

This intense feeling for the past (as he saw it) was a trait which influenced Cobbett deeply. However, it was not the same as Burke's sublime mysticism. Both men felt strongly about the values of ancient institutions and the necessity of preserving their integrity. Yet Cobbett, although claiming to detest Bentham and his followers, applied what were essentially utilitarian standards and did not accept these institutions for their own sake as Burke did. He was convinced that monarchy and parliament were fundamentally good because they had worked for his ancestors and would be just as valuable in his day if only the political and financial evils which afflicted the country could be swept away. The conservative thought of the time, formulated by Burke and implemented by such figures as Eldon, considered that society had evolved gradually over the centuries and must not be interfered with for fear of dire consequences. "Whatever is, is right" might have been the motto of this school. It was this belief which led to the Duke of Wellington's famous defense of the constitution as it stood in 1830. Cobbett, although an upholder of the past to such an extent that his enthusiasm frequently distorted its reality, believed that reform was necessary because a once happy England had been corrupted. He did not desire the glacial change permitted by Burke but insisted rather upon a restoration of English institutions in all their former purity. This reformer was in the position of being, in effect, more reactionary than his opponents and it is necessary to remember his motives in examining his specific proposals for change.

Comparing the condition of England in his time with its former state, Cobbett noted that "We were a nation famed throughout the world not less for the goodness of our dress, the plenty and solid quantity of our food, the decency, neatness and comfort of our household staff and our dwellings, than for our freedom and our valour. English hospitality; the roast-beef of Old England; the Englishman's beer and beef and the Frenchman's soup-meagre and frogs . . . were common, proverbial sayings." [4] This happy situation, he argued, had been destroyed by the products of the Glorious Revolution: paper money, high taxes and a large national debt, plus the resulting political corruption. The new government was characterized by acts dispensing with trial by jury and by the establishment of barracks throughout the country. Thus Cobbett could persistently claim that ". . . I have had too much opportunity of studying men and things to be led astray by any *wild theories about liberty* . . . I want to see no *innovation* in England. All I wish and all I strive for is *The Constitution of England,* undefiled by corruption." [5]

Nor did Cobbett desire any social leveling. Less than two years before he died and long after he had adopted a belief in universal male suffrage and had subjected the Church, the Royal Family and other established institutions to scathing attacks, he could claim that he never endeavored to teach the "ridiculous" doctrine of equality of rank or estate.[6] Dozens of times he insisted that he did not wish for anything new and attempted to assure the aristocracy that its position would be safe. "As naturally as the sparks fly upwards, the mass of any people will prefer superiors to equals in all cases where trust is to be reposed and where their choice is free." The superiors would include men of both fortune and talent.[7] The

4 P.R. (5/9/18), col. 509.
5 P.R. (4/15/09), col. 550. Similar avowals may be found in P.R. (5/16/07), col. 859; P.R. (2/15/17), col. 211; P.R. (11/13/19), col. 384; P.R. (11/22/34), col. 475. This is a long way from his declaration "REVOLU-TION . . . is nothing more than ALTERATION," *The Porcupine* (2/16/01), p. 3, but after 1806 Cobbett does adhere to his contention.
6 P.R. (8/24/33), col. 458.
7 P.R. (11/1/17), col. 937.

picture which he drew of an enlightened Lord Lieutenant
on the style of the Duke of Richmond, just and impartial in
administering the law, an agricultural improver and a pa-
tron of field sports, was certainly appealing to him. He was
definitely out of sympathy with Bentham's republicanism.[8]
If the great families of the kingdom would join with the
people in a program of political reform, the grievances of the
people against them would be forgotten and the traditional
pattern of social distinctions would prevail. Yet blind, un-
critical adulation of the aristocracy was not a part of Cobbett's
character. His ideal was the type of enlightened nobleman
just mentioned: a man of such outstanding character and
ability that his tenants and laborers could defer to him without losing their self-respect. Cobbett's followers could not
appreciate these distinctions and this is one reason why he
was not a greater working class leader.

The aristocracy was only a minor consideration in his insistence that while parliament must be reformed, it must not
be mutilated to conform to some novel scheme. The constitution for which Hampden and Sidney died was still fundamentally sound and its worth was testified to by the actions
of the Americans in preserving the Magna Carta, Bill of
Rights, habeas corpus and English legal forms after their
separation. Cobbett never told the people that there could
be a better government than King, Lords and Commons. For
him, the real innovators were in the boroughmonger government.

> I know of no enemy of reform and of the happiness of the
> country so great as that man, who would persuade you that
> we possess *nothing good,* and that *all* must be torn to pieces.
> There is no principle, no precedent, no regulations (except
> as to mere matter of detail), favourable to freedom, which
> is not to be found in the Laws of England or in the example

8 P.R. (11/13/19), col. 384. Bentham was regarded by Cobbett as a
dreamer with impractical and dangerous ideas.

of our Ancestors. Therefore, I say we may ask for, and we want *nothing new.* We have great constitutional laws and principles, to which we are immovably attached. We want *great alteration,* but we want *nothing new.* Alteration, modification to suit the times and circumstances; but the great principles ought to be and must be, the same, or else confusion will follow.[9]

What, then, was Cobbett's image of the good society? As we might expect, it was not one which exalted political liberty as the highest good. "What is independence to a wretched being, whose dinner is an earthen pipkin of chestnuts and whose bed is a handful of rushes, heath or stubble?"[10] Or, addressing the "Working People of the Whole Kingdom" on the subject of parliamentary reform.

> Now I am for no visionary, no fanciful, no refined benefit; no mental advantage; nothing so very fine that we can neither see, hear, feel, nor touch it; and, if it could be proved that this reform would bring no real, substantial, aye, and bodily, good to the millions of the people, I should say, at once, that it was good for nothing. The *words* rights, liberty, freedom, and the like, the *mere words,* are not worth a straw; and very frequently they serve as a cheat. What is the sound of liberty to a man who is compelled to work constantly and who is still, in spite of his toil, his vigilance, his frugality, half naked and half starved! In such a case the word liberty is abused: such a man is a slave, whatever he may call himself . . .[11]

This passage reveals Cobbett in a bitter mood, after most of his life's plans had failed and before his disappointment was somewhat assuaged by election to the reformed parliament. The reference to poverty visiting even the frugal and hard working testifies to Cobbett's refusal to blame the plight of the workers upon carelessness or lack of industry. But the statement as a whole has a truculent, class-conscious tone,

[9] P.R. (11/2/16), cols. 454–55.
[10] P.R. (1/4/12), col. 12.
[11] *Two Penny Trash* (5/1/31), cols. 241–42.

which is more appropriate to a later decade. Still, it does reveal what Cobbett thought about an ideal society.

Tracing in detail Cobbett's specific views about the role which government was to play means encountering difficulties, for he was inconsistent in what he wrote. At times, particularly when excited by economic injustice, he could demand an active, paternalistic role for the state.[12] On other occasions he was almost Gladstonian in his desire to use government only to remove injustices and not as part of a positive program of reform.[13] Although he lived in an age when many placed faith in legislation to banish evil, Cobbett believed that men had problems which no law could reach. His basic philosophy forbade talk of building a new Jerusalem. Very much a materialist in evaluating any plan for reform, his own wants were simple. He expected all those whom he desired to help to have a similar outlook. A way of life consisting of hard work, rough fare and simple pleasures was a blessing and not something to escape from. Cobbett did not live long enough to observe the skilled workers demand and receive a standard of living approximating that of the middle class. If he had done so, he would surely have subjected them to the same scathing denunciations which he used against the tenant farmers who attempted to live like aristocrats. Since he was not sure in his own mind, now swayed by evidence of suffering to claim an active role for government, now captivated by his own romantic notions of what was ideal, Cobbett could not evolve a clear picture of what part government should play in the lives of its citizens.

With reference to the more tangible questions of the form which government was to take and the related topics of election procedures and political parties, Cobbett could be more explicit. An episode which helped to shape his thinking in this respect more than anything else was the Honiton

---

12 P.R. (5/31/23), col. 522.
13 P.R. (6/23/21), col. 809.

election of 1806. Honiton was a borough in Devonshire whose representative had accepted a sinecure and thus was compelled to stand for re-election. Cobbett vowed to oppose him and although he withdrew his candidacy in favor of the sailor, Lord Cochrane, his experiences at Honiton made a profound impression. Witnessing those eligible to cast ballots in the borough openly selling their votes shook his belief that the country might be regenerated by reform operating through the existing parliamentary system and made him realize that corruption was even wider in extent than he had thought. The ills of the country were not confined to fiscal abuses and a few politicians at Westminster. The ponderously moralistic tone of his writings at this point, with their biblical references and promises never to receive public money for whatever services he might render testifies to his shock.[14] A political structure which could accomplish what he thought England needed began to emerge in his writings.

Although Cobbett was certainly not a man who adhered rigidly to any statement of principles, a basic point of view developed after 1806. The type of government which Cobbett held desirable consisted of a hereditary monarchy, a House of Lords constituted in the traditional manner, and a House of Commons chosen by the people. While tempering his harsh early criticisms of a republican form of government,[15] he never recommended anything but a monarchy for England. The ruler would exercise his prerogatives in the interest of the people, whose welfare should be his major concern and whose good will would be the foundation of his strength. Alert to the needs of his subjects, the monarch should be a man of inexpensive habits and simplicity of manners. As in

[14] P.R. (6/7/06), cols. 833–35; P.R. (6/28/06), cols. 968–73. See Cole, *op. cit.*, for a discussion of this election and an evaluation of its effect upon Cobbett's thought, pp. 113–18.

[15] Compare P.R. (2/5 to 2/12/03), col. 192 with his feelings nearly twenty years later in *A Year's Residence in the United States of America*, passim.

the Middle Ages, he should hear the people's complaints personally and intercede for them when they were oppressed.[16] What was pricking Cobbett here was, obviously, the behavior of the royal family. Further, there was no room for empire within his idea of monarchy. "Where did you pick up that new-fangled slang," he inquired. "To what half-foreign jargon-monger have you been to school? This is a kingdom, that is to say, a commonwealth, a political mixed government, having a king for its chief. We acknowledge no *imperial sway.* . . ." [17]

The members of the lower house must be public spirited, industrious and absolutely incorruptible, chosen by the people and not nominated by the House of Lords. Cobbett claimed that the quality of the members of the House of Commons had deteriorated in recent years. The natural magistracy, to use a phrase of Hume's which Cobbett borrowed frequently, whose character often remedied the mode of their election, had been extinguished. Their place had been taken by a group of lawyers and "placemen" (office holders) who owed everything to the government and were subservient to it.[18] He persistently opposed the seating of placemen and pensioners in Commons. Although he once felt that the integrity of the House of Commons would best be preserved if men of property were elected, he eventually supported manhood suffrage. Yet Cobbett never lost his respect for property or "the dignity and privileges of the peerage. . . ." Despite the immoderation of his attacks upon members of both houses, he could not discard life-long beliefs about the efficacy of property (even though he wanted "sensible tradesmen" elected in place of country gentlemen).[19]

16 P.R. (8/9/26), cols. 187–89, *Cobbett's Register and Lectures,* "Eleven Lectures on the French and Belgian Revolutions," n.p., n.n., n.d., pp. 1–8.
17 P.R. (2/8/17), col. 165.
18 P.R. (9/7/22), col. 595; Amer. P.R. (2/3/16), cols. 129–30.
19 P.R. (10/8/31), col. 89; P.R. (3/2/33), cols. 149–50. In the *Register* article which contained probably his first mention of the necessity for universal male suffrage, he complained that the Speaker of the House of Commons held no property by inheritance. Amer. P.R. (4/27/16), col. 519.

It is in his discussions of the method by which the government should be operated that Cobbett revealed that detachment from reality which rendered him incompetent as a popular leader. No one can aspire to lead people unless he has some grasp of the circumstances of the age in which he lives. This, Cobbett never had. Holding in his mind an ideal that resembled the actual structure of government at the time of Queen Anne, he was out of touch with a society which was changing politically as well as in other respects.

The influence of Blackstone is seen in Cobbett's rigid separation of the executive, legislative and judicial branches of the government. The King should have the right to choose his "servants" (ministers) but they should be excluded from Commons. By harking back to the Act of Settlement in this way, the King might dissolve parliament or change his ministers at will without commotion and parliament might discuss the issues of the day freely. While acting through his ministers the King should be checked by parliament, which would express its power by impeachment or by withholding money.[20] This concept, which did not allow for a treasury bench or even political parties, became more fixed in his mind as he grew older, especially after his quick disillusionment with the reformed parliament. It especially included a denial of the cabinet system on the grounds that this was an innovation in the constitution and that a man could not serve two masters.[21]

Ignoring the technical difficulties inherent in making it work, we might wonder at a scheme that would have prevented parliament from ever becoming supreme. It can be considered only as an expression of the frustration which Cobbett felt over the venal and arrogant conduct of parliamentary business

[20] P.R. (3/28/07), col. 495; P.R. (4/11/07), col. 557; P.R. (1/14/09), cols. 36–40; *History of George IV*, ch. II.

[21] P.R. (4/8/09), cols. 517–19; P.R. (1/14/09), cols. 33 ff.; P.R. (11/29/34), col. 515; P.R. (1/24/35), col. 207.

in an age when there were no meaningful parties and an automatic majority allowed the ministry to treat dissent with contempt. Yet the modern parliamentary system with its ministerial responsibility and cabinet government was gradually evolving even as he wrote. E. T. Williams has listed four incomplete trends in British politics from the turn of the century until the Reform Act: the gradual expulsion of the Crown from the control of policy, the resultant development of the idea of a prime minister, the growth of a functional cabinet which directed a Civil Service, and increased ministerial responsibility.[22] With all these trends except the first, Cobbett was out of sympathy. He pinned his faith, not in a patriot king (for he did not trust the Hanoverians enough for that) but in a return to what he believed to be the system of government of the later Stuarts.

To illustrate by a specific example his determination that the branches of government should be kept separate, in 1807 the ministry withdrew a bill after the King signified his objections to it. Cobbett expressed the view that whether or not the King disapproved of a measure, parliament must act upon it. If the King attempted to proceed in an arbitrary manner, the Commons should exercise the right of withholding supplies.[23] This is consistent with Blackstone, who reserved for the King the right to veto legislation *after* it had been passed by parliament. Yet, as Halévy has pointed out, in practice the King had never had to use the veto because either the ministers were reluctant to provoke a constitutional crisis or he preferred to dissolve parliament and call for a new election.[24] A more emollient method of adjusting disputes

22 E. T. Williams, "The Cabinet in the Eighteenth Century," *History*, vol. XXII (1937), pp. 240–52.
23 P.R. (3/21/07), col. 439; P.R. (3/28/07), cols. 491 ff. In a similar fashion he took a negative position toward Ellenborough, the Lord Chief Justice, holding a seat in the cabinet in a *cause célèbre* in 1806 on the grounds that the judicial and legislative branches of government should be kept separate at all times. P.R. (2/15/06), cols. 193–94.
24 Elie Halévy, *England in 1815*, London, Ernest Benn, 1949, pp. 12–13.

between the King and parliament than veto on the one hand and a refusal to grant supplies on the other had gradually evolved. As the resources of the King were steadily diminished, the power of parliament rose correspondingly. The considerable influence wielded by George III is properly ascribed to a combination of circumstances, including his threatening insanity, Pitt's refusal to press for legislation which he personally believed to be desirable, and the weakness of the parliamentary opposition. Most of all, it was due to the French war, which cast its baleful shadow into every nook and cranny of English life, and, with the other causes, created this disinclination to interfere with the King's crotchets.

These were circumstances which Cobbett did not understand. The extraordinary rigidity of the *ad hoc* system of government which had emerged after the Glorious Revolution made it inevitable that changes would have to be made for it to operate at all. These alterations were made gradually and informally and not for the most part by statute. What had developed by 1799 was a viable but very expensive and corrupt administration badly in need of reform. Cobbett, with the eyes of a true believer, could not see the almost imperceptible changes which were moving it in the direction of economy and greater honesty. His response to the need for improvement was to urge a return to the pristine quality of the constitution as it had once existed. This tendency can be seen again in his attitude toward the places and sinecures which the government used to reward its supporters. A more equitable franchise, a party system, the development of both ministerial responsibility and the cabinet, with the latter controlling administration, were needed to remedy the problem. With the exception of a wider franchise, Cobbett never cared for evolutions of this type. Yet more to the point, he never objected to the sinecures as an institution. Violent in his denunciation of the manner in which they were granted, his solution for the abuse was to have them awarded only for real public service.[25] He evidently did not consider that such a venerable institution, whose roots extended far back into English history, must always be a source of corruption. In this case he favored only a modest reform instead of sweeping changes. Sinecures were useful as a reward of merit, provided that they were administered by a reformed parliament. Once again he proclaimed his faith in the possibility of old wine's being contained in new bottles.

The election system which Cobbett held necessary to secure this type of government for the people took form gradually in his mind. After the Honiton election he began setting forth plans concerning voting procedures and suffrage. In 1810 he proposed allowing male householders the franchise. To ensure an end to corrupt election procedures he would have had the voting take place in one day and subdivide each county with one vote being allowed each parish. The elections would be supervised by a parish officer using voting lists. The parish officer would forward the results to the sheriff, who would draw up the general return for the county and send it to the Lord Chancellor. Parliament's term would be shortened to "a constitutional duration." Cobbett felt that under this plan corruption would be eliminated by substituting respectable property owners for impecunious vote sellers. Men of substance—farmers, yeomen and tradesmen—would "naturally choose *gentlemen of fortune* and of *good character*." The great families and the landed interest would still wield their influence but would no longer be able to buy votes.[26] This strongly Whiggish program was similar to that offered by Sir Francis Burdett, the member of parliament whom Cobbett most admired at that time. He later modified and expanded this method for securing the integrity of elections. County

25 P.R. (3/1/06), col. 315; P.R. (9/10/31), col. 641.
26 P.R. (4/21/10), cols. 601–03.

members should be apportioned by population so that non-taxpayers would have some weight and there should be no pecuniary qualification for members. Voting by ballot was to take place in one day and voters were to cast ballots for all county members in a manner reminiscent of the American General Ticket Plan of which Cobbett certainly knew. Cartwright had proposed election districts but Cobbett was not prepared to agree to so advanced a step. The churchwardens should draw up an alphabetical list of persons eighteen years or over and put it on the church door one month before election for possible correction. After the day of election, the churchwardens, who were to oversee the elections, should submit their returns to the sheriff, who would then make out the county return and send it to the Crown Office.[27]

Within a few years of urging a franchise based on property as a means to remove democratic corruption, we find Cobbett demanding universal male suffrage. He proceeded to this stage after calling for taxpayer suffrage and justified it by allowing that the property of the working man was his labor. With all the zeal of a former sinner who suddenly discovered salvation in religion, he turned upon his former associates and began to accuse them of hypocrisy. In taking this step, which marked him in the public eye as an advanced radical, Cobbett had followed the advice of the "Father of Reform," the ancient Major Cartwright. But, in defending himself a year later when he demanded annual parliaments as well, Cobbett cited Sir John Fortescue and Blackstone in support of universal male suffrage! [28] It was his altered position on the question of suffrage which placed Cobbett briefly at the head of the small, fragmented English reform movement. By this time his private

[27] P.R. (10/19/16), cols. 383 ff.; P.R. (10/30/30), cols. 554 ff. His transition to a more radical position may be compared in these two *Registers*. Where there was conflict, the sentiments in the 1830 issue are indicated.

[28] P.R. (2/22/17), cols. 231–35; P.R. (11/13/16), col. 346.

program of popular political education, begun at Honiton, had become inseparable from his numerous writings on social and economic questions. The years after 1817 did not bring forth many new political views. Generally, Cobbett was content to restate his old ones, often in a more irritable manner.

VI
Law and society

The tendency to be dominated by faith in the validity of past institutions shaped Cobbett's thought with reference to the legal system as well as politics. Although his relations with the law have consistently attracted the attention of his biographers, apart from the Game Laws and the 1834 Poor Law, comment has been confined primarily to his personal problems, especially the several trials and bankruptcy proceedings. Little has been written about Cobbett's position regarding the criminal law as an institution or the subject of crime and punishment. As we would expect, he never attempted to discuss in a sustained manner the legal code of England. Nevertheless, many references scattered throughout his work are interesting for the light they shed upon his entire personality. These references allow us to see a person who was inconsistent concerning specific principles. They also display Cobbett less as a plain man spontaneously giving vent to his feelings than as an ideologist.

Of all the institutions of English society the one which most eloquently reminds the mid-twentieth century observer of the gulf which separates the contemporary world from life as it was lived in England one hundred and fifty years ago is the law. Few social attitudes have changed as much as that regarding crime, its causes, prevention and punishment. To visualize life at that time is to imagine living in a society in which there were well over two hundred offenses (the exact figure is uncertain) punishable by death, with little discrimination on account of the age of the offender. It was a society where a person might legally be put to death for destroying the heads of fish ponds, picking pockets in the amount of twelve pence or over or for merely being in the company of gypsies. Nor was the situation due to a glaring legislative oversight on the part of parliament in failing to remove scores of bizarre anachronisms from the criminal law code. Any attempt to reduce the number of capital offenses met with adamantine opposition. Significantly, the number of crimes deemed punishable by death actually increased considerably during the latter half of the eighteenth century.[1]

It is difficult to reconcile this situation with the pride in English justice held by articulate members of society, even though the burden of the harsh code did not fall on them. Furthermore, despite the practice of continental writers in holding English personal freedoms up to the admiration of the world, England was in reality falling behind the advanced theories of penology being worked out there. The reign of

[1] The reformer, Sir Samuel Romilly, once remarked, "Agreeably to the genius of modern politics, which estimate [sic] property above life, though scarce a tax bill escapes solemn and repeated discussion in Parliament, yet every novice in politics is permitted without opposition to try his talents for legislation by dealing out death among his fellow creatures; and laws of this kind commonly pass as of course without observation or debate." Quoted from W. L. Mathieson, *England in Transition, 1789–1832*, London, Longmans, Green and Co., 1920, p. 115.

George III saw an average of more than one capital offense placed on the books per year. Only the refusal of many juries to convict despite clear-cut evidence of guilt, plus the fact that only a small number of those condemned to death were actually executed, mitigated the ferocity of punishment.[2] Yet in spite of these severities crimes such as kidnaping and manslaughter were inadequately punished, and there were glaring anomalies in laws relating to other offenses such as arson. The growth in the number of offenses punishable by execution was accompanied by an increase in crime, but most men in authority saw no solution to a rising crime rate other than to make the laws even more stringent.

This latter fact demonstrates that little was known about the causes of crime. Confronted with a rising number of offenses, the reaction of parliament was to extend the scope and intensify the severity of the criminal code. Naturally, other factors contributed to the seemingly callous attitude of the members of parliament in this respect: the lack of an efficient police system which made detection of crime uncertain and the unsatisfactory provisions for secondary punishments. Also, with respect to the law, the influence of the French Revolution created an atmosphere that fostered fear and suspicion and inhibited reform. Neither transportation nor imprisonment, the two major alternatives to capital punishment, were regarded with enthusiasm either as deterrents or penalties. But, of course, in the eighteenth and early nineteenth centuries, the major factor influencing thought about the civil and criminal law was the exalted place given to private property. The remark of Romilly reflects upon this subject and is not an exaggeration of the prevailing state of mind. Opinion in Cobbett's time was reflected by the apology

---

[2] From 1800–1810 only one person in seven convicted of a capital crime was actually executed. Leon Radzinowicz, *A History of the English Criminal Law and Its Administration from 1750, The Movement for Reform, 1750–1833.* New York, The Macmillan Company, 1948, p. 152.

for the established criminal code provided in William Paley's *Principles of Moral and Political Philosophy*, published in 1785. This enormously influential work, a textbook in Cambridge University, expounded that the object of punishment is "not the satisfaction of justice but the prevention of crime." [3] The major consideration influencing the choice of punishment for a crime was, therefore, its value as a deterrent. By stressing difficulties in the apprehension of criminals and ignoring the adjustment of punishments to suit the degree of the crime, this theory provided an ideological basis for existing practices. It also adapted to the prevailing emphasis upon property rights and to the widely accepted view of Locke that the state existed chiefly to preserve these rights.

The foregoing remarks apply only to the criminal law. But the condition of this branch of the law indicates the difficulty of effecting changes in the legal system generally. Harsh penalties for minor crimes, the persistence of the pillory and whipping post, inhuman methods of preventing theft of game, all bore against the weak and helpless. It would seem necessary that whoever would champion the cause of the common people must attack this method of keeping order in society all along the line and seek redress everywhere. Yet Cobbett, here as elsewhere, was highly selective about what he desired to be reformed. He ignored certain abuses and preferred that others continue.

Specifically, despite his own incarceration in Newgate, no well of sympathy was created in Cobbett for the convicted criminal. He never made prison reform a part of his program, nor did he support the work of Elizabeth Fry and others who tried to end the hideousness of the jails. The pillory was described as "this old and gentle and good-humoured mode of chastisement." [4] Under this "appeal to the people" the helpless felon might be pelted with dead cats, rocks or filth

[3] *Ibid.*, p. 250.
[4] P.R. (1/7/32), col. 69.

and emerge sans teeth and eyes, but Cobbett could sometimes be stoic when the suffering of others was concerned. What did vex him was the change in the law relating to suicide after Castlereagh took his own life in 1822. Prior to this, the law compelled a suicide to be buried at a crossroads with a stake driven through his heart and this was followed by confiscation of the goods of the deceased. A series of suicides by prominent persons (who were all judged to be insane and thus exempt from the law), culminating in Castlereagh's, resulted in its drastic alteration. Cobbett treated of both the pillory and suicide in an article which was written when he was living in America because of his own persecution by the government. "The punishment of the pillory was *humane* and singularly *just* and *proper*. It put the offender before the *people,* who had been already duly informed of his crime. It gave *them* an opportunity to shew *their* feeling on the subject." On suicide, he remarked, "Men are to endure the ills of life with fortitude. They are not permitted to fly from them with impunity in this disgraceful manner." [5] The occasion of Castlereagh's death was celebrated in no uncertain terms by an open letter to a political prisoner named Swann. "MR. SWANN, CASTLEREAGH HAS CUT HIS OWN THROAT, AND IS DEAD! Let that sound reach you in the depth of your dungeon; and let it carry consolation to your suffering soul! . . . As to compassion; as to *sorrow,* upon this occasion, how base a hypocrite I must be to affect it! nay, how base a hypocrite to disguise, or attempt to disguise, my satisfaction!" [6] Cobbett was more concerned that posthumous punishment of suicides be carried out to the letter of the law than he was in crime generally.

Crime in Cobbett's eyes was merely a symptom of the

[5] P.R. (4/17/19), cols. 929–30. A few months before he died similar sentiments were indicated. P.R. (2/7/35), cols. 323–24.
[6] P.R. (8/17/22), col. 385 and col. 421.

general evil caused by taxes.[7] When the debt and the extravagances afflicting England were eliminated, taxes could be reduced, the people would have plenty to eat, and crime would diminish. In other words, in Cobbett's romantic imagination there was no permanent problem. In terms of present reality he was alarmed that suicides of the highly placed could evade the law; a clear case of favoritism. An article entitled "Softening the Criminal Code" revealed his complaint against Sir James Mackintosh and other legal reformers. These people, he felt, could not be truly humane since they did not concern themselves with persons accused of political offenses; instead, their attention was monopolized by felons. (Cobbett, of course, was exactly the opposite.) With the savage repression of the Labourers' Revolt of 1830 in mind, Cobbett ridiculed Mackintosh for efforts which had resulted in little more than the repeal of laws against witches.[8]

This suspicion of the legal reformers and general disinterest in mitigating the harshness of the criminal law code demonstrates Cobbett's belief in radical reform or none at all, just as it does his frequent lack of proportion. The "System" held him fast and prevented his joining any movement dedicated to substantial or procedural law reform. As a person with many blind spots, Cobbett could ignore enormous cruelty. The lack of vision which he exhibited here is characteristic of his tendency to see only what he wanted to at times which were convenient to him. Cobbett could rage for many consecutive columns in the *Register* over the sufferings of political reformers who had been jailed by the government. His anger concerning the game laws was rooted in his soul. Yet this compassion was severely circumscribed. His dream of a better world was as different as possible from that of totalitarian visionaries of our own day; yet, like them, he was the

7 P.R. (2/16/28), cols. 202–11.
8 P.R. (9/17/31), cols. 722–24.

prisoner of an idea and consequently ignored much that cried out for immediate attention.

In the estimation of this utopian fanatic, the laws which governed England for centuries were basically sound. Had not the country grown great while the statute books were loaded with the fruit of medieval jurisprudence? It was the recent accretions: the game laws and the repressive legislation of Pitt and his followers which were evil and should be swept away. When they had been eliminated, there would be no need of general law reform. At the present time, the need was for impartial administration of the statutes. Justice meant the uniform administration and execution of laws regardless of the situation in life of those brought before the bar of justice. "The law may be very *lenient* or very severe, and equally *just* in both cases." [9]

Possessed by an imaginary English past, Cobbett saw a return to a happier epoch as the solution to the country's needs. He did not, therefore, feel the need to elaborate on a type of legal system which would have worked more equitably in the present circumstances. When his dream was realized and England was as she had been centuries ago, these details would be unimportant. Here is the reason for his opposition to prison reform, special courts to try juvenile offenders and more humane methods of punishment. Beyond this, he was not in general favorably inclined toward the extension of government influence. As early as 1808 he deplored the too frequent use of the courts for legal redress and blamed the funding and taxation system for making the people "completely lawyer-ridden." [10] As he grew older and noticed the effect of government action, Cobbett became less and less favorably inclined toward the extension of its influence. Although he spoke oc-

---

9 P.R. (7/27/22), col. 194. See also *Thirteen Sermons*, No. 5, passim.
10 P.R. (8/6/08), cols. 193 ff. Cobbett's dislike of lawyers ripened into hatred and became one of his most prominent crotchets. Lawyers were too closely identified with the "System" to suit him.

casionally of the duty of the government to ensure the well-being of its citizens, as an old man Cobbett was persuaded that it should confine itself to removing conditions which impeded a person from working out his own destiny. Except in certain cases such as the Poor Law and, eventually, factory legislation, the government was not to pass laws to provide for the people's happiness. "There must be something left to the pulpit,—there must be something left to the parents,—there must be something left to the moral teacher." [11]

Cobbett's refusal to believe in the efficacy of legislation tended to estrange him from most other reformers. For him, the place to develop character was the home and he was not disposed to allow the State even the limited role that James Mill was prepared to accept. He was opposed to Bentham ". . . with his quaint and unintelligible language and mode of stating and reasoning . . ." because the great legal reformer had found the common law "at the end of twelve hundred years . . . so utterly worthless, that, with the assistance of Dr. Black, he apparently hopes to be able entirely to rub out the recollections of the people of this country." [12] Of course, Cobbett was not alone in his concern over the growth of the power of the central government. The country gentry were also worried about this trend which was gradually putting an end to the administrative localism that formed the basis of eighteenth-century politics. They, too, were fond of wrapping the mantle of Old England about them as they cherished a "hallowed tradition" which had existed for only a little more than a century.[13] Mutual dislike of the growing power of the central government was not enough to bring Cobbett and the gentry into an alliance, for they disagreed

[11] Great Britain, 3 *Hansard's Parliamentary Debates*, XXIII (1834), 1363.

[12] P.R. (12/12/18), col. 359; P.R. (8/18/27), col. 492.

[13] See J. Steven Watson, *The Reign of George III, 1760–1815*, Oxford, Oxford University Press, 1960, pp. 51–56 for the local basis of politics at the time. Also, Halévy, *England in 1815*, pp. 36–37.

about conditions on the land. But he was more opposed to the Benthamites, with their iconoclasm and concern for quantitative measures of progress. His outlook here was, in fact, singular. It was noticeable only because his powerful pen brought it to the attention of thousands who were impressed with his vigorous attacks upon the "System" but showed no disposition to accept the remedies which he proffered.

Basic to his contention that the liberties of the people were being destroyed by the government was a belief that the powers of the jury were being transferred to judges, who, in turn, were losing influence to a rising class of magistrates. There were grounds for this fear. More and more justices of the peace were being chosen out of the ranks of parsons and nouveau riche manufacturers and, since the accession of George III, they had been granted greater powers particularly with regard to the administration of the poor laws. In addition to the traditional justices of the peace, there was a new class of police magistrates who, like the justices of the peace, were chosen by the ministry of the day, but, unlike the judges, could be removed at will.[14] The difficulty was that the ministers, as was their practice, were attempting to cope with the problems posed by a new industrial civilization by utilizing the techniques appropriate for a decentralized agricultural society. Authorities from the ministers down to the justices of the peace were inhibited in their understanding of the nature of the changes transforming the country because of their background and training and because of the fear of change produced by the French Revolution. Therefore, their only response to unrest was to increase the severity of the laws and to intensify efforts to root out dissent. This applied to crime as well as to politics.

In 1804 Cobbett calmly pointed out the increasing power of the justices of the peace in relation to army recruitment,

[14] Halévy, *England in 1815*, pp. 41, 44, 378.

the poor laws, and game and revenue laws. He praised them as a class but expressed concern about possible future developments and suggested a curtailment of their power. In the early 1830's he was still inveighing against the increasing power of this group of men, so dependent in their tenure upon the ministry, at the expense of the judges who had been appointed for life and were presumably independent.[15] The harsh practices of the justices in routine, non-political cases intensified a dislike which had its foundation in their frequent oppression of all those lying within their power who had the courage to call for changes in the political system. It was also a source of continual fear to him that the system of London police magistrates would eventually extend to the countryside.[16]

This tendency toward the centralization of government would also weaken the jury system. It is probable that Cobbett's opinion of the jury system as "the wisest institution that ever was thought of by man" was due in part to his knowledge of Blackstone's *Commentaries,* which portrayed it as the very foundation of British liberties. He fought strenuously against any attempt to subvert it in favor of the judges, just as he consistently opposed police magistrates assuming the functions of judges. In 1819, angered by the biased summing up of evidence by judges in political cases, he wrote an article reminding potential jurymen that they alone were to decide the verdict. Therefore, they should ignore all of the judge's speech except that which related to the issue at hand. In the same article in which the above quotation appears, he said that the principal object of a jury was to protect the weak against the strong and that it had the duty to be impressed only by actual evidence.[17] In this and other articles in the

15 P.R. (6/16/04), cols. 946–49; P.R. (7/23/31), cols. 200–02; P.R. (1/7/32), cols. 69–72.

16 See White, *op. cit.,* pp. 108–09, for a more sympathetic account of the justices of the peace.

17 P.R. (1/16/19), cols. 506–12.

Register, Cobbett stressed the need to maintain the purity and impartiality of the jury system. "Juries, like all the other institutions, intended as safeguards of freedom, become, if perverted from their purpose, not only no safeguards at all, but the instruments of *greater tyranny than would have been practised, if they had not existed."* [18] Naturally, the tyranny he feared was political and the jury system, a product of the Middle Ages, was a bulwark against it.

As the demand to establish a police force grew stronger, Cobbett once again demonstrated opposition. Actually, such a step was a radical innovation, indeed, opposed by many in all walks of life. Even the Whig, Sir Samuel Romilly, for many years parliamentary leader of the movement for legal reform, accepted with reluctance the fact that a mitigation of the harshness of the laws could only come in conjunction with a full-time professional police force. In 1824, Sir Robert Peel carried without debate legislation which abolished the death penalty for approximately a hundred offenses and then proceeded, in a series of bills, to consolidate the laws of the country. The canny Peel had stolen the thunder from the Whig reformers. Five years later he established the metropolitan police force, an act for which Cobbett did not forgive him. For Cobbett, who was not excited about the severity of the criminal code, could regard Peel's police force only as a French inspired instrument of repression, another example of "this age of improvement—this march of mind." [19] Of course, Romilly, Mackintosh and the Whig reformers inside parliament, as well as the humanitarians outside it did not share Cobbett's desire for widespread change. He would be more opposed than they to an efficient police force partly because of his greater dislike of the government but, in ad-

18 P.R. (12/16/09), col. 905. See also P.R. (5/28/25), cols. 513 ff.
19 *Cobbett's Register and Lectures,* "Eleven Lectures on the French and Belgian Revolutions." Lecture VIII (9/27/30), pp. 8–9; Great Britain, 3 *Hansard's Parliamentary Debates,* XVIII (1833), 1254–60.

dition, his faith in radical reform led him to believe that such a body was unnecessary.

Another aspect of the law which drew Cobbett's attention during the 1820's was the increasing number of statutes relating to the protection of game and the ever-greater severity of punishment for their violation. The complexities of urban crime might leave Cobbett baffled and disinterested, but he was concerned with the countryside and the problems of its common people. The new class of nabobs, stock-jobbers and city merchants whom Cobbett regarded as driving out the old landed aristocracy jealously sought to protect their hunting privileges against the casual poaching which had been routine practice for centuries. By means of fences, spring-guns, gamekeepers and especially by legislation, they attempted to secure their selfish sport against the depredations of the humbler classes of rural folk. The new game laws substituted long-term transportation for the former punishments for poaching, the pillory, or a few weeks' imprisonment. They came at a time when that masterpiece of irony, the 1815 Corn Law, which was supposed to protect rural interests, was causing hardship among the agricultural laborers as well as the urban workers. By preventing the laborers from eking out their meager diet by poaching, the game laws and attendant apparatus intensified suffering. It must be noted that in 1823 Cobbett was becoming the enemy of the landlords. He attacked the principle and the substance of the game laws which made all of the people pay taxes to support the enforcement of the pleasure of a few and had turned "the country into a hell." Striking out at the hypocrisy of those who hunted for sport and then marketed the kill, he bitterly railed at making the firing on a gamekeeper a capital offense.[20] It was a subject to which he turned again and again, using it

[20] P.R. (4/6/22), cols. 4-15; P.R. (3/29/23), cols. 769-97; P.R. (5/17/23), cols. 408-24; P.R. (4/3/24), cols. 24-25; *Rural Rides*, Vol. I (8/29/23), pp. 204-05.

as a platform from which to make attacks on the government but he was also concerned about the welfare of the laborers. Here was yet another example of the "hypocrisy" of Mackintosh and the legal reformers, whose efforts were directed into other channels.

However, not even the game laws aroused his interest or captivated him as completely as the Poor Law controversy. The bitter struggle which he waged against attempts to change the structure of poor relief reached a peak near the end of his life and actually formed the subject matter of the last article which he wrote for the *Register*. Before this Cobbett fought strenuously against the Philosophical Radicals and the Malthusians who were furnishing a rationale for those who wished to be relieved of the burden of the poor rates, regardless of the social effects which this would have. No other side of the law makes Cobbett appear so sympathetic to our eyes. The game laws were a parochial issue and could be repudiated by anyone not possessing a vested interest in them. They were only made possible in the first place by a landlord–dominated legislature. However, the campaign against poor relief was carried on in the spirit of the latest economic knowledge, and those defending it needed to call upon a reservoir of traditional concepts of society in order to combat the attackers. Whatever success Cobbett might have enjoyed in the intellectual confrontation, in this case there is no doubt of his generous sentiments. This is especially true because he was a small landowner himself and before 1834 bore more than his share of the burden of taxation for poor relief. Although Cobbett made his own defense of these laws, he was in agreement with a minority of Tories led by Lord Shaftesbury on several points. Together with the Factory Act of 1833, the opposition to the Poor Law Bill of 1834 provided the humanitarian Tories with their finest moments in history.

Still, even many radicals, before and after 1834, have admitted that something had to be done about the system of poor relief. This was based upon the Elizabethan Poor Law of 1601, which provided relief from the parish rates for the helpless poor. The cost of administration had reached almost £8,000,000 three years after the war. Because this administration was a responsibility of the parishes and because the charges were levied against the occupiers (not the owners) of landed property, the burden fell most heavily upon the tenant farmers. This generally prosperous class was squeezed by adverse economic conditions after 1815 and could ill afford a tax of this proportion. The Speenhamland Act of 1796 had modified the 1601 act by granting the laborer a minimum standard of subsistence based on the price of wheat and the size of his family. However, its provisions for supplementing inadequate wages through the rates invited employers to cut wages and the act had the double effect of increasing the poor rates and of demoralizing the workers. Although it kept people alive, the system did put a premium on indolence and bastardy. It remained in effect primarily because no one could devise a scheme to cope with the problem of poverty that would be acceptable to the propertied interests and also because of the fear that revolution would occur if it was done away with entirely.[21]

Cobbett answered those who asserted that the poor had no right to expect relief by categorically stating that the right of the poor to receive relief from their wealthier neighbors was a prescriptive right enjoyed in all times and ages. Both the law of nature and the law of God insist that no one should starve while there is food in the land. In the *Poor Man's Friend* and in the *Political Register* he examined the problem theoretically within the unfamiliar framework of the concept of a Law of Nature. According to this law, all things in the world belong equally to everyone; there is no private property. When men join a civil society, they give this up and establish rights

21 See R. E. Prothero, *English Farming Past and Present*, London, Longmans, Green and Co., 1917, pp. 329-31 and p. 436.

of private property the basis of which is labor. The land belongs to those who had initially cleared and cultivated it. This change from a state of nature to civil society was intended to benefit everyone and it was never meant that all of the land should become the property of a few people and that the rest should be impoverished. Therefore, "arrangements" were made for the care of the poor, with the owner of the land being charged with that responsibility. Discussing the change which Christianity made in the lives of the people, which is the next step in his analysis, allows Cobbett to indulge in one of his dithyrambs about the Middle Ages with the clergy seen as trustees of the poor. After the Reformation, the nobility were eventually forced to agree to the Poor Law of 1601, an unsatisfactory substitute for the charity of medieval England,[22] but at least a firm contract that the poor were to be maintained. This was the basis for his repeated contention that the maintenance of the poor was not a gift but a right to be enjoyed under the law.

Since a system, however imperfect, of poor relief had been founded, Cobbett wanted it maintained in all its integrity. All his life he steadfastly resisted attempts to dilute it in any way, especially by changing the composition of the vestry in order to favor the large landowners. Answering the charge that under the existing system the poorer voters had the power of giving away the money of the wealthier ones, Cobbett exclaimed, "It is *not* the money of others. . . . The maintenance of the poor is a charge upon the land, a charge duly considered in every purchase and in every lease." [23] The real problem, as he saw it, was not any innate desire on the part

22 *The Poor Man's Friend or Companion for the Working Classes*, London, H. Stemman, 1826, Letters 1 and 2; P.R. (11/14/29), cols. 619–21. Also, see *A History of the Protestant Reformation in England and Ireland*, London, Charles Clement, 1824, Letter XI, and *Cobbett's Legacy to Parsons*, London, n.n., 1835, passim. The position which religious institutions took toward charity was a major factor in his evaluation of them.
23 P.R. (8/29/07), col. 329.

of the laborers to collect poor relief rather than work as had been alleged. Instead it was the weight of taxation which was at fault. Since the American Revolutionary War, the taxes had increased, forcing the farmers to pay their laborers a pittance where they could afford to hire them at all. The solution to the problem was to reduce the nation's debt, eliminate sinecures, cut salaries, and prevent the laborer from starving by maintaining wages and allowances granted under the Poor Law. This was his answer to those who wanted to economize at the expense of the laborer.[24] Another way in which he felt that the laws were being circumvented was through the use of private charity. Cobbett always opposed anything which smacked of paternalism (except his own brand). He never troubled to distinguish between the charity of the Middle Ages which he admired so greatly and the "comforting" efforts of the Hannah More school which he loathed for demoralizing the poor and making them content with their lot. In his mind the point of difference would probably be an ulterior motivation among the latter, who were, perhaps, more concerned with preserving the existing form of society than with aiding the poor. Nor did he grasp that the concentration of people in northern cities would throw too great a burden on the antiquated poor laws in time of distress. He was furious over voluntary appeals to charity for supplemental assistance, believing that they were intended to relieve greedy landlords of their legal obligation.[25]

In addition to defending the English Poor Law, Cobbett sought to extend it to Scotland and Ireland as well. Appalled by the poverty which he saw in 1834 on his only visit to Ireland he urged its introduction in order to ameliorate the poverty of the people.[26] His observations on Ireland were devoted to

24 P.R. (9/28/16), cols. 277–88; P.R. (8/9/34), cols. 331–50.
25 P.R. (7/16/08), cols. 73–78; P.R. (1/6/27), cols. 95–100.
26 *Three Lectures on the Political State of Ireland,* Dublin, P. Byrne, 1834, passim.

denunciations of Irish poverty and praise of the Poor Law. There is little in the way of an analysis of political and economic conditions in Ireland, and it may be doubted whether the economic arrangements of Irish agriculture would have made such an extension of the English scheme feasible. Cobbett's sympathy with the Irish was no doubt genuine but he had a tendency to use Ireland as a horrible example.

Just before he went to Ireland he had waged a vigorous step-by-step struggle against the Poor Law Amendment Act of 1834. Beginning in 1833 with the report of the parliamentary commission appointed to investigate the workings of the Elizabethan system of poor relief and culminating only with his death in 1835, Cobbett's speeches in parliament and articles in the *Register* attacked every phase of the radical new legislation. It was his last great campaign, for even the Irish trip was motivated by a desire for fresh ammunition against the newly-enacted law. The Whig reluctance to change matters once they were in office did not extend to the system of poor relief. Their commission, dominated by those who sincerely believed that poverty was basically the pauper's own fault, brought in a report which recommended that the existing outdoor relief be terminated in favor of compulsory residence in a workhouse. The administration of assistance was to be made more careful. Three commissioners in London were charged with operating the plan, which was deliberately designed in its details to make public support so unattractive that the poor would avoid it at almost any cost. Undergraduates today are frequently amused despite themselves at the rigor of the final act, thinking it peculiar to the age of *Oliver Twist*. Yet it has an impersonal, business-administrative aspect and is really more appropriate to a later period. Many nonradical elements in 1834 such as *The Times* and a minority of the Tory party were horrified. The coldness of the measure convinced Cobbett that it would dissolve the bonds which

held society together. "Pass this bill and you destroy the constitution as far as it relates to the necessitous." [27]

Cobbett struck out vigorously, tying in this proposed legislation with the game laws and the police by warning of the
likelihood of a Napoleonic style police state designed to en-
slave the many in the interests of the few. Frustrated by the
logical analysis of the proponents of the bill, he abandoned
his "Law of Nature" theories and concentrated upon the
themes of potential despotism and the prescriptive right of
the laborer to receive poor relief in time of need. He was
unable to advance any new arguments against the bill. Cobbett was, in fact, a beaten man. The last article that he wrote
for publication after the fight had been lost, states his conception of what the struggle had been about.

> Not a desire to overturn the Government on the part of the
> people; not a desire to disobey the settled laws of the country;
> not any revolutionary desire; not any desire to touch any one
> of the institutions of the country. [But a desire] to maintain
> the laws of their country, as they were settled at the time
> when the *present church of the country was established;* to
> maintain those laws which formed the foundation, the very
> fundamental principles of the Government; and which are of
> two hundred and forty years' standing.[28]

Therefore, of the various aspects of the English legal code,
Cobbett was primarily interested in eliminating the series of
acts designed to protect the hunting privileges of a wealthy
minority and in the preservation of the Elizabethan Poor
Law. In these two respects, Cobbett was deeply involved because they were close to his experience, and even the latter
concerned the land, which Cobbett saw as the basis of society.
He cherished the poor law and tried to curb the growing
power of the landed magnates. At the same time he advanced

[27] P.R. (7/12/34), col. 85.
[28] P.R. (6/16/35), col. 340. See also P.R. (4/6/33), cols. 22–24 and
almost any issue of the summer and autumn of 1834.

his demand for reform. In the new society, which would be one with present abuses stripped away, there would be no want or misery. Much of the criminal and civil law codes would disappear (one is tempted to say "wither away"), along with the lawyers. Until this had happened, attention must be focused not upon the law in the hope of winning at least a measure of reform, but upon the "System." With reference to the law, then, Cobbett again demonstrated a tendency toward thoroughgoing change and at the same time a belief that the institutions of Old England were perfectly valid.

VII
Political economy

The preceding chapters indicate Cobbett's reaction upon learning that the English government, which he had supported so loyally in America between 1793 and 1800, was actually engaged in destroying a way of life which he cherished. The fact that he did not grasp the nature of the subtle economic transformations which affected the government's policies, coupled with his vision of a bygone rural paradise, contributed to his frustration and rage. If he had possessed a greater understanding of events, he would have been a more successful popular leader. But an aware, prescient Cobbett would not have been the fascinating, perplexing person that he was: prejudiced and violent but almost always original and even at his worst moments having a residue of selfless interest in a better England. His country was being transformed from a rural to an urban nation and its society was becoming less paternalistic and more individualistic. The alteration was so gradual that Cobbett's ignorance was shared and sometimes exceeded by that of the government. His distinctive point of view is best seen when dealing with specific matters of political economy, public finance and agricultural and industrial changes.

The increasing importance of the doctrines of political economy as a factor in shaping government policy and as a topic of serious discussion is testified to by the augmented space which Cobbett had to devote to the subject in his writings. During the first decade of the *Political Register* there was little attempt to deal with economic matters except with reference to charts of commodity and stock prices. Later, as the problems of government finance came to occupy a large part of Cobbett's attention, he was attracted by related topics. The system of finance, comprised of paper money, the funds and high taxation, was most important to him because he believed that it was the major prop of the ruling group. Yet he was concerned with trade and commerce also and on occasion even dealt with economic theory. For the new economics was in the air. Its savant, Ricardo, his student, McCulloch, and parson Malthus were household names. Of course, the great prophet, Adam Smith, was almost canonized and was the subject of an ode by, of all people, Lord Sidmouth. Cobbett was caught up in this atmosphere and found himself in the unfamiliar position of dealing with the dismal science.

It is not surprising that a person of Cobbett's vivacity would find the subject of political economy dry and its practitioners loathsome—the products of a strange new world. "There is a coldness in their principles and opinions that I hate . . . The gain . . . of the thing is all they appear to look at."[1]

Still, Malthus, Ricardo, McCulloch, and the other political economists of the day were significant because those parts of

[1] P.R. (9/5/07), col. 365.

their theories which appealed to the ruling classes were seized upon and implemented (other parts, including Smith's injunction that the laborer must be tolerably well-fed, clothed and housed were ignored). The fact that these men were fashionable added to Cobbett's hatred and derision of them. How he detested the aloof tone of their lucubrations, which to him must have stunk of lamp oil and the musty odor of government documents. Much better to get out in the fresh air and ride about to see how the people *really* lived. Yet for all his aversion to them, the political economists were not the objects of his supreme disfavor. Despite what Professor Cole has said,[2] that dubious distinction must be awarded to members of his own agricultural society, landlords who had betrayed their trust. In his second and last sustained work of fiction, the play, "Surplus Population," the villain of the piece is not Peter Thimble, Esq., a confused, humorless pedant but not altogether an unsympathetic character. It is Sir Squire Grindum, Bart., the lecherous landlord.

Nevertheless, the political economists occupy conspicuous places in Cobbett's rogues' gallery and he fought their ideas tenaciously. Theory and speculation were never Cobbett's way although on several occasions he did attempt to justify the Elizabethan Poor Law in the economists' own terms.[3] Before the age of accurate economic data, it was inevitable that men like Ricardo would eschew an empirical approach in favor of deductive analyses. Cobbett disposed of the theories themselves as follows. " 'Received doctrines of *Political Economy.*' Received *by whom?* . . . And, what is this *'Political Economy'*? The writer speaks of it as if it were an *Act of Parliament,* or, some great *public cause,* or *institution.* Who would think, that he meant a heap of rubbishy paragraphs, written by a man who 'made half a million of money by *watching the turn of the market'*, and another such a heap, written by a Parson,

2 *Op. cit.,* p. 11.
3 P.R. (5/8/19), cols. 1025 ff.; P.R. (8/28/19), cols. 45–46.

who proposed to starve the *working people,* to cheat *their breeding children?"* [4]

The individual last referred to was Thomas Malthus who, along with Pitt and William Wilberforce, composed Cobbett's unholy Trinity. Cobbett branded Malthus' ideas as being the products of an unfeeling hypocrite. The fact that Malthus was a parson in the Church of England certainly reinforced Cobbett's intense dislike for the clergy of that body. His views on religion clearly indicated that his ideal of a good clergy-man was one who devoted his energies to improving the physical well-being of his flock. How far short of this ideal both Malthus and Wilberforce fell! It is true that he had praised Malthus.[5] However, once the latter's ideas were applied to a specifically English situation, there was a complete revulsion on Cobbett's part. Cobbett's antagonism toward Malthus was shared in differing ways by the conservative Coleridge, the liberal Hazlitt and the radical Godwin. The latter, whose view of a limitless human progress had been challenged, attacked the premises of Malthus' argument. Hazlitt, a man of common sense, saw some merit in Malthus' contradiction of overly optimistic views about the effects of population growth but believed that, in addition to faulty reasoning, Malthus had carried his argument too far and thus provided comfort for reactionaries. Cobbett was closer to Coleridge, whose organic view of society made him refuse to turn his back on the hungry. To both Coleridge and Cobbett, the cold Malthusian analysis must have been as disturbing as the actual conclusions.

[4] P.R. (4/9/25), col. 116.

[5] P.R. (2/16/05), cols. 230–31. In an otherwise valuable article, Charles H. Kegel, in "William Cobbett and Malthusianism," *Journal of the History of Ideas,* Vol. 19 (June, 1958), pp. 348–62, overlooks the fact that Cobbett was using Malthus' ideas in reference to the West Indies natives, with the intention of justifying the slave trade. In Cobbett's mind this was completely distinct from problems affecting English laborers. As late as April, 1808, he agreed that population always treads closely upon the heels of subsistence, but disagreed with Malthus about checking it. P.R (4/23/08), col. 646.

Cobbett's attitude toward the Surrey rector was emotional, based on an instinctive loathing which he felt in the marrow of his bones.

Somewhat modified, "beastly" Malthus' ideas won a partial acceptance by many radicals, but these men were spurned by Cobbett. The countenancing of population limitation by birth control or even by continence (or, as it was euphemistically called, "moral restraint") incensed him.

> . . . for, as to preaching the Malthusian doctrine of restraint to the country girls, only let the nasty *feelosofers* go and state the doctrine to them IN PLAIN TERMS; let them state the unnatural, the beastly, the nasty ideas in PLAIN, UNVAR-NISHED LANGUAGE; let them do this, and see how soon their heads will be tied up in their aprons, and their filthy brains knocked out against the posts of the cowcribs.[6]

In his major attack on Malthus, written in 1819 after the passage of a bill in parliament which increased the influence of large landowners on the parish vestries, Cobbett's immediate concern was for the poor laws. The existence of these laws was threatened by the application of Malthusian ideas and Cobbett, an ardent champion, defended them with all the skill he could command. After an attack upon Malthus' character, principles and reasoning, Cobbett stated, ". . . it is not my intention to waste my time on your abstract matter. . . ." and then launched into an impassioned critique of Malthusian suggestions to prevent the poor from marrying. Here, and in the eleventh of his "sermons," Cobbett makes an eloquent and humane defense of the right of the laborer to marry and to enjoy subsistence while there was one morsel of food left in the kingdom. The laws of nature "written in our passions, desires and propensities; written even in the organization of our bodies . . ." compel mankind to procreate

---

[6] P.R. (4/9/31), col. 79. Also see P.R. (4/15/26), cols. 136–39 for a denunciation of Richard Carlile, the radical journalist who had advocated "mechanical means."

and they are reflected in the scriptures and the articles of the church which "you [Malthus], being a PARSON, care little about. . . ." They take precedence over all man-made laws and to deny them is unnatural and atheistic. "Without woman, what is a man? A poor, solitary misanthropic creature; a rough, uncouth, a hard, unfeeling, and almost brutal being. Take from the heart the passion of love, and life is not worth having: youth has nothing to enjoy and age nothing to remember with delight." [7] The only surplus population that Cobbett could see was composed of idlers who lived off the people's taxes, but the Malthusians did not suggest that *they* practice "moral restraint."

Although he was a vigorous defender of marriage as an institution and of the right of the poor to enjoy it, Cobbett did agree with Malthus on one point. It was that early marriage among the laboring classes was a great evil. While he insisted that they had a *right* to marry at any time, he also claimed that misery and hopelessness about bettering their situation drove them to make hasty attachments. When he was young, he said, both male and female laborers lived in the house with the farmer's family. An example of morality, sobriety and thrift was thus set. Intermarriage among the farming and laboring classes was common, as was the desire to save a little money before marriage. This style of life, so dear to Cobbett's paternalistic heart, was now a thing of the past for the farmers had taken on aristocratic airs and had driven the laborers from the house to find lodgings elsewhere.[8] He also took exception to Malthus' main point, that population, unless checked, will outstrip the food supply. To Cobbett, subsistence must precede population, for the workers create food, clothing, and so on in proportion to their numbers. The only way that a surfeit of people can occur is when the govern-

---

[7] P.R. (5/8/19), cols. 1019 ff.; *Thirteen Sermons,* cols. 244 ff.
[8] P.R. (4/7/21), cols. 13–15.

ment interferes and takes subsistence from those who work and gives it to those who do not. The latter, the "surplus population," increases while creating poverty for the laborer and making it appear that there are too many people for the country to support.[9] There were ample provisions in England, according to Cobbett, for all those who wanted to work. It was the pensioners, sinecurists and other idlers who were "redundant." Hadn't England supported her population during the Middle Ages in comfort and dignity? And weren't the inhabitants of the country (despite the lies of the census takers to the contrary) greater in number then than at this time? The problem obviously was rooted in a corrupt borough-monger government, which drained the wealth created by the laboring classes to support a tribe of drones.

A good deal of merriment has been occasioned by Cobbett's insistence that the population of England had actually de-creased since the Middle Ages, and it does seem odd that such a claim would have been so persistently advanced in the face of obvious facts. Yet it was just these "obvious" circum-stances which led him to make his statement "that not a single soul has been added to our population since the time of Queen Elizabeth." [10] He did allow that Lancashire, parts of Yorkshire and, of course, the London area were more populous than ever before but believed that this increase had taken place at the expense of the rural population. His evidence consisted of signs of cultivation in deserted acres, abandoned farmhouses, and the presence of large churches in small vil-lages. The latter especially attracted his attention and he occupied himself on his travels with estimating the capacity of these churches and comparing his findings with the present population of the surrounding area. What motive, he asked, could there have been to make these enormous buildings if

9 P.R. (6/4/31), col. 572.
10 P.R. (6/8/22), col. 615.

there had not been people to fill them? [11] His incredulity toward census reports demonstrating the rapid rise of population in recent years [12] and his belief in rural depopulation was shared by many contemporaries. Actually, the increase in population was caused in part by a rise in the birth rate and also by a fall in mortality due to improved food, sanitation and medical care. The fact that no rural county fell behind in gross population between 1801 and 1851 answers the charge that agricultural changes were responsible for depopulating the countryside.[13] Yet the signs of decay were there and Cobbett is not entirely to blame for trusting the evidence of his eyes—many others made similar mistakes.

In these observations Cobbett demonstrated his penchant for seeing only what he wanted to see, that tendency of his to fix upon one factor in a complex situation and then explain everything pertaining to it on this basis. His notion of a "System" is only the most obvious example. This characteristic helps to account for his tremendously over-simplified views on all phases of English life, including, in this case, political economy. One might judge harshly and say that Cobbett's observation on churches reveals him to be a fool or a liar; but in all probability, Cobbett had simply jumped to a conclusion congenial to his prejudices and then convinced himself of its accuracy. Unable to believe that population could actually be increasing in a society which he believed to be deteriorating, he interpreted the vast size of the churches in proportion to the current population as evidence that he was correct. Although he prided himself on his common sense, Cobbett did not always use it—especially if it would mean relinquishing a cherished prejudice. Hating theory as he in-

11 *History of the Protestant Reformation*. See especially letter XVI; P.R. (4/12/23), cols. 69 ff.
12 "Bang! Bang! Bang! Let the world produce us the like of this if it can." *Ibid.*, col. 100.
13 See T. S. Ashton, *The Industrial Revolution, 1760–1830*, London, Oxford University Press, 1957, pp. 3–4 and p. 61.

sisted he did, he was nevertheless an inflexible doctrinaire if these prejudices were touched.

Cobbett was on surer ground when he pointed out specific abuses and when he condemned the practice of measuring a people's prosperity by statistics. Determining the aggregate of the nation's taxable income, or the increase in exports and imports, or the amount of road building and using these figures to demonstrate the growing wealth of the country was generally accepted by the affluent. It was very comforting to them. The figures annually became more accurate, the analytic techniques more sophisticated and the reassurance they afforded increased accordingly. England was rapidly becoming more prosperous, her people generally better off than at any previous time. Cobbett was quick to deny these assertions. An increase in excise taxes, he claimed, does not mean prosperity (except for those who live on taxes). The measure of national prosperity is the happiness of the great mass of the country's inhabitants, and this happiness means plenty to eat, drink and wear. "Our situation is of a very singular character. We make a figure of brilliancy [sic] that astonishes the world; and we have, at the very same time, the most miserable people that ever saw the light of the sun. We have a metropolis which receives annually an *addition* in houses, in population, and in riches, equal to the metropolis of an ordinary state; and we have a country, the great mass of the people of which are clad in miserable rags, and are, almost literally constantly crying for food." [14] He thus posed the problem of poverty in the midst of plenty, which had been ignored by those mesmerized by statistics. The blame for this ambiguous situation was not hard to locate. "The place and pension list, the thundering standing army in time of profound peace, the intolerable deadweight, kept up for the breeding of Gentlemen and Ladies, the Military and Naval

[14] P.R. (8/21/24), cols. 449–50; P.R. (9/29/21), cols. 708–09; P.R. (11/3/21), cols. 1028–29.

Academies, the enormous pay to Ambassadors and Envoys, the Debt, the Taxes, that drain away all the substance of the people who labour: here is the cause, and the sole cause of all the misery; and until this cause be removed, the misery will continue to increase." [15]

His argument supplied a healthy corrective to the too-hearty optimism indulged in by many of his contemporaries. It is unfortunate that Cobbett and others who felt the same way did not have more impact upon influential opinion, for they would have focused attention upon the plight of large numbers of people whose share in the growing wealth of their country was indeed meager. England would have been a healthier place and her subsequent domestic history would have been happier if the comfortable classes could have been persuaded to forego their fixation with figures and look at existing conditions instead. Yet if these people were blind to certain facts, so was Cobbett. For England *was* gaining in wealth and, although the distribution of this wealth was unfair, some benefits were beginning to trickle down to the laboring poor. It is probable that there was a rising standard of living which affected all classes. This was the major importance of these figures, not the fact that the taxes themselves were frequently used to benefit idle "tax-eaters"—a problem which would be resolved in time. Cobbett could see signs of this increasing prosperity represented in the pianos, sofas, and other household furnishings of the tenant farmer. Yet he ascribed this to a desire on their part to live like the landlords and rejected it as an example of better living, just as he railed against sugar and tea in the houses of the laborers.

Since Cobbett did not believe in the inevitability of progress under laissez faire (or even accept the implications of "progress"), he urged the government to protect the welfare of the people. His paternalistic social attitude would permit government action in this situation. Of course, the Tory government

15 P.R. (8/21/24), col. 482.

of the time did not envision itself as an active defender of
the economic well-being of the common people. Even when
confronted with evidence of misery and starvation, it contended
that nothing could be done to alleviate the situation. Supported by the economists, Tory politicians solemnly denied that
prosperity could be produced by interfering with the natural
working of economic laws. Indeed, in the final analysis, it
was God himself who dictated prosperity by determining
whether or not the harvest would be bountiful. No earthly
hands should attempt to interfere with what had been divinely
ordained. The people had better resign themselves to privation,
pray for a good harvest and patiently wait until their condition
improved. The government, which enforced the Combination
Acts against trade unions, refused to pass effective legislation
to regulate factory conditions, and repealed the income tax
at the conclusion of the war, was not the type to promote
the happiness of its humbler citizens. Cobbett denied that
the government had to remain helpless in the face of depression and pointed out instances where it had legislated for the
advantage of certain groups. Citing examples of abundant
harvests which coincided with starvation, he maintained that
privation was the fault of man, not God. Hadn't the government founded the debt, raised an army and levied taxes? All
of these brought unhappiness to the people but might be
eliminated by legislation. The Tories had also shown a willingness to tamper with economic laws by passing legislation
for the benefit of the fundholder and the Bank of England.
Surely it could do the same for the oppressed taxpayer.[16]

Here Cobbett had assumed a position opposite from what
was to be orthodox economic dogma for generations afterward. Just as he believed that the prosperity of a country was
not to be measured by figures on charts or lines on a graph,
he also insisted that the state had the capacity and the duty
to act to prevent the people from suffering. "Is not *the happi-*

16 P.R. (1/22/20), cols. 646–47; P.R. (2/19/20), cols. 1 ff.

ness of the people the idea that precedes all others? Do we not contemplate the absence of the misery and the degrading vices thereon attendant? Do we not please ourselves in thinking of a healthy, well-fed, well-clad, cheerful, and, in a great degree, independent labouring population?" [17] Twenty years later, in an impassioned *Register* article, Cobbett denounced starvation in the midst of plenty; the system "which takes from those who labour, and gives to those who do not labour." He asked "the Pretty Gentlemen of Whitehall" why this should be so. "Are not these matters worthy of the attention of statesmen?" Selfish extravagance among the ruling class had helped to impoverish the people, yet "you are afraid that the poor, suffering creatures should imagine that they have a right to receive back, in a time like this, some small portion of those taxes, which they have been paying out of their sweat the whole of their lives." [18]

Set against the values of the time, this consideration of national prosperity in terms of higher living standards for the laboring poor is salutary. This, of course, is Cobbett at his best—the Cobbett with whom we are most familiar. And yet, ignoring the fact that Cobbett always viewed prosperity in material terms and the unsubtle environmentalism of this last *Register* article, he reveals once again generous indignation rather than feasible proposals for change. Cobbett's mind was fixed on the evils of taxation and he never comprehended the extent of the connection between economic interest groups and the Tory ministers. Rhetoric aside, all he could suggest was that the government reduce the tax burden by repudiating a large part of the debt and making economies so sweeping as to be completely unrealistic. Cobbett's explosions of wrath sounded like bombast and irritated influential opinion.

A logical corollary of this domestic laissez-faire economic policy was the attempt by merchants and manufacturers to

[17] P.R. (4/5/06), col. 491.
[18] P.R. (5/6/26), cols. 322 ff.

"liberalize" foreign trade. Confident in their ability to manufacture goods cheaper and better than anyone else in the
world, these men tried to end the centuries-old system of
protection which had *pour raison d'état* restricted commerce.
A struggle, waged by the political economists and manufacturers, resulted in major victories for their cause in the
1820's—the repeal of the Navigation Acts. England was by
then well on the way to becoming a free trade nation. Among
the ministers, Robinson and Huskisson at the Board of Trade
were disciples of the new economics and even the Tory Prime
Minister, Liverpool, lent crucial aid to the passage of this
legislation.

Opposition on the part of the shipping interests was expected as their monopoly was menaced. In addition, there
were those who took up the cause of the Navigation Acts for
other reasons. These venerable laws, dating back to 1381,
had outlived their usefulness as a protector of English industry; indeed, they had assumed an opposite effect and
inhibited the sale of goods abroad. However, the Navigation
Acts contributed to the strength of Britain's navy, and this
argued for their retention. This is the main point which
Cobbett made in justifying them. He consistently maintained
that the safety of the country depended upon British sailors,
trained in British ships, and he lamented that the government
would abandon this necessity for the sake of the private profit
of a few individuals.[19] On mixed economic and naval grounds
he also exalted the coastwise trade over foreign commerce.
"It has been most clearly proved, that, for *our* navy, the
nursery is our *coasting* trade." [20] These laws, the product of
the "wisdom and labours of successive ages," represented to
Cobbett the old self-contained England which reminded him
of his childhood. They strengthened the navy, fostered do-

---

[19] P.R. (3/6/02), cols. 205–09; P.R. (5/12/21), cols. 371–74; P.R.
(3/6/24), col. 583.
[20] P.R. (7/15/09), col. 40.

mestic industry and insulated the country from contamination by foreigners. If the Navigation Acts were necessary for England's safety and prosperity, then the arguments of the economists must be false. Cobbett did not believe their contention that all nations would best be served by free exchange of the commodities which each could produce most efficiently. Although he sometimes gave qualified assent to bilateral trade, most of his references were hostile.

Because of this, he not only opposed the principles of free trade but wanted exports from England prohibited as well. The idea that all nations might gain by mutual trade was to him "vulgar" and fatuous. "Nations are *essentially enemies of each other,*" he insisted and went on to say that treaties, including treaties of commerce, are made to gain an advantage and that foreign commerce is of no use unless it adds to the strength of the country.[21] Cobbett commented upon the relation between trade and national policy.

> Feeble nations have always been the strenuous advocates for *free trade and neutral rights.* Powerful nations, on the contrary, have always been for restricted commerce; for hard bargains with their neighbours; for ensuring greater gains from them than they were to receive in return; and in war for the strictest rules relative to contraband; for the most rigid observance of blockades and of every thing tending to make commerce yield to power: powerful nations have always endeavoured to keep their poor neighbours still poor, and their feeble neighbours still feeble. Powerful nations have never talked of sweet reciprocity: Those only cry out for reciprocity that see their neighbours better off than themselves.[22]

Here was an obvious attempt to dispose not only of the free traders' economic arguments but also their idealistic belief in trade bringing about peace between the nations. Although not a cynic by nature Cobbett was always suspicious

[21] P.R. (3/4/26), cols. 613–15.
[22] P.R. (8/2/28), cols. 131–32. See also P.R. (1/13/27), cols. 135 ff.

of foreigners' motivations. He refused to agree that any
lasting good could be achieved by cooperation between countries. In a somewhat different sphere he remained one of the
great mass of Englishmen who never comprehended the foreign
policy of Castlereagh. The very fact that the free traders,
whom he hated, believed in world peace through unhampered
commercial intercourse made Cobbett's negative attitude all
the more pronounced.

Since England could not trade with other countries with
profit or safety, she must find markets within her borders.
A "bountiful Providence" had given Britain the means to
support her population. Her people simply needed the tax
burdens lifted from their shoulders to become the best possible
market. Those engaged in foreign trade and in making articles
for export would be absorbed by agriculture (to the benefit of
their morals and health). The resulting increase in produce,
combined with more skillful farming, would make the country
self-sufficient. Necessary naval stores could be purchased with
savings made at the expense of the East India Company and
the sinecurists.[23] Such was Cobbett's scheme to rid the country
of the burden of its foreign commerce. He usually wrote on
this subject in a heat of anger at conditions which he saw
about him. Hunger and misery on the land and the horrors
of the towns whose inhabitants were absorbed in turning out
goods for export were all visible. They must have seemed
an ironic commentary upon the boasts of national prosperity
through foreign trade. Urban conditions also served as a
contrast to the lavish estates which he saw on his travels.

The East India Company served Cobbett as a fitting symbol
of the commercial movement, although it was really an
anachronism by this time. Until 1813 when parliament took
away the monopoly of the company in the trade with India,
he attacked it as a state within a state, corrupting politics

23 P.R. (11/28/07), cols. 836 ff.; P.R. (3/9/11), col. 589.

in England with its wealth, draining away the country's resources and plundering the inhabitants of India, all for the
advantage of a body of great merchants.[24] The philosophy
and practice of the company's business operations were already
obsolete. However, the complexity and uniqueness of the
situation in India aided in preventing the final clipping of
its claws until after the Indian mutiny. Actually the East India
Company was a symbol, not of modern commerce as Cobbett
believed, but of the mercantilist philosophy of trade with
which he had found so much in common. His writings on the
subject do not indicate that he understood the dilemma in
which he had placed himself. Yet this prejudice is significant
for it undoubtedly contributed to his negative opinion of
business in general. On the basis of the actions of this company and on the pattern of living set by some of its representatives who were his neighbors in Hampshire, he generalized
about all those engaged in commerce. This is unfortunate,
for many had taken advantage of the unprecedented opportunity afforded by the times to raise themselves by their
own exertions, as Cobbett had done himself. Their business
bore no comparison to the East India Company and the way
of life of these frugal, cautious, self-made men was often quite
different from that of the flamboyant "nabobs" who had risked
life itself in the Orient in a successful gamble with fortune.
Placed in unwilling proximity to the latter group soon after
he had returned from America, Cobbett's experience gave him
a somewhat false perspective from which to view the rising
entrepreneurial and merchant classes.

If Cobbett was hostile to those involved in trade with
colonies, he was also antagonistic toward the colonies themselves. With the sole and conspicuous exception of the West
Indies, he regarded them as hindrances which drained off
the mother country's men and money for an inadequate re-

[24] P.R. (1/30/13), cols. 129 ff.; P.R. (2/8/06), cols. 172–73.

turn. A true "little-Englander," he could not even consider them valuable as a source of raw materials. In 1831 he suggested selling Hanover and Canada to gain enough revenue to pay the debt.[25] He also opposed attempts backed by Wilberforce to turn that fruitful source of slaves, Sierra Leone, into a colony.[26] Part of his bias against this scheme was due to a fear that it would produce the immigration of Negroes into England. Similarly, his tenderness toward the interests of the West Indies planters may have been a means of expressing hatred of the East India Company. In contrast to the latter, he praised the West Indies interests because their lands were cheap to administer and did not engage in wars. Besides, the islands employed British ships and sailors while keeping them within reach in time of war.[27] There does not appear to be any other substantial reason for this extraordinary concern, which at times favored the sugar planters at the expense of the English consumer. However, in 1821, Cobbett noted his displeasure with the opposition on the part of the planters to reform in England. Although he maintained their right to own slaves, heaping ridicule upon the Evangelicals and others who wanted emancipation, he later reluctantly voted for emancipation in parliament in deference to the wishes of his constituents. Nevertheless, he voted against compensating the former slave owners from taxes.[28] This action and his insistence that the duty on West Indian sugar be maintained marked the end of his unusual tenderness.

Commerce and political economy represented to Cobbett a set of impersonal, antisocial theories and attitudes. They contributed to the corruption of the morals of the people by fostering the growth of cities and supported tyranny by an alliance with the boroughmonger system. Theory and statistics,

[25] P.R. (8/6/31), col. 338.
[26] P.R. (8/27/03), col. 280; P.R. (3/24/04), col. 438.
[27] P.R. (2/16/05), col. 237; P.R. (10/1/31), col. 3.
[28] P.R. (8/4/21), col. 146; P.R. (6/15/33), col. 674; Great Britain, 3 Hansard's Parliamentary Debates XX (1833), 204.

overseas commerce and colonies, then, were objects of intense dislike not simply in their own right but because of their identification with a government which he hated. He never deceived himself about the tendencies of political economists, as he did those of the agricultural landlords. As a younger man he had been involved with landlords and even the politicians, but not with the economists. These persons he always regarded coolly and his early references to them, at the time of the Treaty of Amiens, were almost as hostile as his later ones.

Long before his opinions on matters of politics had taken on that degree of relative clarity which we may regard as "final," he was noting that commerce led to the corruption of parliament through bribery and the purchase of seats.[29] The original patriotic animus was quickly reinforced. Also, he had never identified the welfare of the commercial classes with the good of the country as a whole, as so many Tories, in government and outside of it, tended to do. One may ask who was the true conservative—Cobbett or those who were adamant against government intervention in the interests of the poor but sympathetic when merchants and manufacturers requested assistance in times of depression? [30]

In all this we see a way of life passing and a representative of that life fighting a last ditch battle against the forces of change. To a considerable extent, although confused about details, Cobbett realized the general nature of the struggle and was more aware of the consequences than the Squire Jolterheads and other members of the landed interests whom he vainly tried to rouse. He sensed that economic life was bound up with politics and perceived that economic changes were the cause of the altering of the condition of England. On certain occasions he used his eyes to measure change and what

29 P.R. (12/12/07), cols 900–01.
30 Cobbett was never deceived about the flexible interpretation which the commercial classes gave to laissez faire. P.R. (12/6/06), cols. 867–68; P.R. (3/9/11), cols. 585–86.

he saw disturbed him profoundly. Having strong prejudices he was not always willing to do this, for he was not a peripatetic empiricist as some have claimed. Although many of Cobbett's observations were inaccurate and his biases were often gross he did see this problem in human terms. Some of his enemies did not.

VIII
Public finance

The image of a man devoted to a way of life which was passing, his face set against change, is supported by Cobbett's struggle in the field of public finance. For over thirty years he looked upon the entire body of financial institutions with incomprehension and mistrust and constantly waged war upon them. No other topic was the subject of as many *Register* articles as public finance. Nothing else reveals Cobbett as being so thoroughly misinformed, the victim of both his lot as a weekly publisher compelled to write on all matters, as well as of his obtrusive prejudices. On this subject and political economy as well, Cobbett was handicapped by their complexity. But here, too, Cobbett had company in the form of many individuals charged with the responsibility of governing the country.

Cobbett was opposed to the entire arrangement of public

finance. Debt, taxes, funds and the "paper-aristocracy" who manipulated them were to be extirpated root and branch. After spurning a government offer to make a profit at loan-mongering immediately after his return to England in 1800, Cobbett was led to examine this unfamiliar problem. At once he understood that the funded debt was a menace because it diverted the attention of the government creditors (or fund-holders—the term which Cobbett applied to them) away from the good of the country as a whole and made them preoccupied with their selfish interests. The lack of military ardor, as seen in the support of the fundholders for the Peace of Amiens, and concentration upon pecuniary affairs disgusted Cobbett with this class. His earlier strictures reveal a patriotic bias rather than an economic one.[1] At this time he was a sensitive patriot, urging *guerre à outrance* upon the French and was galled at the concern of these men for their pocket-books.

The softness which Cobbett believed that Pitt's ministry felt toward the problems of merchants and bankers was a factor in his growing radicalism. Distrust soon ripened into hatred and he perceived what seemed to him grave social consequences attending the rise of the new monied class. He expressed resentment at "the system of rendering *every thing* commercial; of making merchants and bankers into Lords . . ." The importance of finance and commerce to the war effort was reflected in the growing influence of this class in government, and Cobbett did not like it. He looked with horror upon the "gamblers" and "speculators" whose influence was replacing that of the aristocracy and the church.[2] Although enemies, the French deserved congratulations for their almost exclusively agricultural economy as well as their small national debt "and, which is the same thing, she [France] has no paper money; none of that sort of property which gives

[1] See, for example, A.R. (11/6 to 11/13/02), col. 608.
[2] P.R. (1/11/06), col. 41.

to its owners an interest at variance with the rest of the country. . . ." [3]

By the year 1800 the tempo of change in England was increasing. Economic pressures were operating ruthlessly to undermine the position of those groups unable to meet the stress of new conditions. Not only the hapless agricultural laborers and handloom weavers were victims of this process, but various landed interests, secure for generations, were now unable to keep abreast of rising prices and increased taxation. Cobbett was aware of this and aware also that what he described as a new class of arrogant, wine-drinking, fox-hunting farmers, with novel-reading daughters and sons aping young squires, and "a house crammed up with sofas, pianos, and all sorts of fooleries. . . ." had arisen. [4] The change had been going on for some time but war conditions had accelerated it and made it more visible. The precise causes of this change were too concealed for Cobbett to appreciate them. Yet his strictures against ". . . the numerous and powerful body of loan-jobbers, directors, brokers, contractors and farmers-general, which has been engendered by the excessive amount of the public debt, and the almost boundless extension of the issues of paper-money . . ." have point.

As early as 1804 he warned that the chief domestic danger did not consist of democrats or anarchists, but the excessive quantity of bank notes which had produced this "paper-money aristocracy" to the detriment of the landed aristocracy and the country at large. [5] For the rest of his life he was to denounce those who made a living "by watching the turn of the market." Over twenty years later he wrote: "Of what *use* are a banker and his people to the public. They do no work of any sort; they produce nothing, nor do they improve the

3 P.R. (2/11/04), cols. 180–81.
4 P.R. (12/16/15), col. 330.
5 P.R. (9/8/04), cols. 370 ff.

worth of any thing that is produced by others." [6] The financial class, without values save those concerned with making money, with their households of French footmen and Italian singers, was not only destructive itself, but it also provided a bad example. The City of London, that great "Wen" which, Cobbett claimed, produced nothing but consumed more than half the food raised in England, was their monument. City and country were sharply divided, in Cobbett's mind, because of his preoccupation with agriculture. But his attempts to alert the traditional leaders of English society to their danger were futile because there were no really clear-cut lines dividing the landed aristocracy from the mercantile class. Unlike the Continent, England had no *noblesse*. Individual landowners, like Sir Thomas Beevor, supported him but the majority, with financial, social, and often family connections among the commercial groups, did not.[7] Also, the absence of political parties in a modern sense meant that the landed interest was spread among each of the two nominal parties. There was thus no real political confrontation of the two groups. It was, in fact, the determination of those calling themselves Whigs to continue the funding system while in office in 1806 which sent Cobbett a long way down the road to radical opposition. It also created the never-to-be-eradicated opinion that there was only one major political grouping in England.

The war against France dominated public finance at the time when Cobbett was beginning his career as a journalist and its fiscal effects continued to plague England for years after Waterloo. This conflict, of unprecedented scope and intensity, had tremendous impact upon English monetary

6 P.R. (4/1/26), cols. 3–4.
7 Cobbett had some awareness of this. At the time of the marriage of Ellice, a City of London merchant, to Lord Grey's sister, he noted, "There is one of the numerous instances, which the pride of the Aristocracy has been bent down to an alliance with the 'CHANGE'." P.R. (3/25/20), col. 96.

policies as well as upon the more frequently discussed aspects of domestic politics and trade. Not only was Britain compelled to expend great sums for her own forces, she also pursued the policy of subsidizing Continental allies in order to keep them in the field against the French. The result was a rise in public expenditure from a total of £26,200,000 in 1790 to a peak of £174,070,000 in 1813. In 1815, the total debt, including debts incurred for the Emperor of Germany and for Portugal, was £832,197,004. The Liverpool ministry never wavered in its intention to pay this debt which, although enormous, was not as large as it might have been, thanks to Pitt's policy of reducing the amount of money raised by borrowing. His introduction of a graduated income tax in 1799 and the increasing of other taxes made possible an average ratio of revenue to total income of 46.8% for the years 1793–1816.[8] The income tax was an innovation, made palatable to those affected only by the nature as well as the severity of the struggle which Britain was waging. The sums raised by land and income taxes were, however, minor in comparison to the yields of the indirect taxes. These taxes fell heaviest upon the poor and forced them to bear a disproportionate share of the financial cost of the war.

Six years before the war began, Pitt proposed to reduce the national debt by means of a sinking fund. A group of independent commissioners were appointed to buy up outstanding government stock on an allowance of one million pounds per year, plus a small additional amount raised by accumulated interest on the redeemed stock. An oddity of the scheme was this latter feature, which was intended to take advantage of the workings of compound interest. A high

[8] For a defense of Pitt's financial policies, see Norman J. Silberling, "Financial and Monetary Policy of Great Britain During the Napoleonic Wars. I Financial Policy," *The Quarterly Journal of Economics*, Vol. 38 (February, 1924), pp. 214–33. The figures cited above referring to public expenditure and the ratio of revenue to total income are from this source. See also Halévy, *England in 1815*, ch. 3.

interest rate on government securities was, therefore, regarded as desirable because it enabled the fund to accumulate more quickly. Amid all the controversy engendered by the plan, one thing was clear. There would have to be peace abroad and economy at home so that the budgetary balance could be maintained and the fund allowed to accumulate.[9] Another essential element was seen in Pitt's insistence upon the inviolability of the fund. Payment to it had to be made, even at the cost of raising money through taxation or a short-term loan in times of deficit. During the war, this led to the ludicrous situation whereby money was borrowed at a high rate of interest to pay loans made at a lower rate. Peace, prosperity and the integrity of the fund were therefore necessary criteria for its success. Of course, under these ideal conditions almost any device for debt reduction might work. However, this one was not to receive a fair chance, for in 1793 a twenty-two-year war with France began. To his admirers the greatness of Pitt lies in his determination to subordinate everything else to winning the war. This overlooks his sinking fund scheme which continued its costly operations, although somewhat modified in its details by his successors, while taxes were oppressing those lacking the good fortune to be government creditors. In his defense, however, it has been argued that by allowing the fund to continue, Pitt insured that money could be borrowed at low rates of interest.

Taxes and borrowing were necessary for the government to function during these years of war and its aftermath. There was also one other element in British finance which was just as important in maintaining the country's ability to carry on the struggle. This was the government's decision to suspend specie payments by the Bank of England in February, 1797. The resulting measure, which was bitterly opposed by Fox,

[9] For a discussion of the background to this scheme, see Carl B. Cone, "Richard Price and Pitt's Sinking Fund of 1786," *The Economic History Review,* Series 2, Vol. 4 (Nov., 1951), pp. 243-51.

Sheridan and others of Pitt's political enemies, relaxed the currency to allow for the unprecedented expenses incurred in prosecuting the war.[10] Depreciation of the Bank of England notes was an inevitable consequence.

Taxes, paper money and the national debt formed the basis of Cobbett's resentment of government finance. He was to struggle against it all his life, devoting to the subject as a whole, or parts of it, more space in the *Political Register* than to any other topic. Sometimes, in exasperation, he would refer to the intricate financial system as "The Thing," a characteristic attempt to simplify a situation and register disgust simultaneously. This term would also include the widespread corruption in political and social life stemming from the operations of the country's financial organization. "A loan was not the bringing of money to the Government: it was the writing of a name that constituted the loan in the first instance. Then came a shuffling about of the paper money; and after the bonuses, discounts and allowances of one kind and another, the thing amounted to little more than the lending of the gains arising from the various workings of the thing." [11]

Appalled by the growing size of the country's debt to the fundholders and dismayed at the government's persistence in treating it as sacrosanct, Cobbett concluded that the debt must be repudiated if England were to survive. He suggested that this was not the heinous thing that repudiation of a private debt would be, for the first duty of the country was to preserve itself, and the good of the individual must give way before the good of the community. Painting an unconvincing picture of a greedy fundholding widow, he tried to show that debt repudiation would harm only the covetous.[12] Yet this simple suggestion of 1806 was considerably modified ten years

---

[10] See Norman J. Silberling, "Financial and Monetary Policy of Great Britain During the Napoleonic Wars. II Ricardo and the Bullion Report." *The Quarterly Journal of Economics,* Vol. 38 (May, 1924), pp. 397–439.

[11] P.R. (6/22/22), col. 723.

[12] P.R. (1/25/06), cols. 97–110.

later. In a series of *Register* articles he changed his earlier position to allow for an "equitable adjustment" of the fund-holders' claims. This new attitude permitted the compensation of the fundholder in proportion to the value of gold at the time the money was lent. Furthermore, the account with the fundholders should not be settled until every sinecure and pension not merited for any real public service was abolished and every government salary reduced to the standard of 1788. Also, economies should be made in the allowance granted to the royal family, the standing army in England should be discharged and the East India Company held to a strict finan-cial accounting. It was the officeholders and boroughmongers who made the war and profited by it, and they should be made to disgorge before the "innocent" fundholder had to accept his reduced portion.[13]

This change of attitude reflects Cobbett's increasing (but not yet permanent) disillusionment with the landlord borough-mongers. Appeals to them for radical reform had been use-less. The landlords, although hurt by adverse economic conditions, had placed their faith in the 1815 Corn Law, which greatly restricted imports of grain, to get higher prices for their products. Although Cobbett was not alone in his demand for "equitable adjustment," there was no widespread disposition for radical solutions.[14] His efforts to come to an agreement with the landlords continued until 1823. A frus-trated Cobbett addressed appeals to them to repudiate the debt during the same period from 1816 to 1823 that he was seeking the favor of the fundholders by promising only an "equitable adjustment." This search for assistance also con-tributed toward Cobbett's placing himself in the forefront of agitation on behalf of the rights of the common laborer.

[13] P.R. (8/17/16), col. 172; Amer. P.R. (6/8/16), cols. 722–36.
[14] See Halévy, *The Liberal Awakening*, p. 113, for evidence of unrest among some members of parliament. This volume clearly indicates the preoccupation of the ministers with financial matters during the postwar years.

Cobbett was now driving at a reform of parliament on a popular basis and saw the fundholders as a class separate from the boroughmongers. The latter were now the enemy— all others, potential friends. He professed to believe that the fundholders would listen to reason and settle for partial compensation by a reformed parliament rather than risk losing all at the incompetent hands of the boroughmongers. Economies effected by this reformed parliament through retrenchment and the confiscation of boroughmonger property would allow the government to make this adjustment with the fundholders. In subsequent years Cobbett returned to this theme. His hatred of the landed interest became a major feature of his writings.[15] Here his hostility toward compensation of the government's creditors took second place to the loathing which he felt toward that amorphous cluster of privilege and corruption which he called the boroughmonger system and identified with the agricultural interests. Of course, his reasoning about the willingness of the fundholders to join forces with the radicals against the landowning boroughmongers was confused. There was no watertight separation between fundholders and boroughmongers and, besides, not all boroughmongers were landowners. The fundholders wisely relied upon the importance of credit to the country and the reluctance of the Liverpool government to introduce innovations in contracts to secure them full compensation.

In the confusion of the debate over government financial policy, to which Cobbett contributed dozens of articles and tens of thousands of words, two items of legislation provided an axis about which discussion could develop. They were the Bank Restriction Act which suspended gold payments by the Bank of England in 1797 and Peel's Act of 1819 which provided for a return to gold payments in several stages spread over a period of three years. The former act was followed

15 See P.R. (10/20/21), cols. 902–06; P.R. (7/15/26), cols. 148–50. Also, see P.R. (9/9/26), cols. 641 ff. for a philippic against the landed interest.

by an increase in paper money, inflation and greater misery for the working classes. The latter resulted in a contraction of notes and falling prices, in addition to signifying that faith with the fundholders was to be kept, even at the expense of paying off a debt in coin that had been contracted in inflated paper.

Cobbett's attitude toward all this was hostile. As far as the debt was concerned, in the course of his argument for "equitable adjustment" he noted that a lender could not expect solid gold coin in return for depreciated paper. The fundholder must only be paid a sum sufficient to purchase as much as the pound would have bought when the money was lent. As usual, he used an analogy from agriculture to clarify his position. Those who lent money between 1793 and 1815 should not attempt to secure 4¼ bushels of wheat for every 1¾ bushels they lent.[16] He refused to admit that the "industrious classes" were bound to pay debts incurred before their time any more than a child was bound to pay debts of a father who had left him nothing. Here was a reflection of Thomas Paine's notion of separate and distinct generations.[17] Furthermore, he denied the practicability of Peel's scheme. Cobbett could not conceive how a debt contracted in an inflated currency could be paid after deflation had been legislated. This was the basis of his famous "Gridiron" prediction, in which he volunteered to be broiled alive over a fire by the ministry if Peel's bill could accomplish its purpose.[18] He was wrong (but never admitted it) because a gradual return to a cash basis was made possible by a great increase in trade. The resulting revenue enabled the government to keep faith with the fundholder. For years Cobbett maintained that the government was about to renege on its promise, and every temporary difficulty was hopefully viewed as the beginning

16 P.R. (6/22/22), col. 728–29.
17 Great Britain, 3 *Hansard's Parliamentary Debates*, XIX (1833), 31.
18 P.R. (11/13/19), col. 364.

of the end.[19] Naturally the failure of the agricultural interests, who were adversely affected by deflation, to follow his lead increased his fury toward them.

As for paper money itself, its natural tendency "is to draw property into great masses, to make a few persons very rich, the community in general very poor, and totally to destroy the harmony and happiness of the people." [20] In his major work on the subject, *Paper Against Gold,* Cobbett castigated the entire system of public finance. Paper money, the national debt and Pitt's sinking fund, the system of taxation as well as the new financial aristocracy which manipulated all of this were the objects of abuse.[21] He later claimed that his enforced leisure in prison gave him time to study finance and write about it, but he had written in a similar vein on previous occasions.[22]

Perhaps his point of view was expressed most succinctly as follows:

> That paper-money, and, indeed, that money of no sort, can *create* any thing valuable, is evident; and that it cannot *cause* it to be created, on a *general* scale, is also evident; for, all valuable things arise from *labour,* and, if an addition to the quantity of money sets labour in motion in one place, it draws it from another place; that is all that it does. If its nature and operation be such as to cause new and fine houses and carriages and "grand dinners" to make their appearance, it takes away the means of furnishing the houses of the most numerous class, robs them of their bedding, their food, their drink and their raiment. Nothing is *created* by it. It is not value *in itself;* but merely the *measure of value,* and the means of *removing valuable things from one possessor to another.*[23]

---

[19] In 1833 he proclaimed the gridiron prediction "completely fulfilled." P.R. (6/8/33), col. 581.

[20] P.R. (2/8/34), col. 326.

[21] *Paper Against Gold and Glory Against Prosperity* (2 vols.), London, J. M'Creery, 1815, passim. *Paper Against Gold* was originally published as a series of *Register* articles in 1810–1811 while Cobbett was in Newgate.

[22] P.R. (11/16/16), cols. 514–15.

[23] P.R. (5/26/21), col. 509.

His facile observations ("Money is nothing but a thing to *measure* by; and, surely, that is the *greatest* measure that will hold the most wheat.") [24] divert attention from the dry analyses of the economists and the obscurities of government financial policy. Regardless of their inaccuracy, they seem to be "well meaning," proof that Cobbett "had his heart in the right place." As such, they have helped create the familiar picture which we have of Cobbett—a Jove hurling thunderbolts of denunciation at the oppressors of the common folk of England. His misunderstandings, misleading analogies and downright ignorance have been brushed aside, sometimes by historians who, like Cobbett himself, had no use for a money economy.

The part that credit played in the new economic system, which was Britain's major source of strength, was a closed book to Cobbett and he could only visualize the notes flooding the country as so many promises to pay. All that he knew was that paper money depreciated the value of currency and consequently raised prices. His copious writings are a medley of shallow analyses, dubious advice to his readers, and attacks upon the whole foundation of government finance. Cobbett's native shrewdness prevented him from being completely wrong, but his work is generally jejune, derivative (he showed, but seldom acknowledged, his debt to Thomas Paine and Horne Tooke), and sometimes downright silly. Cobbett was unfitted by background or training to understand the complicated paper money system which was shaping the economy. Yet he was forced to examine it and he commented decisively and confidently upon problems which few others really understood, least of all many of the government ministers. Cobbett was forced to examine other problems, too, but in the case of agricultural developments and political liberty, he had the advantage of that greater personal experience which was imperative if he was to make any sense at all.

[24] P.R. (11/3/21), col. 1049.

Poor as the quality of *Paper Against Gold* and his other writings concerning money are, it is in the area of taxation that Cobbett is most incoherent. His confident assertions consist of shallow nonsense and prejudice, motivated primarily by his hatred of "The Thing." Here, too, he displayed his physiocratic bias in the insistence that agriculture was the basis of the economy. "From the earth comes every thing that we eat, drink, and wear. The earth is the source of all the necessaries of life: of all that man wants. He who does *nothing* to make the earth produce, either directly or indirectly, must eat and drink and wear to the *loss* of those who labour." Land and labor were the bases of the country's prosperity and this prosperity could not be destroyed as long as it remained established upon them, even by a wholesale burning of bank notes and dividend certificates.[25]

From the point of view of one who aspired to be the tribune of the common people, the problem of taxation was formidable. Even after the introduction of the income tax (on a graduated basis, with incomes under £60 exempted), the greater part of the country's revenue came from traditional excise, customs and post office duties, plus the land tax. The tax burden pressed most heavily upon the poor. For many years Cobbett insisted that *all* taxes ultimately bore upon labor. Edmund Burke, in one of his complacent homilies, compared taxes to dews which were raised from the whole surface of the ground and then sent back in enriching showers. Cobbett denied this and said that taxes were raised by those who labored and benefitted those who did not.[26] Insistence that the poor shouldered the tax burden alone led him to claim that taxes on necessities such as salt were best and that a tax on draught horses would be better than a tax upon

---

[25] P.R. (9/11/19), cols. 117–18; P.R. (11/7/07), col. 711. This attitude was displayed again in his chronic suspicion of trade, but Cobbett perversely rejected one element of physiocrat doctrine: a laissez-faire economy.

[26] P.R. (8/9/17), col. 600.

pleasure horses.[27] This attitude was eventually forgotten, as was his early insouciant attitude toward the subject generally ". . . who ever heard of a *light* tax? The growling of the multitude, about the rise in the price of porter and of grains, will certainly be despised by the ministers. . . ."[28] The citizens' willingness to bear wartime taxation is usually proportioned to his interest in his country's struggle, and Cobbett was not an exception. As his disenchantment grew, he began to strike out at those he felt were waging war against Napoleon in order to stifle English liberty, and he proposed that they pay the cost of the war.

By the 1820's he no longer claimed that all taxes were, in the final analysis, raised from the laboring class and advocated a drastic revision of the excise taxes in order to benefit the poor. He urged that the salt tax which he once praised be repealed, along with the tax on malt.[29] Apart from being a burden, he later claimed that the malt tax was instrumental in changing for the worse the manners and character of the rural population. The expense of malt not only prevented laborers from making their own beer, it also had the undesirable social consequence of helping to expel single laborers from the houses of the farmers.[30] The heavy duty thwarted Cobbett's ideal of having every family brew its own beer and thus be as self-sufficient as possible. This is another reflection of Cobbett's belief that a principal reason for the disruption of life on the land, as he had once known it, was the increase in taxation. Even if the farmer did not attempt to ape the style of living of his new fundholder neighbor, he could not, in many cases, afford to continue to support his laborers in

27 P.R. (3/9/05), 382–87.
28 P.R. (4/10/02), col. 378.
29 P.R. (6/9/21), col. 692. Taxes on tea, spirits, coffee, and tobacco should remain in force, as those using these hateful commodities deserved to starve.
30 Great Britain, 3 *Hansard's Parliamentary Debates* XXI (1834), 902.

his house. Taxes were helping to create a new class in society at the expense of social values which Cobbett cherished.

Eventually he advocated a quarterly tax on all houses, lands, mines and other real property in the kingdom. He felt that the tax would be certain in amount and easy to collect. Nor would it fall exclusively upon the owner of property, as it would be distributed by the owner to his tenants and the consumer. How this scheme, in which the owner was to redistribute his taxes to the poor, was to benefit the latter, Cobbett did not say. An interesting feature was that the tax should not be graduated, for Cobbett felt that this would bear hardest against the industrious and the skillful. The man who had one thousand acres must pay a thousand times as much tax as the man who had but one acre but not proportionately more.[31] Cobbett did not want any scheme of taxation that smacked of levelling, or which might be confiscatory. Even at this late stage of his career, long after he had come to accept universal male suffrage and had doubted the necessity of the royal family and the House of Lords, he was unable to reconcile himself with the social changes on the land which his political program would necessarily bring. All he wanted to do here was to shift some of the tax burden from the shoulders of the poor by lightening the indirect taxes. At the same time he repeatedly urged the common people to hoard gold, hoping to bring "The Thing" down in that way. This, not trade unions, was Cobbett's way of improving the lot of the urban worker. Actually, much of the fiscal confusion of the 1820's was caused or intensified by the weakness of the country banks. Although Cobbett persisted in regarding these banks as tools of the Bank of England, it was only when the Bank of England monopoly was broken to allow the establishment of joint-stock banks that an end could be put to the chaos caused by the frequent failure of these country banks.

[31] P.R. (2/11/32), cols. 437–38; P.R. (3/30/33), cols. 789–90.

In 1830 Cobbett reviewed the financial policy of the government as he saw it. He blamed the government for causing the
value of money to fall while allowing taxes to remain sta-
tionary. Warning of future consequences, he renewed his call
for the reduction of expenses on the army, the church, the
civil list and the interest on the national debt.[32] The complaints were familiar, but futile. Whether Whigs or Tories
were in power, the debt was going to be paid and the country
was going to have a system of finance which would be ad-
vantageous to the propertied classes.

Just as the country banks were, in Cobbett's imagination,
tools of the Bank of England, the latter was the instrument
of the government. For Cobbett, to whom issues were seldom
complex or motivations subtle, regarded this institution, like
the Protestant Reformation, as engendered by a beastly lust.
The object, naturally, was not the same, being in this case
a desire for lucre. Begun with the national debt after the
Glorious Revolution had fixed boroughmonger rule on the
country, the two had grown together. Bank of England notes
and the debt had increased in proportion to each other over
the years, and both worked to the impoverishment of the
people.[33] Firmly convinced that the Bank of England and the
government cooperated to the detriment of the people's interests, Cobbett regarded the former as a pernicious influence
upon the life of the country. "A Bank, such as ours is, and
necessarily must be, is a most powerful instrument in the
hands of men at the head of affairs; it corrupts public morals,
it creates a fallacious appearance of wealth, it induces men
to look to trick and speculation rather than industry for the
means of rising in the world, it sets a whole people upon
the notion of living upon trust; and, above all things, it

---

[32] *An Accurate Report of Mr. Cobbett's Lecture Speech on the Present
Distresses of the Country and their Remedies, etc.*, Halifax, N. Whitley,
1830, passim.
[33] *Paper Against Gold*, Vol. I, pp. 11 ff.

tends to render a government, in a great measure, *independent of the people*." [34] No wonder he was suspicious of its role in the life of the country and warned Americans to avoid the English example and not establish a banking system of this type.

It has frequently been said that monetary nostrums have often attracted political extremists and cranks of all sorts. Cobbett never had any "monetary nostrums." All he wanted was to return to the day when a man could throw a solid gold coin on a counter, hear it ring, and receive an equivalent amount of goods without worrying about scraps of paper. He never seemed to realize that the time was past when the country's economy could survive without bank notes. As he reiterated time and again, the root of his antagonism against the financial system was social, not economic. In this, as in his hatred of banking interests, the cities, and laissez-faire economic doctrines, Cobbett resembled an American populist of the 1890's. Although their specific remedies differed, both were aware that the agrarian way of life which they treasured seemed to be increasingly irrelevant in the world in which they lived. Each proposed drastic measures to preserve it. The qualities of rage and frustration are apparent in Cobbett's voluminous writings. In his mind, paper money had brought war, debt and pauperism to a once free and happy England. As he said himself, the end of the paper money system would not be catastrophic. "No: the corn and the grass and the trees will grow without paper money; the Banks may all break in a day, and the sun will rise the next day, and the lambs will gambol and the birds will sing, and the carters and the country girls will grin at each other, and all will go on just as if nothing had happened." [35]

These are nice words but more was happening on the land

---

[34] Amer. P.R. (1/13/16), cols. 34–47.
[35] *Paper Against Gold*, Vol. II, p. 35.

than Cobbett could comprehend. The destinies of carters and country girls, landowners, tenants and laborers were all affected by the health of the banks, and in the countryside there were other developments which were just as confusing and frustrating to the former ploughboy.

IX
Society on
the land

The eighteenth century witnessed so many major advances in farming that authorities insist there was a "revolution" in the agricultural methods of the period as well as in industrial production. Whether there was anything truly revolutionary about what occurred on the land at this time is doubtful; it is more probable that existing tendencies were accelerated. What resulted after changes in virtually the entire system of cultivation were more varied crops in greater abundance and larger and more useful livestock. Like the substitution of machine labor for hand labor in manufacturing, the long-run result of the agricultural improvements was not only of benefit to the people of England but absolutely essential to the survival of their nation. Also like the Industrial Revolution, the agricultural changes were accomplished at such a terrible cost to large numbers of people that the beneficial effects have tended to be overlooked by some. It is worth noting again, however, what has been emphasized by many others: that the growing population could not depend upon foreign sources for most of its food supplies; the great bulk had to be raised at home. Had England, despite generally poor harvests, not been able to feed her vast army of industrial workers, the Napoleonic wars could not have been won. During the eighteenth century the population nearly doubled and the fact that England could continue to provide subsistence for her people with little aid is the major fact which must be remembered when examining the question of agriculture in detail.

There was great enthusiasm for improved methods of agriculture before and during the early years of the reign of "Farmer George." Conditions demanded greater efficiency on the land and interested parties responded with innovations or a more intensive use of proven formulas for increasing output. Crop rotation, extensive use of fertilizer, livestock improvement, experimentation with grasses, long leases for tenants who would improve the land, were all characteristics of the famous system of the skilled cultivators of Norfolk. These men were joined by enthusiasts in other parts of the country and the result was an exciting break-through in agriculture. The consequences were as important as the more widely known intensification of industrial production, which was occurring simultaneously. Notwithstanding all this progress, in order that increased agricultural production could be achieved it was necessary that there be large holdings worked by skillful, progressive farmers. The necessary improvements were too costly for the small cottager, even if he were disposed to favor them. The result was a great increase in the rate of enclosure, especially after 1793, when the war with France commenced. This process, in which landowners, by eliminating small holdings and fencing off the common lands, converted their property into one large area, had begun in the thirteenth century and during Tudor and Stuart times had been used to facilitate sheep raising. Now enclosures helped to bring about changes in the means of cultivation of the soil.

The economic efficiency of this consolidation of scattered strips of land is unquestioned today. Those who had the money and the skill to take advantage of the new conditions prospered. For those who lacked these requisites, the effect was catastrophic. Squatters, without legal title to the land they tilled, lost everything. Even small farmers who had rights to property might find that their allotment was too small to pay the cost of fencing it, especially since the elimination of the commons meant an end to the grazing of animals and gathering of fuel there. Conditions were made worse by a rise in the cost of living and increased taxation toward the end of the century. A traditional mode of living was breaking down under the impact of technological change and numerous bewildered victims suddenly were made destitute. Those who could not, or would not, adapt to the new circumstances sold what they had and joined the ranks of the landless agricultural workers who were needed to perform tasks on the improved farms. Some, it is true, became factory operatives but most stayed on the land and helped increase the population there. Many of the social effects of the enclosure movement were deplored even by those who supported it and were enthusiastic about the greater quantity and quality of the yield in crops and livestock.[1]

Of all the changes taking place in England during his lifetime, none were as familiar or as important to Cobbett as the ones so briefly sketched above. A successful yeoman farmer in an age when this class had almost disappeared, Cobbett never lost faith in the agrarian life and was usually happy

---

[1] For a description of conditions on the land, see Arthur Young, *A six weeks tour through the southern counties of England and Wales*, etc., London, W. Strahan, 1772. Also, R. E. Prothero, *op. cit.*

working about his own farm. He believed that his own character and success were a testimonial to farming. "This way of life gives the best security for health and strength of body. It does not *teach,* it necessarily produces, *early rising;* constant forethought; constant attention; and constant *care of dumb animals.* The nature and qualities of all living things are known to country boys better than to philosophers.[2] Because he was always sensitive toward what would affect the rural interests, it is not surprising that agricultural matters form a conspicuous part of his copious writings. However, despite numerous insights, much of what he wrote does not measure up to what one would expect from an observer with Cobbett's background.

This is primarily because Cobbett, without sympathy for change during a time when the whole country was in rapid transition, failed to overcome his prejudices sufficiently in order to permit an accurate analysis of what was happening. Even the traditionally stolid pattern of rural life was undergoing transformation. Cobbett realized that something was occurring on the land but never appreciated its extent, nor did he have more than a dim realization of the reasons for it. In addition, his lack of enthusiasm colored his judgment. Cobbett's agricultural writings reveal his agitation and disturbance about matters which concerned him far more intimately than any other subject to which he addressed his pen. Yet we are left unsatisfied. Nothing else so clearly displays Cobbett at both his best and his worst: generous and vengeful, perceptive and blind, altogether a prisoner of his prejudices.

Much of Cobbett's vehemence of expression arose from simple bafflement. To cite one example, he persistently misunderstood the collective temper of whole groups during this time. When the landlords and tenant farmers refused

---

[2] P.R. (3/17/21), col. 731.

to behave in the manner which Cobbett thought was both traditional and desirable, his disappointment made him react with redoubled ferocity. In considering his attitude with regard to the landlords and tenant farmers, it must be realized that Cobbett firmly believed that union among all agricultural classes against interference from outside had been dictated by nature. Landowner, tenant and laborer, although separated by rank and station, should nevertheless be as one in all matters pertaining to agriculture. A goodly portion of his writings were directed toward urging the landlords to live up to their responsibilities concerning the land and its people. He recalled the benevolence of this class in former times ". . . having still in my recollection so many excellent men, to whose grandfathers, upon the same spots, my grandfather had yielded cheerful obedience and reverence, it is not without sincere sorrow that I have beheld many of the sons of these men driven from their fathers' mansions, or holding them as little better than tenants or stewards, while the swarms of Placemen, Pensioners, Contractors, and Nabobs . . . have usurped a large part of the soil. . . ." [3]

This remark, coming in 1816 at the height of the post-war agricultural crisis, may be interpreted as both a genuine expression of respect and as a warning. Conditions on the land had deteriorated after Waterloo and many once prosperous proprietors had been forced to sell out to men from the city. Yet to Cobbett's dismay the legislature never wavered in its determination to repay every penny of the national debt. This insistence upon full reimbursement of the fundholders against what seemed to Cobbett to be their own interests was, of course, one of the major decisions of the landlords who dominated parliament during these years. Cobbett was shocked that nothing could persuade them to repudiate the debt and join with their "natural allies," the tenant farmers and rural

[3] P.R. (12/21/16), col. 775.

laborers, in a struggle to overthrow the "System." It was upon this point that his whole subsequent policy turned.

Time after time he warned the landlords that unless the debt was repudiated they would lose everything and be replaced by the very class which their fidelity had saved.[4] He coaxed, threatened, and pleaded with them to forego "good faith" with the fundholders and align themselves in their proper position at the head of the agricultural interest. It was in vain; to Cobbett's surprise and disgust, the wealthy landowners, for economic and political reasons of their own, chose to trim their sails to the prevailing trade winds and remained loyal to the nation's creditors. In 1822 he addressed a "Farewell Letter to the Landlords" in the *Register*. "Engrafted upon your native want of feeling is the sort of military spirit of command that you have acquired during the late war. You appeared, at the close of that war, to think that you had made a *conquest* of the rest of the nation for ever. . . ."[5] However, his abuse became more violent the following year after parliament had rejected the "Norfolk Petition." This was a wide-reaching proposal for reform that included the partial reduction of the debt or at least reduction of interest. Because this petition had the support of a number of landowners Cobbett had put great faith in it. Its failure came shortly after Cobbett's lack of success in gaining a seat in parliament at Coventry and the bankruptcy which this political campaign helped to bring on. The Cobbett who wrote the following words was a wretchedly disappointed man.

These incomparable cowards; these wretched slaves; these dirty creatures, who call themselves country gentlemen, deserve ten times as much as they have yet had to suffer. They are the makers of their own ruin; and that, too, from as bad motives as it is possible to imagine. Their own injustice towards the people; their own insolence; their employment of the vilest

[4] P.R. (1/18/23), cols. 142–43; (3/31/21), cols. 865–66.
[5] P.R. (4/6/22), col. 2.

wretches on earth to calumniate and betray the people. Their shocking subserviency to men in power and their agents; their incomparable meanness; all these mark them out as worthy of that fate which awaits them.[6]

Although Cobbett never lost his conviction that there could be no real justice ". . . unless the people be governed by that natural magistracy which grows out of the long-settled proprietorship of land. . . ."[7] it was with anguish that he observed one more aspect of the England which he loved breaking down. The old ties of affection between landlord and tenant, based on respect on one hand and consideration on the other, had loosened. Personal communication between them was replaced by a system of attorneys, stewards and land agents and the landlord knew little of the problems of those beneath him. The halls where landlords used to sit at the head of their tenants became "objects of wonder" as to what they were used for.

What Cobbett said had a good deal of accuracy[8] although, as usual, he was inclined to exaggerate the happier aspects of the past. Whatever community of feeling had existed on the land was weakening. Changes in the methods of agricultural production were partly responsible for this, both because they made land cultivation a business and because the increased profits enabled the owners to live better than before. Also, the landowning and business classes were drawing together socially and professionally and this was changing the outlook of many proprietors. To Cobbett's dismay, cosmopolitan tastes were becoming more prevalent, resulting in a widening gulf among the various ranks on the land. He noticed this estrangement, testified to by the game laws and watchmen to protect the estates of the nobility, and blamed much of it on the "totally new demeanour" produced by

6 P.R. (5/24/23), cols. 477–78.
7 *Two Penny Trash* (10/1/31), col. 79.
8 P.R. (1/13/27), col. 131.

the war.[9] Cobbett was largely correct here but it was probably a determination to preserve these new standards and not simple ferocity which was responsible for the new spirit which he deplored. He pointed out in the same article that economic conditions had resulted in the appearance on the land of men who were not farmers. These men were London businessmen following the time-honored English tradition of investing in land for reasons of social advancement after compiling a fortune in trade. This was the class which had benefitted enormously during the war and which continued to profit from their investments in the funds after it was over, while the agricultural interests were depressed. Many found themselves in possession of estates which had formerly been in the hands of one family for generations. Cobbett earnestly implored the landlords to make common cause with their tenants and laborers against these interlopers while there was yet time. As the 1820's wore on, he could see that his pleas were to be unavailing, for the large landowner was now protected against catastrophe by the Corn Laws. The tenant farmers and especially the laborers bore the brunt of the hard times. Incensed at what he regarded as the callous attitude of the landlords toward those for whom they should have felt an obligation, Cobbett subjected them to the rage of a frustrated prophet, bewildered at the unsympathetic obstinacy of those who ignored his message. These men "contain in their breasts, carry about constantly in their bosoms, a greater quantity of contumely, arrogance, tyranny, and insolence, than . . . all the rest of mankind." [10] They are "The most cruel, unfeeling, brutally insolent and base of God's creatures." [11]

Two important policies of the landlord-dominated legislature which Cobbett opposed were the enclosures and the Corn Laws. Both contributed to his hatred of proprietors

[9] P.R. (8/20/31), cols. 454 ff.
[10] P.R. (3/17/27), cols. 708–09.
[11] *Rural Rides,* vol. II (8/30/26), p. 370.

and parliament. In the case of the enclosures his opposition was early and consistent and his reasons were varied: enclosures were a violation of private property; they granted too much power to the government; they would not lead to efficient farming. But his main concern was for the welfare of the small farmer. He thought that a system of small, independent owners and self-respecting tenants was essential to the health and safety of the nation. The part enclosures played in dispossessing them for the sake of the landowning aristocracy, or worse, fundholders who were newly settled on the land, was pernicious. Cobbett approved of enclosures only if they could be implemented without injuring those with established interests upon the land.[12] His regard for the prescriptive rights of those in possession of property and his refusal to introduce changes except where everyone concerned would benefit demonstrates a healthy conservatism. It was left to the avowed disciples of Edmund Burke to upset tradition in the interests of efficiency and the greatest benefit of the greatest number. Even on the point of efficient farming, Cobbett questioned enclosing land. He claimed that too much land was often fenced off by one person to make for good farming and suggested that the remedy was more intensive cultivation of existing acreage. Besides (and this point is related to his concern for the inhabitants of the land and the strength of the country) "waste" land was not useless. Instead, it provided pasture for animals and thus contributed to the farmers' independence. Still more significant, it allowed children to grow up vigorous and strong in healthy surroundings.[13] In one of Cobbett's last efforts, *Legacy to Labourers*, he tried to trace the history of land tenure in England to demonstrate

12 P.R. (8/18/04), cols. 244–45; P.R. (3/5/08), col. 367.

13 Even Arthur Young, the great apostle of the enclosure movement, deplored the disappearance of the commons, although it did not affect his belief in the ultimate rightness of the movement. See Prothero, *op. cit.*, p. 215. Cobbett opposed Young but paid tribute to his talents and allowed his space in the *Register* to express his views.

that the rights of the landlords were not absolute: that the poor had the right of assistance in times of travail and should not be cheated out of their inheritance by enclosure acts.[14]

Two of Cobbett's limitations are once again clearly evident: his general inability to grasp the long-range significance of a policy and his tendency to see only what he wanted to see. Despite the soundness of some of his judgments, he was unable to realize the necessity of the enclosure movement. Convinced that "not a single soul has been added to our population since the time of Queen Elizabeth," [15] he would naturally fail to understand the necessity to end subsistence farming. In this respect, too, Cobbett was curiously blind to reality.

As for the Corn Laws, the supreme example of the ability of the landlords to impose their wishes on the rest of the nation, Cobbett registered only an inconsistent opposition. On the surface his policy was based upon a belief that millions are "doomed not only to incessant and uncompensated toil, but, in large part placed in danger of perishing with hunger . . ." [16] However, as in so much of Cobbett's thinking, the "System" was not far away. Although the Corn Laws extended far back into British history, it was only in the period after 1815 that they had any major significance as a factor affecting prices.[17] But the act of 1815 was another matter. By curtailing the importation of foreign grain this act at times forced the majority of people to eat dear bread in order to maintain the standard of living of a small but politically powerful class of landowners, and its importance in the life of the country was very great. Without it, the

14 *Legacy to Labourers*, London, William Cobbett, 1834, passim. This is a strange book. Written in simple language so that barely literate men could read it, it contained some of Cobbett's attempts at political and economic theory as well as numerous quotes from Blackstone.

15 P.R. (6/8/22), col. 615.

16 P.R. (8/5/26), col. 340.

17 Donald Grove Barnes, *A History of the English Corn Laws from 1660–1846*, New York, F. S. Crofts and Co., 1930, p. 93. Also, Prothero, *op. cit.*, p. 270.

suffering of the working class during the postwar depression would not have been so intense and, correspondingly, their agitation would have been less pronounced. On the other side, the great landlords might have listened more attentively to radical remedies such as those which Cobbett proposed.

His own attitude toward the bill was not as simple as has generally been believed.[18] True, he referred to it as ". . . one of the most outrageous attempts on the rights of mankind that ever was entertained" and noted that "There is something so monstrous in the idea of compelling people to purchase their food dear, when they can purchase it cheap, that human nature revolts at it." [19] But the real problem was the debt. As long as it existed high prices would be necessary to pay the consequent taxes. The government was aware of this and the Corn Bill was intended to prevent a fall in prices.[20] In other words, "It is the GOVERNMENT, and not the FARMER, who stands in need of high priced corn." [21]

On this issue, too, Cobbett was fundamentally concerned with paper money and high taxation. His writings during the months when the Corn Bill was under discussion make abundantly clear the fact that he was still primarily interested in striking a blow at the fundholders and that he opposed a tariff on grain in 1815 because this would prevent the fall in prices which was a necessary first step toward the repudiation of the national debt. The real remedy for the country's ills was to cut taxes.[22] Cobbett refused to place the blame for the bill where it belonged: squarely upon the

18 See Cole, *op. cit.*, pp. 193–94 and W. Baring Pemberton, *William Cobbett*, Harmondsworth, Penguin Books, 1949, p. 86, for examples of a misunderstanding of Cobbett's position. To say, as Pemberton does, that "Cobbett came out in vigorous denunciation of the Corn Laws" is telling less than half the story.

19 P.R. (10/22/14), col. 513 and col. 519.

20 P.R. (5/21/14), cols. 657–62; P.R. (5/28/14), cols. 684–90; P.R. (6/4/14), cols. 705–26.

21 P.R. (1/28/15), col. 107.

22 P.R. (1/28/15), cols. 100–10; P.R. (2/11/15), cols. 161–64; P.R. (3/25/15), cols. 353–57.

shoulders of the landlords. What is also evident is the fact
that he was primarily concerned not with the effect of the
bill upon the people but instead with eliminating paper money
and high taxation and thus striking a blow at the "System."

Cobbett tended to treat the landlords gently because he
hoped that they would realize that their real vocation consisted in being his allies in the struggle against the "System."
After 1823, when he realized that this was not to be, he gave
vent to his frustration but did not take up the cause of Corn
Law repeal. He continued to insist that the problem was
financial and, while not supporting protection as intrinsically
good, declared it necessary if the debt was to be paid. Since
the debt was not to be repudiated and taxes lowered, there
was no alternative other than high prices.[23] Except for a
brief reversal of this position in 1826 after a look at conditions in the industrial North, for the rest of his life Cobbett
frequently went on record as opposing repeal.[24] This policy
included a negative view of William Huskisson's significant
step toward free trade in corn, the sliding scale which permitted the entrance of corn at a nominal duty when the
price reached 73 shillings per quarter.[25]

Pro-Corn Law agitation was not merely representative of
a selfish desire on the part of the landlords and major tenant
farmers to preserve newly-won luxuries which Cobbett hated:
their "gig, musical instruments, parlour, bell to call servant,
and some other things in the way of dress; but, above all
things, *wine upon table after dinner.*" [26] Many landowners,
like the Abbé Sieyes in another situation, were happy just to
survive and had no thought of buying pianos or sofas for

[23] P.R. (4/30/25), cols. 257–300. P.R. (4/23/25), cols. 198–202; P.R.
(5/14/25), col. 395.
[24] P.R. (3/10/27), cols. 673–78; P.R. (11/23/33), cols. 452–53.
[25] P.R. (3/3/27), cols. 577–96; P.R. (7/7/27), cols. 85–88. All of this
is ignored in Cole, *op. cit.*, p. 311.
[26] P.R. (6/28/23), cols. 779–84.

their parlors.[27] Cobbett was aware of this and also of the plight of the common people on the land and in the factory. But it was his concern with the "System" which determined his position on the Corn Laws, and he persistently refused to consider this legislation on its own merits. "Encouraged by high profits, approved by economists, justified by necessity, agriculture advanced rapidly on the new lines of large farms and large capital." [28] This statement concisely sums up the major trend in agricultural production during the late eighteenth and early nineteenth centuries. Its effect upon the two largest agricultural classes apart from the landowners was profound. Of these two classes, the tenant farmers and the laborers, the former were much less numerous, though more powerful. Since the yeoman farmer, of which class Cobbett was the major living representative, had largely disappeared by the time he was born, the tenant farmers were the only rural group of any real importance to which he might appeal. His inability to influence the tenant farmers in the direction he desired and to become the spokesman of this significant but almost inarticulate class was a major factor in Cobbett's life. Exhortations to them, couched in the language of an older England which was almost extinct even during his youth failed because he did not comprehend the aspirations of a group which, as a whole, had ambitions to rise in society. Few of his writings reveal his being so out of touch with his times as the ones directed toward these tenant farmers whose average standard of living was so much higher than that of tenants in Ireland or even America.

It is noteworthy that Cobbett did not treat the tenant farmers seriously until several years after the war. Up to that time most of his not-very-frequent references portrayed

27 The Corn Law of 1815 did not represent the maximum protective demands. See David Spring and Travis L. Crosby, "George Webb Hall and The Agricultural Association," *The Journal of British Studies,* vol. II (Nov. 1962), pp. 115–31.

28 Prothero, *op. cit.,* p. 214.

the typical farmer as a somewhat shrewd but rather comic rustic of limited ambition and comprehension. There were undoubtedly many of these "Farmer Grubs" in England at the time but there were others as well who wanted, and were successful in getting, a way of life unprecedented for their class. For these people Cobbett had no message. He recognized that the tenant farmers consistently supported the government in its policy of repression of the laborer out of fear that their property and social status was threatened by the latter. Like many other radicals Cobbett was more adept in pointing out shortcomings in the action of others than in persuading them to change their minds.

> You, the farmers, have not only been deficient in point of view of public spirit; you have not only shown a willingness to support a system, which has at last brought even yourselves to the verge of destruction; but you have voluntarily aided and abetted those by whom the system has been carried on; and, what is still worse, you have appeared to take pleasure in the persecution of every man, whose zeal has urged him forward to oppose that system. You are, therefore, not proper objects of compassion: all of us suffer, but you merit your sufferings.[29]

The reader of this passage may well smile when he learns that the intention of the article, as a whole, was to win converts to reform. The following passage is even more explicit: "Yes, and I *shall* see the scarlet hunting-coats stripped from the backs of the farmers. I *shall* see the polished boots pulled from their legs: and I *shall* see the forte-pianos kicked out of their houses . . ." [30]

The problem with the tenant farmers, as Cobbett saw it, was that having had a taste of better living during the war, they acquired a desire to become gentlemen. That a few farmers ought to become gentlemen Cobbett did not deny: "This is the natural soil to produce gentlemen." But a whole

[29] P.R. (1/6/21), col. 4.
[30] P.R. (3/17/21), col. 757.

body of farmers dressed in top boots and scarlet jacket and approached by laborers with cap in hand would create an unnatural situation. As Cobbett pointed out with more candor than tact, the business of a farmer was not beyond the level of most laborers. Surgeons and physicians, he conceded, because of their limited numbers and patient study, may become gentlemen, but to make a comfortable living and rear a large family was about all that most farmers could expect. England could not be free and happy if farmers in general wanted to lead a life resembling that of a gentleman.

To the very end Cobbett urged the farmers and their families to return to "those habits of industry, care, utility and a due sense of their station in life, all of which they were sublimated out of by the *yeomanry cavalry* dreams, and by the accursed system of banking and paper money." [31] It was all unavailing. Few farmers listened to his remedies of lower taxes and rents, which were to be created by a reformed parliament. More were interested in achieving prosperity through protection and by the lowering of the poor rates.[32] Nor were their wives and daughters in a mood to forego their pianos and busy themselves with preparing dinner for the laborers.

The following quotation reveals so much of Cobbett's romantic aspirations.

> Each considerable farmer used to have one head carter, and one under carter at the least, a couple of threshers, a shepherd, a cow-boy, a couple of young women, and a girl or two, *all in the house;* and all *sitting at the same table with the master and the dame.* These took the head of the table, had the first cut, perhaps; but all sat at the same board. Here was a group of young people bred up under the eye and in the company of those who were so well able to teach them their various duties, and whose *interest* it was to see them perform those duties with regularity, and in the very best manner, and whose

31 P.R. (12/1/27), cols. 591–92.
32 P.R. (8/15/29), cols. 193–211; see P.R. (3/23/22), cols. 706 ff. for Cobbett's plan to aid the farmers through radical reform.

example must necessarily be powerful. Here was *education*. Here were early rising, industry, good hours, sobriety, decency of language, cleanliness of person, due obedience . . . This was *England:* this was an English farm-house . . .

In the farm-houses there used to be a long oak table, three inches through, at which the whole family sat. The breakfast was by candle-light in winter; and it consisted of beer, bread, and bacon or other food, prepared by the dame and the maids, while the men and boys and masters went out to feed and clean their horses and cattle by lantorn-light [sic]. It was not a mess consisting of *tea-water* and *potatoes*. When the men went out, they had their bottles of beer and their luncheon bags . . . at night all assembled again, and all were in bed four hours before midnight. This was *education*. This was *good-breeding*. From this arose the finest race of people that the world ever saw. To this the nation owed its excellent habits. All was in order here. Every one was in his place. These were the breeding places of sober and able workmen. This supplied the cities, occasionally with their most active and successful tradesmen and merchants; and it supplied the fleet and army with *hardy* men, fashioned to due subordination from their infancy.[33]

This vision of a rural paradise was certainly a travesty of the state of relations between master and man at the time Cobbett wrote it. No group had suffered more severely in physical terms than the agricultural laborers in the South of England. Enclosures, competition of the machine in producing items which were once the prerogative of cottage economy and the high cost of living combined to reduce the marginal standard of living of this class. For some time the problem had caused grave concern. As early as 1795, when starvation threatened in one locality, the magistrates at Speenhamland, in Berkshire, decided to use the rates to supplement the

[33] P.R. (4/7/21), cols. 10–11. This was part of an attack upon the paper money system, which he believed to have destroyed this way of life. See M. E. Seebohm, *The Evolution of the English Farm*, London, George Allen and Unwin, Ltd., 1952, p. 334 and p. 339 for support of Cobbett's observation that the farmers refused to have their laborers lodge in their houses.

laborer's earnings in proportion to the price of bread and the size of his family. This practice was speedily copied elsewhere and was sanctioned by an act of parliament the following year. The inevitable tendency was to lower wages and use the poor rates to supplement them. This, in turn, weakened the character of the farmers as well as the laborers. The incentive of the former to pay a decent wage was lessened as he knew that he would simply be benefitting other farmers who were less scrupulous. The laborer was encouraged to be improvident, for only a pauper could receive relief. In the North, however, the need of the factories for help kept up wages, and Cobbett himself pointed out that the economy of the region was not exclusively agricultural. He noted that conditions within the two sections varied so greatly that Lord Grey and other members of the government who lived in the North could not judge conditions elsewhere.[34]

It has been suggested that Cobbett left out the sordid aspects of country life as he remembered it from his childhood. There is good evidence that conditions on the land were blacker than Cobbett painted them: grasping landlords, unsanitary hovels, and overwork were not unknown in the eighteenth-century rural scene.[35] The tendency for a person, confronted with an unpleasant reality, to shrink from it by finding refuge in a mental image of a former, happier time must not be overlooked either. Yet even those who criticize Cobbett for doing just this admit that he probably knew the English countryside better than anyone else in the early part of the nineteenth century. One must be careful not to say that this acknowledged expert on the land and its people did not understand what he was talking about. It seems probable that Farnham and the surrounding area, with its rich soil,

[34] *Rural Rides*, vol. III (9/26/32), p. 714; (10/2/32), p. 732.
[35] For an interesting picture of England in the eighteenth century which casts doubt upon the "golden age" theory, see M. D. George, *England in Transition: Life and Work in the Eighteenth Century*, London, George Routledge and Sons, Ltd., 1931.

importance as a corn market and fine yield of hops was better
off than most sections during Cobbett's youth.[36] Later, the
laborers in the part of the country with which Cobbett was
most familiar, Hampshire and Wiltshire, may have suffered
most.[37] In Wiltshire he saw "Fine fields and pastures all
around; and yet the cultivators of those fields so miserable!"
Yet, the next day in neighboring Gloucestershire "The girls
at work in the fields (always my standard) are not in rags,
with bits of shoes tied on their feet and rags tied round their
ancles, as they had in Wiltshire."[38] These observations concerning the effects which poverty and the type of charity
afforded by the Speenhamland system were having on the
physical well-being and character of the laborer originally
began to appear in the *Register* in 1821 under the title "Rural
Rides." Later published as a book, they reached a wider
audience. Today, the many editions of *Rural Rides* contain
Cobbett's best known writings and form the principal basis
of public appreciation of him. Most of *Rural Rides* was
written from notes made while Cobbett travelled around the
countryside on business. The information contained in the
work gives the sense of veracity. His comments are terse and
pungent, generally free from theorizing, and they reveal Cobbett at his best.

Part of the appeal of *Rural Rides* lies in Cobbett's penchant
for interjecting extraneous remarks about the standard of
living of the people and the state of cultivation within a
paragraph concerning, say, the style of church building in a
parish. Or, the sight of a field of ripe wheat could prompt
him into a diatribe against Malthus. The rich soil and lovely
landscapes of southern England drew from Cobbett warm

[36] H. C. Darby (ed.), *An Historical Geography of England Before
A.D. 1800,* Cambridge, Cambridge University Press, 1936, p. 474 and
p. 542. Also see Young, *op. cit.,* pp. 208–09, 261–62.

[37] See G. M. Young, *Early Victorian-England, 1830–1865,* vol. I, London, Oxford University Press, 1935, p. 135.

[38] *Rural Rides,* vol. I (11/7/21), p. 615 and (11/8/21), p. 17.

emotion, but the visible poverty of its people made him cry out in wrath. Even before 1815, although the agricultural prosperity created by the war blunted the sharp edge of poverty for the laborers, there was enough evidence of evil conditions for Cobbett to comment upon low wages and a breakdown in habits of frugality and industry among these workers.[39] Of course, he placed the blame for their plight upon the boroughmonger government, whose taxes resulting from its war against the freedom of the French people (this was the way he viewed it) impoverished England. We know that the end of the war, which should have meant a lifting of their burdens, brought increased misery to the agricultural laborers. Since the boom was over and the farming interest had entered upon a twenty-year depression, the condition of these people grew worse. It was a terrible time for so many people on the land and those farmers who were suffering the traumatic effects of falling prices for their produce were generally not tender toward the interests of those under them. Farm prices were cut drastically while taxes remained high and one result was a great change of ownership of land as thousands of owners and tenants lost everything and often abandoned their farms. Forced more and more to rely upon the rates, many laborers became little better than slaves rented out by the parish to whoever would employ them. Men embraced pauperdom so as to be awarded at least a pittance which would keep them from starving; women were encouraged by the system of allowances for each child to have as many children (in wedlock or outside of it) as possible. This degeneration of a whole class was recorded by Cobbett with burning sorrow. Even today it makes melancholy reading.[40]

"What an *Englishman's castle* that must be where the

[39] P.R. (2/8/06), cols. 133 ff.; P.R. (7/16/08), cols. 73 ff.

[40] See J. L. and Barbara Hammond, *The Village Labourer, 1760–1832*, London, Longmans, Green & Co., 1919, chs. VII, VIII, IX and Prothero, *op. cit.*, chs. XIV and XV for a discussion of conditions affecting the agricultural laborer during this period.

kettle is not boiled! Talk of *security;* talk of freedom; talk of *rights and liberties:* talk of *glorious constitution* to a people in *this state*! It is the grossest mockery, the basest insult, that ever was offered to the mind of man." [41] Of all the terrible conditions brought about by the "System" the impoverishment of the agricultural laborers was by far the most evil. Cobbett saw taxes and tithes, raised to satisfy government creditors and the Church, stripping the laborer of his food and clothing and reducing him to a hungry, cowering pauper.

> What injustice, what a hellish system it must be, to make those who raise [food] *skin and bone and nakedness,* while the food and drink and wool are almost all carried away to be heaped on the fund-holders, pensioners, soldiers, dead-weight, and other swarms of tax-eaters! If such an operation do not need putting an end to, then the devil himself is a saint.[42]

These laborers were Cobbett's people. He was anguished to see others thriving while they suffered, and anguish led to outrage which produced violent polemics. Cobbett glorified (and in many ways personified) the independent meat and bread-eating and beer-drinking English peasant, in whose place he observed a shabby beggar. While Scott and other Tory romantics were dilating on the virtues of the sturdy peasant of the Middle Ages, Cobbett was championing the cause of living men, whose desperate condition roused him to fury.

Always fervently and sometimes eloquently, he defended the laborers, holding their poverty responsible for any crime which they committed, instead of accepting the fashionable view which blamed poverty on crime. He praised them for being so patient, easily satisfied and willing to work ". . . they are industrious, they are virtuous, they are good and true in their very natures; and cursed be the man who is the advocate

[41] P.R. (5/19/21), col. 461.
[42] *Rural Rides,* vol. II (8/30/26), p. 369.

for treating them harshly!" If their children were not so dutiful, it was because they had seen their parents "treated like scum" while "standing outside of a window on a Saturday night, to receive their pay, instead of receiving it in the farmer's kitchen with a mug of beer in their hand." Above all, he reminded his listeners that "the fate of our country, its honour, its independence, the happiness of ourselves and our children, depend on the fate of the labouring people." [43]

It was during the "Swing" riots of 1830 and the repression which followed that Cobbett was at his noblest. Beginning in Kent, violence quickly spread to other Southern counties, leaving behind burning hay-ricks, broken machines and frightened landowners. The causes were economic; threshing machines, which had replaced hand labor, may have been the factor which started the riots. Yet there were also complaints against low wages, inadequate poor relief and the tithes, insofar as the latter prevented landowners from paying sufficient wages. During the time that the laborers held sway, unpopular landowners and overseers of the poor were terrorized and even manhandled, but no one was killed and, on the whole, the laborers presented their moderate demands with courtesy. Cobbett was intensely interested in these developments and devoted himself to trying to secure justice for these men. He staunchly defended their character and, while opposing violence, urged his readers to reflect upon the circumstances of the laborers' lives before judging the actions of "the most good-natured and the most patient" people in the world. Detailing the suffering of the poor and repeatedly insisting that the riots arose out of poverty alone and were not instigated from outside, he observed that "it is no new feeling of discontent that is at work: it is a deep sense of grievious [sic] wrongs; it is long harbored resentment; it is an accumulation of revenge for unmerited punishment; it has long been

[43] P.R. (4/15/26), cols. 148 ff.; P.R. (7/14/32), col. 76; P.R. (2/1/34), col. 266.

smothered in the bosoms of these our injured and suffering countrymen, and it has now *bursted forth* . . ." [44]

These observations, as accurate as they were sincere and generous, came to have a deeper meaning for Cobbett. For in 1831 he was to be tried by the Whig government on the charge of inciting the laborers to sedition. He naturally wished to establish the indigenous nature of the riots. Although the government used extorted evidence, Cobbett handled his cause in a masterful fashion and the result was a triumph for him.[45] Inasmuch as the trial was not held until July, his protests against the policy of repression pursued by the Whigs against the laborers were somewhat circumspect.

Still, although the impending trial made caution imperative, he could not contain his dismay over the savage sentences imposed on the starving rebels. "My heart sinks within me at the thought of the sentences. I sat down to write a petition in my single name; but, upon beginning to put the words *upon paper,* my soul recoiled from the writing of those expressions which are deemed indispensable in such a case. Towards all the sufferers, not actuated by malice, I feel as if they were my brothers or my children." [46] His remedy for the problem urged conciliation on the government and on its agent, the "yeomanry cavalry," ". . . pull off your hairy caps, your party-coloured jackets, and your Wellington-boots. . . ." All offenders should be pardoned and those actually transported should be returned home, the Poor Law administered fairly, the game laws repealed along with Ellenborough's Act, which made it a capital offense to strike a man with a heavy instrument, even though the victim was not killed.[47] The strain on Cobbett was very great, for he was committed to the support of the Whigs in their policy of

---

44 *Twopenny Trash* (11/1/30), p. 98; P.R. (11/27/30), cols. 807–10.
45 See Cole, *op. cit.,* pp. 365 ff. for a short account of the trial.
46 P.R. (1/15/31), col. 151.
47 P.R. (1/7/32), col. 101; P.R. (1/22/31), cols. 207–08.

parliamentary reform. He was not only tormented by observing the cruelty with which the Whigs had met the spontaneous uprising of starving men, he also was faced with the knowledge that upon those who were persecuting the laborers and himself depended the fate of the reform which he had urged for so many years!

Not content to defend the laborer with his potent pen, Cobbett practiced himself the virtues that he preached. To a request for a donation for the poor he replied:

> *My* labourers, Sir, stand in no need of any such largess; they have, *from me,* the means of purchasing bread, meat, and beer, every day of their lives; no parish officer ever sees their face; they are not slaves, but as free as I am myself . . . If all labourers were in this situation, we should have no occasion for subscription for the purpose of feeding the *poor.* . . .[48]

He boasted of giving constant pay in all seasons and weathers and of paying a sick man as much as a well man.[49] Of course, Cobbett was paternalistic but he did have an interest in preserving the self-respect as well as the health of those who worked for him. Although he demanded a solid day's work, his agricultural employees seem to have been well treated and some of them remained with him for years. However, his fussiness in matters of diet must have been trying to those who lived under him. His hatred of potatoes (except as a relish) and of tea are well known. Yet it might be noted that Cobbett's ideal diet, so heavy in what we today call carbohydrates, could have been modified by vegetables, which were then being grown more extensively. This innovation was characteristically opposed by him. He discussed his cures for the ills of the laborers in a vigorous manner between descriptions of the way in which they lived. While he never ceased to maintain that the funding and taxation system was

[48] P.R. (10/21/09), col. 580.
[49] P.R. (7/29/09), cols. 111–12.

basically at fault, he could also make constructive suggestions to aid the rural worker. The remoteness from practical reality which he exhibited in other situations did not affect him as much in this field.

Many of these suggestions are found in *Cottage Economy,* a book which was designed to instruct the agricultural laborer in matters which would enable him to become self-sufficient and thus "set what is called misfortune at defiance." The book contained Cobbett's usual invective against tea, potatoes and baker's bread but also had detailed instructions in the arts of brewing and bread making, as well as livestock keeping. Each member of the family must participate: "Every woman, high or low, ought to know how to make bread . . . ," and instructing a child in the domestic arts took precedence over biblical instruction in one's duty toward God. Cobbett's avowed purpose was to inform the working classes how to manage their own households so that they might regain the abundance of former days.[50] Although much of what he had to say about tea was silly, for example, "I view the tea drinking as a destroyer of health, an enfeebler of the frame, and engenderer of effeminacy and laziness, a debaucher of youth, and a maker of misery for old age," or amusing, ". . . the gossip of the tea table is no bad preparatory school for the brothel," there was good sense as well. The practical advice was, for the most part, sound and economical and he showed his mastery of his craft. A diet of potatoes, baker's bread and tea *was* inferior to one of meat, home-baked bread and beer. If the advice contained in the book had been more generally followed, the laborers might have fulfilled Cobbett's hope and become more independent and bold. Still, the work as a whole was retrograde. Cobbett wanted these people to return to the simple, independent ways of their ancestors, which he saw as replete with roast beef and plum pudding. This was passé in an age when the laborer wanted ready-made items,

50 *Cottage Economy,* London, C. Clement, 1822, passim.

which he could purchase with money, instead of working to produce them himself. Baker's bread, even when it was not adulterated, was certainly less nutritious than home-made bread, yet the workers insisted upon buying their bread instead of making it. Cobbett himself noted that "They will not, even if they greatly gain by it, do anything out of the track of their habits and prejudices." [51] There is some difference of opinion about the cause of this attitude.[52] The interpretation which a historian places upon this refusal of the laborer in the South to eat coarse bread often indicates his answer to the question of whether living conditions were getting better or worse for these people. Did the workers prefer soft, wheaten bread because their systems, weakened by hunger, could not digest properly a coarser variety? Or was it mere fastidiousness, made possible by higher living standards that persuaded them to choose the former? Similarly, the question arises as to whether the popularity of tea drinking was because of an increasing desire for luxury or simply due to a scarcity of milk. George Orwell has pointed out [53] that where people are demoralized by a long period of unemployment and living on a meager allowance, there is a powerful temptation to brighten their drab lives by eating foods which taste good but are not necessarily nutritious. Perhaps the poor in England after Waterloo may have clung tenaciously to their baker's bread, in sullen defiance of their masters' attempts to deny them one of the few pleasures they were able to enjoy, just as slum dwellers a hundred years later persisted in purchasing fish and chips instead of cheaper but less "tasty" items which the government urged them to buy with their dole. The ineffectiveness of Cobbett's proposals in this case may stem not from lack of comprehension of the economic situation but

---

[51] *Rural Rides,* vol. III (10/14/32), p. 767.
[52] See J. L. and Barbara Hammond, *The Village Labourer,* pp. 123 ff. vs. Prothero, *op. cit.,* p. 451 and Ashton, *op. cit.,* p. 159.
[53] *Down and Out in Paris and London* and *The Road to Wigan Pier.*

from obscure psychological factors which he could not appreciate.

When concerned with agricultural problems, Cobbett revealed traits which marked his attitudes concerning all national issues: a penchant for seeking solutions to new problems by turning back to the past, a conviction that a unified society was natural and good, and a belief that all misery was caused by the funding and taxing system which could be cured by a radical reform of the nation's finances. Opposed as he was to enclosures in the form in which they were carried out, he still blamed taxes for impoverishing the people. This relates to a fourth fundamental belief: that agriculture was the foundation of the economy and was always able to provide a living for everyone if it was not subordinated to other interests. It could be restored to prosperity by a removal of the burdens with which it was afflicted, but not as Horner and Ricardo had argued by the increasing wealth of commerce or manufactures.[54] He took a lively interest in the poor who earned a living from the soil and his suggestions have value, even though they were not always accepted. An environmentalist, his concern was with increasing the material welfare of these people. Character improvement would be more likely to occur this way than as a result of Methodist Sermons or religious tracts.

> I will allow nothing to be good, with regard to the labouring classes, unless it makes an addition to their victuals, drink or clothing. As to their *minds*, that is much too sublime matter for me to think about. I know that they are in rags, and that they have not a belly-full; and I know that the way to make them good, to make them honest, to make them dutiful, to make them kind to one another, is to enable them to live well; and I also know, that none of these things will ever be accomplished by Methodist sermons, and by those stupid, at once stupid and malignated things, and roguish things, called Religious tracts.[55]

54 P.R. (2/22/23), col. 491.
55 *Rural Rides,* vol. I (8/6/23), p. 176. Also (9/29/22), p. 97.

The worker must earn his living by honest toil; "benevolence" or "comforting" was degrading to donor and recipient alike. If the weight of taxation were lifted, the land would respond abundantly and there would be no need for charity except in rare cases of hardship.

A fine practical farmer, Cobbett was more at ease writing about agricultural questions than anything else. One reason for his relative accuracy on this subject is that he could observe what was occurring all about him, another was his sympathy for the victim and a third reason was his knowledge of certain agrarian conditions. Where one of the elements of observation, sympathy or knowledge was missing, Cobbett generally presented a somewhat inaccurate or even a grotesque picture of a situation, for he lacked imaginative understanding. He once wrote, "The deplorable descriptions of the distresses in the manufacturing districts, though very afflicting, are not, however, those which produce the most serious impression upon my mind. I am much more deeply affected by the general, though silent distresses of those whom we call the country people . . . I see scores of young men, framed, by nature to be athletic, rosy cheeked and bold . . . I see them thin as herrings, dragging their feet after them, pale as a ceiling, and sneaking about like beggars." [56] The words "I see" are, of course, crucial.

And yet, in assessing Cobbett's impact upon the agriculture of the time, one is bound to be disappointed. Well-intentioned and knowledgeable in many ways, he was unable to take his proper place in the agricultural picture. This is not simply because his desires were not those of powerful interests. The problem is really Cobbett's lack of understanding of changing conditions which rendered his own proposals reactionary. His ability to innovate, which helped him to personal success on the land, did not extend to his schemes to improve the lot of the landless laborer. Furthermore, not only was he unable

[56] P.R. (8/10/16), cols. 111–12.

to persuade the dominant political forces; even in his own field he was bereft of allies. Apart from Arthur Young he had a bad word about almost all of his contemporaries who were connected with agriculture on a major scale. Of course, this does not imply that Cobbett's motives (or even his ideas) were wrong in themselves. It does mean that he was to be generally regarded as a lone and even eccentric voice in an area in which he might be expected to have a very important role.

If Cobbett was deficient as an analyzer of agricultural trends, it is clear that his weaknesses would be even more marked when dealing with subjects with which he had less contact. This was true not only of political economy and public finance but also in the case of industrial development. This he not only never understood but, in general, despised and tried to ignore. Although it is true that he was more aware than most of the economic basis of the factory workers' agitation and was usually sympathetic with their plight, Cobbett never saw this subject in a correct focus. He was too deeply committed to rural values and his mind was shackled by the "System." Cobbett was lacking as a leader of groups living on the land but his relationship with the urban workers was to prove transitory.

X
Industrial changes

No aspect of Cobbett's England has received more attention from modern historians than have the changes in economic and social organization resulting from the replacement of hand labor by power machinery.[1] The most significant part of this work has not concerned the technological development of the period, valuable as research in this area has been. Instead, it is the examination of the very thing in which Cobbett himself was interested that has produced such important results: the effect of the Industrial Revolution upon the lives of the working class. This examination and consequent re-evaluation of the problem by numerous scholars is among the most rewarding and exciting work done in the

[1] For the sake of convenience we will continue to use the term "Industrial Revolution" to signify this profound alteration of the means of production.

field of British history in recent years. It has banished certain shibboleths such as "hungry forties" and has rendered obsolete many cherished conceptions about early nineteenth-century life. New findings have resulted in a fresh approach to the lives of those who were greatly affected by these changes and thus has created a need to reconsider certain of Cobbett's writings.[2]

Considering the enormous impact which industrial changes had upon English society at the time when Cobbett was the foremost popular journalist, it seems surprising that he did not recognize this more clearly. His writings, immense in their volume and widely ranging in subject matter, seem to cover the early nineteenth century like a vast blanket—events, issues and personalities alike. Yet Cobbett devoted relatively little space to the factory system. Furthermore, what he did write reveals that he was often ignorant of the subject, the victim of misinformation as well as simple lack of knowledge. Much of this ignorance was the result of inertia, and the question arises, how could this champion of the common people have been lacking in interest concerning a situation which determined the lives of hundreds of thousands? The answer is not simply because industrial changes were new and strange to him. Commerce and finance were also unfamiliar, yet they formed the basis for dozens of articles as well as being implicitly noted in many seemingly extraneous writings. Gov-

2 See the following revisionist contributions: T. S. Ashton, *op. cit.*; F. A. Hayek (ed.), *Capitalism and the Historians*, Chicago, University of Chicago Press, 1954; T. S. Ashton, "The Standard of Life of the Workers in England, 1790–1830," *The Journal of Economic History*, Supplement, IX (1949), pp. 19–38; Herbert Heaton, "The Industrial Revolution," *Social Education*, Vol. II (March, 1938), pp. 159–65. These writings and most others in their category stress that the standards of material welfare of the worker were generally rising during this period. The following older work reminds us that it would be an error to consider the worker only in relation to his physical environment. J. L. and Barbara Hammond, *The Town Labourer, 1760–1832*. The body of writing on this subject is large and is still growing. For a recent discussion see E. J. Hobsbawm, *Labouring Men, Studies in the History of Labour*, London, Weidenfeld and Nicholson, 1965, chs. 5, 6, 7.

ernment finance, however, seemed to him to be a basic reality of life; it was an enemy, visible and powerful, and it had to be destroyed. On the other hand, Cobbett seemed to regard factories as an exotic manifestation. Bad on the whole, but subordinate in importance to "this accursed paper money system." The aspect of industrial organization which attracted his attention most frequently was the condition of the factory laborers. He wrote intermittently on this subject, usually during times of crisis when their suffering forced itself on everyone's attention. His acknowledged unfamiliarity was reflected in frequent lack of precision.

In his last years, under the tutelage of John Fielden, the Radical manufacturer, Cobbett displayed a more knowledgeable attitude toward the facts of industrial life and his first visit to a cotton factory occurred when he visited Fielden's mill at Todmorden in January, 1830.[3] However, he never grasped the fact that the manufacturing system was not merely a peripheral force, but instead was the dynamic of English society. This is in large measure the reason why Cobbett never came to terms with it and helps account for the irrelevance and antiquated nature of many of his observations. It is nevertheless fair to point out that Cobbett was no different from almost all of his countrymen in failing to understand the new industrial system. Knowledge of factory manufacture spread gradually. If he is to be criticized, it is not because he failed to consider industrialism as later generations did, but because he did not care to investigate it.

It is noteworthy that a disproportionately large number of his comments regarding factories and machinery originally appeared in accounts of those peregrinations through the countryside, which were later reprinted as *Rural Rides*. From the early 1820's these travels took him through sections of the country quite different from the agricultural South with which he was so familiar. He would report to his readers

[3] *Rural Rides,* Vol. II, p. 598.

the conditions under which the working people lived.[4] Harsh as he often was toward the factory system, he could not repress a thrill of pride at the sight of ". . . the iron furnaces in all the horrible splendour of their everlasting blaze," which, in a rare bit of insight, he recognized as a sign of English strength.[5] He was careful not to allow this feeling to develop. Somewhat later, in writing of the manufacture of silk, he announced: "I never like to see these machines, lest I be tempted to endeavour to understand them." As in the case of sun, moon and stars, Cobbett was quite satisfied to witness their effects.[6] These travels in old age widened his point of view in other ways. Although he had twice been refused permission to speak in Manchester (in 1819 and 1826), Cobbett later visited the place several times and in 1832 actually accepted an invitation to run for parliament from there. The reception which he received on these visits from the ". . . thousands and thousands of intelligent, acute, and well-educated men, who reside in this wonderful hive of industry, perseverance, ingenuity, intelligence, and talent of all sorts" delighted him.[7] This appreciation of the town after he had actually seen it is in contrast with previous judgments made from the non-industrial South. Had he lived ten years longer, he might have modified his hitherto hostile attitude and accepted the factory system.

Cobbett's attention was not directed toward industrial matters on a large scale until 1811 when the Luddite riots began. Previous to this the Berlin and Milan Decrees of Napoleon and the American Non-Intercourse Act had closed the European and American markets for British goods. These develop-

4 At North Shields, for example, he noted that the working people were well off; their dwellings solid and clean and the furniture good, "but the little gardens and orchards are wanted." *Rural Rides*, Vol. III (10/2/32), p. 732.
5 *Rural Rides*, Vol. II (1/31/30), pp. 607–08.
6 *Rural Rides*, Vol. II (10/28/32), pp. 817–18.
7 P.R. (1/16/30), cols. 67–68.

ments gave manufacturers an impetus to introduce machinery in order to cut costs. The lack of markets and the technological innovations both threw thousands of people out of work. Driven to desperation by threatened starvation, the workers in the Midlands vented their resentment against the new machinery in riots which soon extended over virtually the whole country. As Cobbett recognized, these disturbances were inspired simply by hunger. Fully sympathetic with the workers' plight he defended their cause in the *Register*. For those who accepted the government's contention that the rioters were lawless elements directed by political agitators, Cobbett had scorn: "He, alas! knows not what it is to feel hunger, and to hear children crying for bread." [8] While trying to dissuade the workers from violence he also urged that the government attempt to find employment for them on the land, even suggesting that the legal expense of enclosing the land be reduced.[9] Although well meant, this was a characteristically reactionary remedy for *industrial* unemployment, but as he was an opponent of the enclosure movement, Cobbett's suggestion does show evidence of sympathy. He became at this time an advocate of the workers' cause and vainly urged conciliation upon the government. In his opinion the existing laws were sufficient to deal with the riots while the workers' grievances were inquired into.[10] His plea was in vain for the rioters were crushed. The ministers, their nerves stretched taut by the prolonged strain of the war, had panicked at the assassination of Spencer Perceval, the Prime Minister (an event unrelated to the riots) and imagined that the spontaneous violence of starving men was a calculated attempt to overthrow law and order. Today there seems to be something ludicrous in the frantic efforts of the government to

8 P.R. (4/18/12), cols. 497–98.
9 P.R. (11/23/11), cols. 652–53; P.R. (4/18/12), cols. 497 ff.
10 P.R. (5/2/12), cols. 546 ff.; P.R. (7/4/12), cols. 11 ff.; P.R. (1/9/13), col. 43.

convince itself that it was dealing with treason. Sealed Bags and Secret Committees, *agents provocateurs* and whisperings of sedition in connection with a purely economic problem suggest the atmosphere of a farce now that time has blunted the consequences of this blundering. However, rather than speaking of bloody executions bringing comfort to the hearts of the ministry and the lashing of the workers back to their hovels, we might instead attempt to comprehend the plight of fallible men, doggedly waging war against an immensely strong antagonist who was then at the height of his power. Weak, but not wicked, somewhat callous, but not cruel, they made wrong decisions, yet also managed to resist importunities from much of the press for a more drastic repression.

Through his residence in London, Cobbett was removed from the disturbances physically, but he was not aloof to them. He had no real knowledge of their background or causes and, except what was revealed by reports of events, was unaware of day-to-day happenings. Yet his insight was more acute than were the reports upon which the government based its actions. His was the triumph of common sense and humanity over fear and inflexible doctrine. Doctrinaire and insensitive as he was in so many instances, an occurrence like this would bring out his best qualities. "I do not wish to justify the woman who, according to the newspapers, committed *highway robbery* in taking *some potatoes out of a cart at Manchester,* and who, according to the newspapers, was HANGED FOR IT. I do not pretend to justify her conduct. But, there is, I hope, no harm in my expressing my *compassion* for her; and, I further hope, that my readers would think me a most inhuman brute, if I were to endeavour to deprive her and her unhappy fellow-sufferers of the compassion of the public; by asserting that she was actuated by a *treasonable* motive. . . ." [11] These words were written and printed while Cobbett was still in Newgate under sentence for sedition.

[11] P.R. (7/4/12), col. 24.

It is not true that 1812 brought home to Cobbett for the first time the situation confronting the industrial laborer. He had long been aware of the effect which excessive hours and unhealthy working conditions had upon the physical well-being of the workers.[12] Still, after the Luddite riots he did not pay much attention to the problem until 1823. For the first time he considered in detail the circumstances under which the factory operative earned his bread. Probably his political disappointments, his bankruptcy and the failure of the Norfolk petition helped turn his attention to this subject as it did toward Irish affairs. For a year or two the *Register* was full of denunciations of factories which were based on information that had been furnished by correspondents. In July, 1824, came his most outspoken criticism. In an article addressed "To The Cotton Lords," he saluted them as "My Lords, Seigneurs of the Twist, sovereigns of the Spinning Jenny, great yeomen of the Yarn . . ." Then followed sarcasm and invective.

> You can look with an eye perfectly calm on the poor souls that are thus toiling for you. You can see the poor children pining away their lives in these hells upon earth; you can see them actually gasping for breath, swallowing the hot and foul air, and sucking the deadly *cotton-fuz* into their lungs: you can, with all the delight of greediness gratified, behold scenes like these in your own country, under your own roofs; aye, and invented and put in practice by yourselves . . .

and

> But, why make the places so very hot? Our summer-heat is only seventy-five degrees; and yet you shut these poor little cotton-fuz creatures up in eighty-four degrees of heat . . .

What makes the above especially interesting to the historian is that these quotations come almost parenthetically in a very long article which was mainly devoted to denouncing the

12 See P.R. (7/23/03), col. 127.

cotton magnates for their search for new markets in South America.[13] Other issues of the *Register* during this period contained similar denunciations of the factories. Impassioned and sometimes eloquent, they may be found sandwiched between maledictions directed toward the clergy, political economists and the government.[14]

Together with descriptions of the sufferings of the workers of "that blood-stained town" (Manchester) are comparisons between their lot and the "fat and lazy and laughing and singing and dancing" Negro slaves in the West Indies. This allowed Cobbett an opportunity to attack the Evangelicals, whom he actively hated and despised. *"Have you ever found a dead Negro with nothing in his belly but sour-sorrel?"*, he asked those who looked with compassion upon the West Indian Negroes while ignoring the plight of their neighbors. Cobbett could be brutally insensitive and here he took out his resentment against Wilberforce and his followers at the expense of the slaves, for whom he felt only contempt. The state of mind of the comfortable, which could display tenderness toward distant slaves while remaining indifferent to their suffering compatriots, was anathema to him. Cobbett was not only a firm believer that charity begins at home, but he was concerned solely (when he was concerned at all) with evils which were visible to him.[15] Polemics against the South American independence movements and the Evangelicals indicate that Cobbett did not see the plight of the factory operatives as a

13 P.R. (7/10/24), cols. 65–110. Cole does not explain this either in his biography of Cobbett or in the book of extracts of Cobbett's writings which he edited with Mrs. Cole. The latter contains a portion of Cobbett's article without indicating the intent of the article as a whole. Cole perhaps overestimates Cobbett's influence over the industrial working class in the 1820's, as well as his sympathy for them. See Cole, *op. cit.*, ch. XVII and G. D. H. and Margaret Cole (eds.), *The Opinions of William Cobbett*, London, The Cobbett Publishing Co. Ltd., 1944, pp. 171–73.

14 See, for example, P.R. (7/10/24), cols. 65–106 and P.R. (1/15/25), cols. 159–75.

15 For example, see P.R. (8/30/22), cols. 513 ff.; P.R. (12/6/23), cols. 582 ff.; P.R. (11/27/30), col. 861.

separate problem, even while writing on their behalf. Everything was a part of the "System."

Except for occasional irritable outbursts, his stand against factories did not extend to machinery. In 1816, during the post-war depression, when large numbers of workers were unemployed and suffering from privation to a degree which was probably never matched in later years, Cobbett addressed a long article to them. This "Letter to the Luddites" contained numerous observations but its main purpose was to tell these unemployed workers that their sufferings were not the result of machinery but were caused by the taxation and paper money system. Citing examples from agriculture and the home, Cobbett tried to prove that machinery made tasks easier and cheaper to accomplish and thus operated for the benefit of everyone, including the worker. The problem was the high taxes, which reduced the purchasing power of the consumers and rendered them unable to buy goods.[16] However, ten years later he admitted that he had considered the problem in the abstract and that the impact of machinery upon the laborers' condition might conceivably differ according to the circumstances. True to his veneration of the past, the type of manufacturing which Cobbett approved of was the ancient one carried on in the workers' cottages. Here there were no evil factory conditions. The worker, surrounded by his family, would divide his time between farm and machine and the former would provide a cushion during hard times. He showed particular favor toward the idea of women and girls doing carding and spinning at home while the male members of the family tended to the farming chores. Naturally, the paper money system was blamed for creating monopolies which caused the working people to mass together in those parts of the country which were least productive of food.[17]

16 P.R. (11/30/16), cols. 562–592.
17 *Rural Rides*, Vol. II (8/30/26), pp. 376–77, (9/29/26), p. 440; P.R. (1/6/27), cols. 69–70.

Cobbett thus reacted against the factory system rather than the machine. Like the agrarians of the East, he wanted to return to a pre-capitalist past—but also to retain the machinery which capitalism had made economically feasible. There is excellent evidence to suggest that he never understood what displacement by the machine meant to the worker.[18] He always retained the ideal of a simple, self-sufficient family based on agriculture. To these people machinery would be a boon. For Cobbett and many others, the evil of a factory lay in that it took the workers from their homes and thus destroyed their independence and close-knit family ties.

The sufferings of the industrial laborers, as well as many other evils afflicting the people as a whole, were blamed by the government on the long war. This war, which was unnecessary in Cobbett's eyes, increased the debt and the taxes and caused prices to rise. His solution, of course, was a reformed parliament, which would set about lowering the debt and taxes and thus allow the hard-pressed manufacturer to pay his employees higher wages. Only with great reluctance did he recommend legislation to reduce hours of labor or regulate conditions in the factories. This constant preoccupation with political causes and solutions of economic difficulties obscured reality for him. Even as late as 1827, he blamed the suffering of the Spitalfields silk-weavers on high taxes.[19] Here was a classic case of technological unemployment, but Cob-

[18] A seldom-reported incident of this nature involved Cobbett in 1831. At that time he refused a request of unemployed printers to stop having the *Register* printed by machinery. Cobbett's reply was that machine printing saved time and money and that he left the technical side of the business to his printer, who had assured him that nothing could be done to accommodate the unemployed hand workers. Cobbett went on to tell the men how little he ate himself and admonished them that walking the streets is more virtuous than living off the labor of others. A touch of the Pharisee? Perhaps, but it is more likely that his attitude was due to inability to grasp an unfamiliar situation. Nevertheless, it is possible to make a justified comparison between Cobbett and the mill owner who washed his hands of his workers' plight by blaming their long hours on economic laws. See P.R. (8/27/31), cols. 567–68.

[19] P.R. (7/7/27), cols. 100–01.

bett could not recognize this although it took place close to him, within the City of London. Yet, his frequent tenderness toward the masters must not be confused with the conclusions of present-day investigators who hold that they were ambitious, frugal men who ploughed back profits into their businesses and drove themselves as hard as they did their employees. This was not Cobbett's view, for at times he denounced them violently. The sympathy which he showed was occasioned by ignorance of industrial conditions and a firm conviction that the debt and taxes were at the root of all evil in the kingdom.[20]

Since Cobbett was convinced that economic problems must be solved by political means, he was not enthusiastic about the workers attempting to better their lot through strikes. Nevertheless, he insisted that the worker had a *right* to strike. Private property was inviolate and the property of the worker was his labor. The worker might withhold his labor (property) if the wage (price) was not high enough, just as other property owners did. This was the basis of the right to strike. The Combination Acts of 1799 and 1800 were unjust in theory as they prevented the worker from exercising his right to contract and in practice since they discriminated between masters and men in their procedure and application.[21] Although often in sympathy with the workers, Cobbett patiently tried to explain that their misery could not be cured by strikes against "Your poor devils of masters . . . ," whom he believed to be suffering from high taxes along with their employees. In 1821, when this was written, he was not as aware of the nature of the factory system as he was to be a few years later. He pictured a warm, intimate relation existing between master and man "(For, I like these words a great deal better than the new-fangled jargon of *'Employer* and *Operative')*" and insisted that the cause of "this unnatural strife" between the two was not the master's avarice. There was, of course, a good

20 P.R. (7/6/16), cols. 6 ff.
21 P.R. (12/19/18), cols. 378 ff.

deal of truth in this assertion, but not in the claim which was based on current economic theory, that the means to secure higher wages were out of the hands of the workers as wage rates were determined by supply and demand. He said that even if the employers could afford to pay more, the increase in wages would only raise prices. Until the organic reform, which Cobbett deemed necessary, had been achieved, the best policy that the workers could adopt was to insist that their wages be supplemented by the poor rates. To him the Poor Law was not charity but a right which all in distress should enjoy without a sense of degradation.[22]

In this argument there is evident again the weakness in Cobbett's approach to economic problems. His captivation by a belief in one great evil, which could only be eliminated by radical reform, his remoteness from the scene of distress and his lack of economic knowledge meant that he was unable to offer constructive advice. All of this was accompanied by that essentially reactionary train of thought which was present in almost everything he wrote. His faith in the poor rates over savings banks is an example. Cobbett could not appreciate an expanding economy or the possibilities of a rising standard of living for all through greater production. He could only visualize the production of a fixed amount of goods each year for a stable population. His ignorance with regard to industrial relations, to use a term which to Cobbett would have been incomprehensible, was later corrected to some extent. But even when he denounced the cruelty of the manufacturers in the mid-1820's, he was focusing his attention on ways to bring down the "System" and urged the workers to forego attempts to raise their wages in the interest of trying to secure a price reduction.[23] Cobbett regarded unions as being almost useless from an economic standpoint and believed that the workers themselves could do little to better their lot by join-

22 P.R. (4/14/21), cols. 90 ff.
23 P.R. (9/17/25), cols. 710 ff.

ing them. Furthermore, Cobbett was usually lukewarm at best toward specific measures designed to help the workers. The deeds of those who attempted to achieve concrete gains for this class usually went unsung in the *Political Register,* just as he ignored reformers in other areas. Sometimes their plans were regarded as a plot to cheat the worker of his earnings and even of his freedom. This feeling extended to benefit clubs and savings banks, both of which were so important in building a confident, relatively prosperous working class aristocracy in the next generation. Ironically, Cobbett felt that these "absurd and ridiculous" institutions would have a bad moral effect upon the worker as they would make him less careful to be sober and healthy. More important, they would tend to weaken what Cobbett regarded as the worker's only salvation in times of trouble, the poor rates.[24] Benefit clubs and savings banks seemed to him to be examples of the "Methodist comforting" which he hated, as it tended to make the worker satisfied with his lot instead of militant, and Cobbett wanted an aggressive working class in order to help carry radical reform, just as he desired unrest in Ireland for the same reason.

Although he objected to comforting the worker when this was done by others, Cobbett himself was paternalistic as he revealed in his defense of the "tommy" system under which the workers were compelled to purchase necessities at a company store. Liking the idea of payment in both money and goods, he noted that if he had a village at his command, no tea kettle would sing and there would be no publican.

Cobbett claimed that it was a master's duty to exercise control over the lives of his servants. All of them, married as well as single, should be taught the virtues of early rising, industry and cleanliness.[25] Cobbett knew about the abuses of the tommy system and had even denounced them. Yet he

24 P.R. (1/7/32), cols. 109–13; P.R. (1/1/32), cols. 155–59.
25 *Rural Rides,* Vol II (5/18/30), pp. 667–70.

defended it in principle because it resembled the beneficent control over the lives of his own workers which he practiced on his farm. He could not understand why a design which insured his own laborers plenty to eat and drink as well as wholesome living conditions could not be applied to industry.

The impersonality and complexity of factory production obviously remained a mystery to Cobbett, whose contacts with industrialists were limited to those who took a personal interest in the welfare of their employees. Cobbett, to whom kind treatment of his laborers was good business as well as a moral obligation, looked at the factory owners from the point of view of a small farmer. He could never comprehend the ruthless drive for profits which animated these men, who were the products of a different way of life, any more than Gibbon could really understand the bad Roman emperors, who were so different from the rational, urbane eighteenth-century Englishman that he represented. It is interesting how much this brief mention of an ideal factory community resembled the actual achievement of Robert Owen. The latter's success as a humanitarian factory owner was discussed, though seldom emulated at the time. Despite this and strong similarities in personality and family life, Cobbett never cared for the benevolent despot of New Lanark. After a visit to Owen's factory, he registered an amused skepticism, praising the physical appearance of the place and health of the people but objecting to the discipline which Owen enforced.[26] Perhaps Cobbett was jealous of a rival for leadership of the working classes or possibly the character traits which the two powerful personalities shared helped to keep them apart.

This adherence to his old opinions continued even after Cobbett had been elected to parliament from Oldham in 1832 and was caught up in the agitation for factory reform. Although he had promised the electors to work for shorter hours of labor in mills and factories, his initial reaction in

[26] *Rural Rides*, Vol III (11/4/32), pp. 839–41.

parliament to such plans was cautious at best. Failure, he claimed, was the result whenever a government tried to regulate relations between "master and servant" by legislating hours of labor. The contemplated bill to limit children's labor would interfere, not with the manufacturer and the children, but with the manufacturer and the children's parents and would advise the world that the latter were cruel. Although this statement begs the question to a considerable degree, it is technically correct, for most minors were not employed directly by the manufacturer but by the spinners or other workmen. The stark poverty which led some parents to oppose limitations on their children's toil was blamed upon his familiar enemy, the overburden of taxes "laid on to support the rich." With rare modesty, however, he went on to acknowledge that he knew nothing of manufacturing and proclaimed his willingness to defer to his fellow member from Oldham, the enlightened manufacturer, John Fielden.[27]

This unusual admission that someone else knew more than he led to one of Cobbett's finest moments. When Lord Shaftesbury's epoch-making bill was introduced in 1833, Cobbett supported it vigorously and resisted attempts to dilute its provisions. Of course, the factory owners, acting in accordance with Nassau Senior's theory that their profit was made during the last hour of labor in the day, tried to prevent the daily hours of labor for children under eighteen from being reduced to ten. At this point Cobbett made what was probably his most effective speech in parliament. Speaking on behalf of the children, he noted that the "reformed" House of Commons had made a discovery greater than all previous Houses had ever made—that the prosperity, happiness and independence of the country depended upon "the labour of three hundred thousand little girls in Lancashire!" Deduct two hours a day from this labour and ". . . away goes the wealth,

27 Great Britain, 3 *Hansard's Parliamentary Debates,* XV (1833), 1294–96.

away goes the capital, away go the resources, the power, and glory of England!" [28] Cobbett's speech failed to accomplish its object but it was one of the most notable made on this occasion. The final bill, an amalgam of Tory humanitarianism and Benthamite utilitarianism, was probably the best which this parliament could produce. Its enactment, however, certainly did not satisfy the workers or the Radicals. Cobbett's hatred of the Whigs and sympathy for the worker was increased during the course of the bill through parliament and he became an enthusiastic advocate of the eight hour day.[29] His doubts regarding the efficacy of government intervention on behalf of the working man had disappeared, but he never lost his conviction that taxes and the funds were the root of all evil.

It is apparent that Cobbett's interest in industry and the urban worker was occasional and always related to his larger objects. Devotion to a belief that a combined political and financial "System" ruled the country prevented him from investigating the problem of industrialization thoroughly. Cobbett never accorded the Industrial Revolution anywhere near the same attention which he gave to agriculture.[30] Even as he deplored the growth of conditions to which industry gave rise, he correctly spoke of the agricultural interests as dominant both in numbers and importance. Agriculture supplied everything which the people needed in food and clothing. The men and boys were to work in the fields and the women and girls were to remain at home performing the tasks which would supply the family's clothing.[31] The farming family of Cobbett's imagination was self-sufficient in articles which he

[28] P.R. (7/20/33), cols. 181–82.
[29] P.R. (12/14/33), cols. 641–42.
[30] Perhaps his observation that the total population engaged in manufacturing was less than one half million, as compared with nearly five million in agriculture, was one reason. P.R. (5/5/21), col. 347.
[31] See P.R. (11/20/24), col. 451. This article contains Cobbett's most outspoken criticism of factory conditions. His description of an ideal society was intended as a contrast.

felt they really needed. There was hard work but also plenty of recreation within the bosom of the family. Like agrarian radicals before and after, Cobbett felt that this was the ideal way of life.

The factory promised hard work too, but could not afford the genial ways of the farm. It was not self-sufficient but had to produce and sell goods to stay in business. Difficulties of raising capital, primitive marketing information, fierce competition for supremacy all ensured that the workers would be driven. An ugly pattern developed which was to become classic in every newly industrialized country. Its seeming inevitability perhaps should exonerate the English factory owners from the species of original sin with which they have been labeled. As for the leisure which all were supposed to have enjoyed on the farm, who are we to deny the accuracy of Cobbett's reminiscence, the arguments of modern economists to the contrary? It should be remembered though that Cobbett was referring only to a family engaged almost entirely in agriculture. He never discussed a situation in which the breadwinner was a weaver or nailmaker working in his cottage with a small plot of land to give him independence. It was this class of domestic laborer which the industrial and agricultural changes hurt cruelly.

Cobbett had been pictured as a man poised on the edge of a new age with his face set firmly in the direction of the past. This posture is said to have handicapped his understanding of the new shape which society was assuming. On the other hand, it intensified his appeal to the uprooted factory workers who, like him, were once peasants.[32] This point of view is accurate, except that it supposes the transition from an agricultural to an industrial England was much more rapid than it was in fact. It also overrates Cobbett's appeal to the factory worker, which was at its peak before he fled to America in 1817. Although he later became much more

[32] See Cole, *op. cit.*, ch. I.

aware of their circumstances, he never regained his influence over these men. This was partly because the price of the *Register* had become more than the worker could afford and partly because his remedies lacked relevance. Finally, the above statement assumes that Cobbett wanted to understand the plight of the laborer in the factory. There is not much evidence for this, even after 1820. Cobbett was sympathetic with these people but was too captivated by his own plans for radical reform and, at heart, too much an agrarian to allow them to dominate his mind for very long. After observing the conditions of the miners, less than three years before he died, he wrote that their work was terrible but that it was not a life of hunger, their rent was free, fuel and a doctor cost nothing. All in all "their lives seem to be as good as that of the working part of mankind can reasonably expect." [33] Compare this with his feeling for the agricultural laborer—for whom nothing was too good!

It is hard for us to realize from Cobbett's writing that these were times when real wages were generally rising and conditions were improving for the mass of the people. Despite future setbacks, most industrial workers were over their worst period by the early 1820's. The greatest suffering was undergone not by the factory operative but by the skilled domestic workers whose standards were being undermined by the machine. Modern investigators have revealed that there was an uneven, but perceptible, increase in the standard of living for the industrial working class during Cobbett's adult years. Yet the evidence which he submits, granted that it is usually not first hand, of poverty and misery is real enough. Bad harvests—still the key to the happiness of all workers—artificially high food prices, even his own pet hates, high taxes and an extravagant government, contributed toward preventing the workers from gaining but a meager share of the wealth which they were producing. Still, apart from the

[33] *Rural Rides*, Vol III (10/4/32), p. 737.

victims of technological unemployment, *on the average* they were faring better than their parents and grandparents. Cobbett could not understand this, in part because he overlooked the sordid aspects of traditional rural life. Also, the Industrial Revolution by fostering the growth of cities did not intensify squalor, but made it conspicuous and created such a menace to health and safety that something had to be done. Poverty in urban areas is much more apparent (and dangerous to society as a whole) than poverty in the countryside. This persistent inability to understand the economic conditions in which he lived would have rendered Cobbett's efforts nugatory even if he had the power to cause them to be adopted.

XI
The role of religion

William Cobbett once wrote, "The Christian religion, then, is not an affair of preaching, or prating, or ranting, but of taking care of the bodies as well as the souls of people; not an affair of belief and of faith and of professions, but an affair of doing good, and especially to those who are in want; not an affair of fire and brimstone, but an affair of bacon and bread, beer and a bed." [1] This statement might be considered his testament on the purpose of religion. There was nothing of the metaphysician or mystic about Cobbett. Religion, as far as he was concerned, was useful in proportion to its positive effect upon a person's conduct, and conduct, not faith, was the measure of the intensity of religious feeling. For the forms and rituals of religion Cobbett had only contempt, and he regarded teaching the history of the jury sys-

[1] P.R. (2/15/34), col. 386.

tem to children as preferable to instruction in the catechism. As far as his personal religious beliefs were concerned. Cobbett was too well-read and had seen too much of the world to be content with the simple faith of his peasant ancestors. Still, although he was acquainted with the writings of the great skeptics of his youth, Hume and Gibbon, he eschewed their total disbelief. While Cobbett's attitude was essentially secular, there is a suggestion of the ethical religion and social gospel movements of the mid-nineteenth century in some of his statements. "To practise justice, mercy, charity and other virtues, is natural to uncorrupted and unperverted human beings. That which strengthens this natural propensity, or arrests the effects of corruption and perversion, and does this through the means of reverence for God and an expectation of future rewards and punishments, is called RELIGION. So that, religion means *virtue* arising from considerations connected with a Supreme Being and with hopes and fears as to another world." [2] Obtaining virtue would seem to depend upon an adequate supply of bacon, bread and beer, for Cobbett could not envision want and sanctity travelling hand in hand.

This worldliness carried over to matters of doctrine and biblical interpretation. Cobbett's real concern, the health of the state, was demonstrated in the case of two of the main religious issues of the time. He opposed both the more general circulation of the Bible and the partial relief of the Dissenters from their disabilities. Although Cobbett regarded the discussions of doctrinal subtleties as barren and useless, he had a firm belief in the necessity both of the Bible and of someone to interpret it. Along with many others, he claimed that there could logically be but one true belief and because of the difficulty in ascertaining it, biblical interpretation had to be in the hands of experts.[3] But in his writings on this issue and

[2] *Thirteen Sermons*, No. 2, pp. 26–27. Also, P.R. (2/8/12), cols. 66–67.
[3] P.R. (9/26/07), cols. 486–87; P.R. (6/12/24), cols. 655–59.

in his opposition to relief for the Dissenters, it is obvious that (as he once admitted) Cobbett was viewing religion with the eyes of a politician.[4] If everyone was to interpret the Bible in his own fashion, it would give rise to ignorant quarrels which might menace social stability. Never a complete libertarian, Cobbett wanted a tranquil society in which there was a consensus upon basic beliefs, both religious and secular. His objection to the Dissenters was due to this and also to a conviction that they were interested only in achieving religious equality and not in the political reform which the country needed.[5]

Cobbett said that he himself remained a member of the Church of England, not because of any attachment to its doctrines or because he thought that belonging to it made him better than anyone else. Instead, the experience of a lifetime convinced him that uniformity in religion was "a most desirable thing." [6] It was enough for Cobbett that the ancient law of the land had made the Church of England the established church, and he resolved never to leave it (just as he never would renounce his country despite his persecution by its government). He did not consider that any church had a monopoly of righteousness. Indeed, in the all-important matter of moral conduct one was as good as another. It was the tendency of the sects to concentrate upon gaining their "selfish security while their country is in danger" that he objected to. To win their narrow objectives, Cobbett claimed that dissenting ministers would support the government in any oppressive act, and this was simply villainous to him.[7] It is true that Cobbett was changing religious ground about

4 See P.R. (1/27/20), col. 759.

5 P.R. (6/5/13), cols. 812–14. It must be acknowledged that Cobbett did not believe in thought control. Consistent with his defense of a free press, Cobbett insisted that liberty of discussion should apply to religion as well as politics. ". . . and, as to religion, TRUTH can never be in *danger, as long as discussion is free.*" P.R. (4/8/20), col. 237

6 P.R. (12/21/33), col. 705.

7 P.R. (1/13/21), cols. 65–81 and 99–110.

the end of the Napoleonic wars [8] during the same period that he became a confirmed exponent of radical reform. The unfailing approval of organized religion for the reactionary domestic policy of the government and its support of Continental tyranny as a bulwark against Napoleon influenced him deeply. The position taken by many important Dissenters was particularly disappointing. For the remainder of his life he was a bitterly hostile critic of most religious organizations and frequently referred to religion in the context of a stalking horse for tyranny.[9]

Although his own Church of England enjoyed great privileges, its position among the people had been weakened, principally by its own lethargy. There were also present more virile church groups on the one hand and, on the other, the rational and skeptical thinkers who were the representatives of the Enlightenment and of scientific thought. They flourished in the spiritual vacuum of eighteenth-century Anglican thought and deed. The Church was extraordinarily complacent, not only toward ideas, but also in the face of new economic and political realities which were altering the complexion of society. An atmosphere of unreality existed about its generally bland attitude. Although the Evangelical branch led in the abolition of the slave trade and attempted to end blood sports and gambling, the image which the Church projected was one of spiritual sloth, seeming unconcern about temporal abuses, and unwillingness to accept the industrial England which was evolving. Secure in its relationship to the state, which protected it from without, the Church enjoyed a general lack of criticism from within the Anglican communion.[10]

---

8 Cole, *op. cit.*, p. 192.

9 P.R. (11/25/15), cols. 225–30. However, he did exhibit anger upon receipt of a letter dated in the "era of the Carpenters son, 1821." Letter, William Cobbett to James Cobbett, (2/23/22), Nuffield College, Oxford, England, Cobbett MSS, No. 164.

10 Halévy, *England in 1815*, pp. 389–401.

Considering the neglect and lack of religious zeal shown by its clergy, the nation displayed an indulgent attitude toward the Church. Perhaps the truth of Cobbett's observation that, politics aside, the clergy were tolerant and well behaved, "good neighbors, good masters, good hunters, and shooters, and famously good and hearty companions" [11] had much to do with this. Certainly Cobbett's own criticisms of the Church usually concerned its support of government reaction and the cost of its upkeep, not doctrine or the personal character of the clergy. Indeed, as late as 1814 he considered the latter to be more tolerant and less bigoted than either the Catholic priests or the Dissenting preachers.[12] More tolerant and less zealous might be another way of putting Cobbett's thought, for with his utilitarian religious ethic, he was impatient with dogma.

Cobbett's manner of addressing the Church changed from hortatory appeals to preserve itself by winning the friendship of the people to denunciation for its support of reaction.[13] His later attitude was linked to his belief that the French Revolution was a purely domestic issue which the government determined to crush for fear that its example would help the cause of parliamentary reform in England. Here Cobbett saw the clergy, fearful that the French expropriation of church property would become the practice in England, cynically defend Roman Catholicism and join with the boroughmongers in their effort to stifle freedom at home and abroad. He was never able to convince the Church that its real enemies were those who would use it for the purpose of repressing the people. He was also unable to make church authorities understand that reform by sweeping away bribery and corruption would be of benefit. The refusal of the Church to accept Cob-

[11] Amer. P.R. (3/16/16), col. 347.
[12] P.R. (6/18/14), col. 797.
[13] Note the difference between P.R. (4/1/09), col. 486 and P.R. (2/14/29), cols. 196–97.

bett's advice and to identify itself with the common people and the immoderate language against reform, adopted not only by the hierarchy but by many of the lower clergy as well, distressed Cobbett at first and later incensed him.[14] But, of course, the terrible fear which the French Revolution had introduced into the minds of propertied groups in England made it useless and even dangerous to talk of reform. While this fear lasted, the Church, which had always identified itself with the powerful, was in a more congenial position as the defender of privilege rather than of the people.[15]

Exasperation which Cobbett felt toward the Church was reflected in his increasingly hostile attitude toward the church establishment after 1815. Where he once hoped that both purity and utility might be restored to it from within, he eventually called for disestablishment and the application of church revenues to the elimination of the national debt. This position was justified by noting that church property was granted originally in consideration of the fulfillment of certain duties. However, in the reign of Henry VIII all this property was taken and given to "protestant parsons" and aristocratic favorites. Since the precedent had been established by one act of parliament, why couldn't another make similar changes, in view of the fact that obligations of the clergy were not being fulfilled? [16] By 1822 Cobbett was writing that the church establishment was unnecessary for the purposes of religion and

14 P.R. (6/27/12), cols. 897–99. He expressed regret at the want of mercy and charity in a message from the clergy of the Diocese of Salisbury to Prime Minister Perceval dealing with discontent among the people and considered it strange that they did not express any compassion for the sufferings of those whose labor supported them.

15 For a discussion of the Church in the 18th century from an Anglican point of view, see N. Sykes, *Church and State in England in the XVIIIth Century*, Cambridge, Cambridge University Press, 1934, passim; J. H. Overton, *The English Church in the Nineteenth Century (1800–1833)*, London, Longmans, Green and Co., 1894, holds that a reformation in the practices of the Church began about the turn of the century; see ch. I.

16 P.R. (6/6/07), cols. 991–92; P.R. (9/21/22), col. 342.

implying that its property ought to be used to liquidate the debt.[17] He carefully distinguished between property given to the aristocracy and to the clergy at the time of the Reformation. Cobbett, who had not given up hope for the aristocracy by 1822 but was to do so very shortly afterwards, allowed them to keep their property if they adopted his attitude toward radical reform. Clearly, keeping faith with the fundholder was more important than preserving the financial privileges of the Church.

He had once contended that the nation was not bound to continue paying the fundholder if it was in danger from foreign countries or if the stability of the state was menaced by domestic conditions. Now he said that faith must be kept with the fundholder until every piece of property not essential to the nation's safety had been applied to the discharge of the national debt. He especially meant the property of the Church. By its aloofness and its neglect of charitable duties, the Church had forfeited its value and no longer contributed to the health and safety of the country. In a lengthy *Register* article written in 1827 Cobbett expressed his frustration and resentment over accumulated rebuffs from many sources. Not only did he consider it legitimate and desirable for church property to be sold to reduce the debt, but he attacked the clergy for neglecting their pastoral duties through non-residence and for the unforgivable sin of social climbing.[18] Of course, Cobbett had not suddenly fallen in love with the fundholders; at the moment they were simply less obnoxious to him than the Church and the landlords, and he especially hated any group or person in which he had lost faith. The Church of England, the landowning class, the Quakers and several prominent personalities all suffered abuse after their respective falls from grace.

[17] See *Two Penny Trash* (1/1/31), cols. 148–50 and 166–67 for a full statement of these views.
[18] P.R. (7/21/27), cols. 209–35.

Two legislative acts which influenced him against the Church almost as much as its views on political and social questions were the supplementing of the salaries of poor clergy by grants from parliament and the voting of £1,000,000 for new church buildings in urban areas in 1818. In both cases Cobbett felt that the Church itself should meet the expenses and not impose on an already overburdened taxpaying public. Historians have treated with irony the solitary effort by the government to ease the distress of the growing industrial working class through building churches. Yet, as G. M. Trevelyan wisely remarked, ". . . students of history are often so much obsessed by the notorious political event of the Peterloo massacre that they imagine the Lancashire factory hand as the typical wage earner of the year 1819; but he was not; he was only a local type . . ." [19] Although Cobbett is considered a spokesman of the working class, it is interesting to note another example of his lack of contact with the new industrial cities as late as 1818. He objected to the appropriation for church building on the ground that if population was increasing so must the tithes. He was either unaware or did not care to recognize that it was the non-tithe paying population that was growing in numbers. Also, he professed not to understand why new churches were needed when the existing ones were generally empty.[20] Actually the Church was able to raise more money for church building through private donations than it received from the government in 1818 and in 1824, when it was awarded £500,000 more. Although Cobbett was free from the coarseness of some of the writers who attacked the enormously wealthy church establishment, he became its bitter opponent in this matter of accepting money from the

[19] G. M. Trevelyan, *English Social History*, Longmans, Green and Co., New York, 1942, p. xi. Sir John Clapham has pointed out that as late as 1830 only one person in eighty in Great Britain worked in a cotton mill. Cited in Fritz Stern, *The Varieties of History from Voltaire to the Present*, Cleveland, World Publishing Co., 1962, p. 310.

[20] P.R. (7/1/09), col. 996; P.R. (6/20/18), col. 704 and col. 710.

government instead of adopting reforms which would allow it to meet expenses. Here his efforts were ineffective, for little was done by the Church to correct abuses and the Whig reforms of the mid-1830's did not go as far as he would have wished. By the time he died, Cobbett was advocating the complete separation of church and state on the twin bases of neglect of duty by the clergy and the expense of upkeep of the establishment. He also changed some of his ideas about the Dissenters and pointedly compared the devotion to duty and morality of their ministers with the attitude of Church of England parsons.[21]

Advancing more deeply into the church question, the two internal aspects which drew his attention most frequently were the tithing system and the non-residence of many of the clergy. Both were subject to criticism by others, within and outside of parliament. Nevertheless, in that property-conscious age, with the memory of the French Revolution still fresh, nothing substantial would be done to alter so valuable a bulwark of order as the Church. Although tithes were a burden to the already over-taxed farmer, and perhaps more than half of the livings were non-resident, persons within the Church who demanded a change were a minority. Of course, for the first quarter of a century those who were most aggrieved, the Catholics and the Dissenters, were politically almost powerless. In Ireland, where the system of tithing and non-residence was aggravated by chronic poverty, there was considerable unrest. It took Cobbett a good many years to evolve toward his final position concerning tithes. The path from adamant defense to qualified approval to reluctant acceptance and finally to outright opposition was long and marked by a hesitancy to introduce innovations into such a hallowed custom. Disgust with the political and social policies of the clergy, their opposition to reform, and what he regarded as their bloodthirsty advocacy of repression of the

21 *Cobbett's Legacy to Parsons,* passim.

poor, was again certainly more important in changing his mind than ecclesiastical abuses. Since the functions of charity and care of the poor, which he asserted were the foundations of the tithe system, were no longer adequately performed, parliament had the right to abolish tithes and apply the revenue to public purposes.[22]

Similarly, Cobbett's attitude took shape gradually concerning the problem of clergymen who did not reside in their livings but who collected the full fee while paying a curate a miserable wage to fulfill the duties of the office. At first, while favoring the enforcement of residence, he believed that if the principle was to be followed faithfully many parishes would not have clergymen due to the small stipend provided. There was no hint in 1802 that a redistribution of church wealth would provide a sufficient salary for all resident clergy.[23] About the same time that he adopted a radically different attitude toward the tithes, he shifted position on this problem as well. In his *Rural Rides* he displayed indignation frequently over the contrast between the opulence of the residences of the higher clergy and those of their poverty-stricken parishioners or the "almost destitute" curates. It was this luxury combined with the lack of religious zeal on the part of bishops, deans, chapters, and colleges that disgusted Cobbett and helped lead him to the conclusion that the higher clergy had forfeited the right to their wealth. The government should assume the property of the Church and pay the working clergy a salary.[24] Cobbett observed that a good part of the burden which the clergy inflicted upon the nation was due to their being allowed to marry. Their children produced "an enormous national evil" as they expected to be kept like

22 P.R. (1/23/19), cols. 549–61; P.R. (8/10/22), cols. 326–39. For an extreme defense of tithes in his early obscurantist style, see *The Porcupine* (1/26/01), pp. 2–3.

23 P.R. (6/5/02), col. 655.

24 *Rural Rides*, Vol. I (8/31/23), pp. 212–13; *Rural Rides*, Vol. II (8/31/26), p. 382; P.R. (9/5/28), cols. 302–03.

ladies and gentlemen. Social pretensions always irritated him, and he was especially moved here because he felt that these children added to the already swollen pension list, as well as causing their father to scurry around to find "suitable" situations for his sons. In making his point for a celibate clergy, he noted that Malthus never tried to stop the breeding of parsons and pensioners—only those industrious persons who supported them.[25]

Apart from the cost of such an establishment, Cobbett refused to admit that the clergy should be better off than average folk anyway. "Did [Christ] depend on the *erudition,* or *cunning,* of the teachers, for the success of that doctrine, which he was teaching? . . . Did he choose, for his Apostles men with immense estates, scores of manors, scores of gamekeepers, and with apparel the most sumptuous that can be conceived? Did he ever say or insinuate, that the success of his saving word depended upon the teachers of it having palaces for their places of residence; having parks well stocked with deer; having retinues of servants. . . ." [26] On principle Cobbett opposed the social aims of many parsons and their families. This was perhaps one reason for his irregular attendance at church. Churchgoing was a practice which to him was a duty, but not as the word is usually interpreted. He was interested in attending because it afforded him "a very good opportunity of making an estimate of the condition of the people." However, attending at the expense of foregoing any of his writing "would be a vile and most criminal affectation and hypocrisy, understanding the contents of the Bible as well as any parson can, and having besides written a dozen of good thumping *Sermons myself.* . . ." [27] The "Sermons" refer to a series of articles in the *Register* which were later published as a book. They were written to answer the tract writers who had turned

25 *Two Penny Trash* (1/1/31), pp. 164–65; P.R. (7/21/27), cols. 220–21.
26 P.R. (7/14/22), cols. 653–54.
27 P.R. (7/14/32), col. 78; P.R. (4/12/28), col. 464.

their talents to the strengthening of authority. In addition to containing Cobbett's views on religion, the *Sermons* abound in sharp observations of society. Strongly critical of the government, they were yet able to circumvent the Six Acts, which permitted "religious" writings to circulate freely. There is nothing in them which displays a devotional attitude. Denying religion altogether, as Robert Owen discovered to his cost, was a foolhardy thing for any prospective reformer to do. Cobbett was, in the final analysis, a prudent person in religion as well as politics. Although he would make violent attacks upon institutions and personalities, he seldom carried them to the point at which he would be subject to retaliation.

Turning to the other religious groups in the country there was a Catholic minority, small in numbers and weak in influence, which looked hopefully upon the late eighteenth-century trend toward the gradual removal of their disabilities.[28] The major political right which they sought was emancipation, a goal which several times during the early part of the following century seemed within their grasp but always eluded them. However, the French Revolution, so inimical to change generally, may have lessened opposition in this case. As Halévy has said to this new attitude, "The modern Babylon was no longer Rome but Paris, Anti-Christ no longer the Pope but Voltaire." [29] The romantic movement in the arts, the plight of the French Catholic refugees and the decline of earlier religious antagonisms all contributed to creating a more favorable environment for the extension of this type of reform. The native Catholic minority was still small although it was beginning to register the effects of the large scale Irish im-

---

28 For the position of English Catholics at the turn of the century, see B. Ward, *The Dawn of the Catholic Revival in England, 1781–1803*, 2 vols., London, Longmans, Green and Co., 1909. Also, Halévy, *England in 1815*, contains a concise discussion of the background to emancipation. See pp. 468–85. A recent work by Ursula Henriques, *Religious Toleration in England, 1787–1833*, London, Routledge and Kegan Paul, 1961, contains a chapter devoted to Catholic emancipation. See ch. V.

29 Halévy, *England in 1815*, p. 476.

migration which was to transform its composition. Composed primarily of scattered groups in remote rural areas and of a handful of aristocracy and their retainers, it had preserved its religion during over two centuries of persecution. This persecution was mild by comparison to what religious minorities on the Continent had to endure and was usually confined to political disenfranchisement and social ostracism. However, the great changes in European politics and religious attitudes since the Reformation tended to make even these disabilities obsolete.

Perhaps a more important obstacle to emancipation than the generations-old conviction among non-Catholic Englishmen—those indifferent to religion as well as the fervent Protestants—that Catholicism was synonymous with an alien tyranny, was the question of Ireland. It is true that even if Ireland had not existed many Englishmen would have hated the Catholic Church,[30] but the most bigoted would have been hard pressed to insist that emancipation would threaten English liberty. However, the prospect of enfranchising a large number of ignorant and potentially disloyal Irish excited prejudices other than purely religious ones and threw the considerable weight of the Irish Ascendancy into the scales against emancipation. The major argument of those opposing emancipation was that Catholics were compelled to divide their allegiance between sovereign and pope. This seemed to taken on more weight when the potential traitors were not merely a few tens of thousands of Englishmen but millions of Irish with a long history of grievances against England. The Irish influence upon emancipation must be considered paradoxical, for while it was the major inhibiting factor it was also the force which ensured the realization of emancipation in 1828.

Insofar as Cobbett's own attitude is concerned, if we are willing to penetrate beneath the crust represented by his

[30] Henriques, *op. cit.*, p. 139.

History of the Protestant Reformation, we will see that his most powerful motive for supporting the cause of the Catholics was knowledge that it was a weapon against the "System." The racy, immoderate style of the *History* contributed to its "phenomenal" sale [31] and it is probably true that Cobbett's polemic aided Catholic relief. Yet the zealous advocacy contained in the *History* should not obscure the fact that he was primarily interested in achieving radical reform. Although Cobbett may have been "carried away," as Cole says,[32] by John Lingard's *History of England,* it was not primarily due to the arguments of this able Catholic scholar that Cobbett assumed the duty of correcting the abuse and falsehood which for 300 years had been heaped upon the medieval church. As he himself wrote:

> All my plans in private life; all my pursuits; all my designs, wishes, and thoughts, have this one great object in view: *the overthrow of the ruffian Boroughmongers.* If I write grammars; if I write on agriculture; if I sow, plant, or deal in seeds; whatever I do has *first* in view the destruction of those infamous tyrants.[33]

Before discussing Cobbett's specific attitude toward emancipation, it is necessary to note briefly the most important events in his life during the years immediately preceding 1824 when he emerged as the outspoken champion of Catholicism and the Catholics. Between 1819, when he returned from the American exile to which the government had driven him two years earlier, and 1823, Cobbett had suffered major reverses. In 1820 his campaign to secure election to parliament from Coventry failed. The cost of this campaign helped to bring on bankruptcy. The following year saw his hopes of striking

---

[31] Quoted from James A. Reynolds, *The Catholic Emancipation Crisis in Ireland, 1823–1829,* New Haven, Yale University Press, 1954, p. 67.
[32] *Op. cit.,* p. 288.
[33] P.R. (8/14/19), col. 8.

a major blow against the "System" crushed when the cause of Queen Caroline collapsed. Cobbett, as we have seen, was closely involved in her struggle to become England's recognized queen. In 1823 the "Norfolk Petition," Cobbett's attempt to unite all classes living on the land, failed. Short of funds, his influence over the workers diminished and with the circulation of the *Political Register* greatly reduced by the operation of the Stamp Duty Act,[34] Cobbett was in need of a new string for his bow. Catholic Emancipation, which was more than ever "in the air" in 1824, thanks to the activities in Ireland of Daniel O'Connell and the Catholic Association, provided Cobbett with a ready-made weapon against the "System."

Until the 1820's Cobbett had a rather consistent but disinterested attitude of friendliness toward English Catholics. A couple of articles critical of Pitt's scheme for emancipation in that fountainhead of Cobbett's erstwhile reaction, *The Porcupine,* were superseded by a *Register* article in 1804 calling for repeal of the Test Act.[35] From that time on, he urged concessions mildly, took pleasure in Lord Grenville's election as Chancellor of Oxford University over the anti-Catholic Lord Eldon ("the triumph of tolerant principles over hypocrisy and bigotry . . .") and tried to assure his readers that the Catholic Church was not a threat to English liberties.[36] It is true that there was a brief exception to this attitude of friendliness. Cobbett was a strong partisan of the Spanish rebels against Napoleon and when the regime of Ferdinand VII was restored by the allies, the *Register* contained numerous articles critical of the Church. However, this phase was mostly confined to a few weeks in 1814.[37] Similarly, his writings

---

[34] Halévy, *The Liberal Awakening*, p. 103.

[35] *The Porcupine* (2/12/01), p. 3 and (2/13/01), p. 3; P.R. (12/29/04), cols. 1061–62.

[36] P.R. (6/13/07), col. 1041; P.R. (12/23/19), cols. 969–72; P.R. (2/13/13), cols. 203–04.

[37] P.R. (9/13/14), cols. 291 ff.; P.R. (9/10/11), cols. 346–49. In 1825 he proclaimed that the Spanish people were better off than the common people of any European country. P.R. (10/8/25), col. 100.

on Ireland and the Irish were friendly. They praised Irish character, spoke out against coercion and urged a generous effort to meet Ireland's protests and thus bind the country to England by ties of friendship and mutual interest.[38] Cobbett's fundamental attitude toward the Irish was that they were countrymen of the English and their land as much attached to the English Crown as were Scotland and Wales. Because of the affinity which he saw between England and Ireland, he held himself in part responsible for the wrongs of the Irish. He took up their cause with the same fervor as he did the grievances of mistreated industrial workers in Lancashire, or even his beloved agricultural laborers of the southern counties. Yet Cobbett did not want simple reform. Instead he said, "It is the whole *state* of Ireland; it is the *system of governing Ireland*" which had to be changed.[39] As in the case of England, he saw the need for complete transformation. When the activities of the Catholic Association, under the leadership of Daniel O'Connell, made the affairs of their unhappy country a major subject of discussion in England, Cobbett saw his chance to attack the "System" through the connected issues of Catholic Emancipation and Ireland.

The record of the next few years reveals that Cobbett's prime motivation here was not disinterested sympathy with the wrongs suffered by English and Irish Catholics but, instead, a desire to strike a shrewd blow at his enemies and, perhaps, to advance himself politically as well.[40] Once he saw his course, Cobbett plunged ahead without inhibitions. In a strong article in the *Register* he claimed that the Church

---

[38] P.R. (10/12/11), col. 457; P.R. (8/1/07), col. 167; P.R. (12/24/08), cols. 971–72.

[39] P.R. (4/18/07), col. 586.

[40] In 1826 he ran for parliament from Preston. One reason for this was that Preston was a borough which, in addition to having a democratic franchise, contained a sizable number of Catholics. Catholics otherwise eligible could vote if the candidates informally agreed among themselves not to object. See Cole, *op. cit.*, pp. 300–05 for an account of this election.

of Ireland had "spread destruction, degradation and misery over that once happy country . . . ," and urged that it be suppressed by law. He accused it of neglect, corruption and oppression and cited facts and figures to support his argument. The sufferings of the Catholics were spoken of sympathetically and their remaining true to their faith despite "coaxing and wheedling, menaces and punishments" was praised.[41] His arguments were impressive and placed him in the middle of the controversy. Cobbett's basic attitude in these writings is not difficult to discern. Mingled with praise of the Catholic clergy and suspicion of the Catholic aristocracy is his insistence that the Irish no longer confine their agitation to their own problems and join with the English reformers to demand radical reform.[42] English and Irish Catholics had ceased to be objects of pity, calling forth occasional expressions of sympathy, and had become allies in the struggle against the corrupt boroughmonger system.

Meanwhile, in Ireland, the Catholic Association, before being suppressed by the government in 1825, had prepared the way for a Whig-sponsored bill providing for Catholic Emancipation to be introduced and passed in Commons. However, two riders were attached to the bill. The first raised the county franchise property qualifications from 40 shillings to 10 pounds; the second provided for payment of the Irish Catholic clergy by the government. Thus, on the one hand, the danger of parliament's being crowded with Irish proletarians would be lessened and, on the other, it was hoped that the revolutionary ardor of the Irish clergy would be terminated. Over the protests of some of his countrymen, O'Connell accepted the riders. Cobbett was vigorous in his opposition to the bill, which he claimed was an attempt to bribe the priesthood and fasten a landowning oligarchy upon the coun-

41 P.R. (5/29/24), cols. 513–48.
42 P.R. (5/21/25), col. 471; P.R. (8/5/26), cols. 346–49.

try. It was with relief that he witnessed rejection by the House of Lords.[43] Cobbett was undoubtedly concerned that O'Connell had been captured in an aristocratic embrace, after the fashion of other radicals before and after. Yet it might be assumed that this conclusion was secondary to his worry that the Catholics might gain their emancipation without a major reform of English institutions. This may be seen in his attack upon O'Connell and the now illegal Catholic Association, which continued after the defeat of the bill.[44]

Although it is not accurate to state that Cobbett "ceased to prosecute the quarrel" with O'Connell,[45] he did ignore the issue for some time. Early in 1827, however, Cobbett's annoyance over the persistence of the Irish in following O'Connell and going their own way apart from the English reform movement led him to a number of irritable outbursts in print. He frankly avowed that Irish Catholics could never expect to gain anything without the support of the English people.[46] In a series of petulant articles he made plain his jealousy of the Irish "Liberator" and was led to the fantastic assertion that if Catholics were to agitate for the repeal of the Established Church and for the use of tithes for the maintenance of the poor, they would have the support of ninety-nine hundredths of the Protestants of England! [47] Fortunately for themselves, the Catholics followed the leadership of O'Connell and accepted the only form of emancipation possible under existing circumstances.

At home his position regarding Catholic Emancipation was

---

[43] P.R. (3/19/25), cols. 716 ff.; P.R. (5/28/25), col. 543.

[44] P.R. (7/23/25), cols. 195–201, cols. 225 ff.; P.R. (8/13/25), cols. 399 ff. Also see the occasionally hilarious play, "Big O and Sir Glory," although it is highly allusive and the somewhat ponderous humor may not be to everyone's taste. "Big O" was, of course, O'Connell, and "Sir Glory" was Sir Francis Burdett, the former ally of Cobbett's who had introduced the bill in parliament. P.R. (9/24/25).

[45] As G. D. H. Cole does, *op. cit.,* p. 293.

[46] P.R. (1/13/27), col. 164.

[47] P.R. (3/3/27), cols. 597–606; P.R. (3/10/27), cols. 655–56.

even more explicit. Although he conceded that some good might be done if Catholics were allowed to sit in parliament before reform had taken place, he preferred that they remain disenfranchised because their discontent would aid in securing what Cobbett really wanted. If Catholic Emancipation passed without a reform of parliament, "it would naturally quiet the most noisy of them for a little; and I want these noisy ones to continue to be noisy. . . ." [48] By this time the Catholic Association had been cleverly reorganized to evade the law. Its continued preoccupation with the cause for which it had been formed drew Cobbett's ire. Although he supported O'Connell when the latter illegally contested the famous Clare election against the government minister, Vesey Fitzgerald, he turned on him when O'Connell did not come to England on the strength of polling the most votes.[49] After the introduction of a new bill in 1828, Cobbett ranged himself on the side of the fanatical Protestants who were exhausting all the stock anti-Catholic arguments in a frantic effort to prevent passage of the bill. He even accused members of the Catholic Association of being "a kind of mongrel Catholics . . ." who would sacrifice their church for personal aggrandizement.[50] The emancipation of well-to-do Catholics without a reform of church and state did not, in Cobbett's opinion, seem enough to make Ireland happy and content. Quite the opposite, it would simply burden the common people with a new set of oppressors. The type of changes which Cobbett thought necessary for both Ireland and England could only be accomplished by a reformed parliament.[51] The satisfying of the demands of articulate Irishmen would lessen the agitation for such a reform. Thus, Catholic Emancipation must be postponed until it could be incorporated into the

48 P.R. (2/7/29), cols. 176–77.
49 P.R. (7/26/28), col. 97.
50 P.R. (11/1/28), cols. 571–72; P.R. (11/15/28), cols. 632–35.
51 P.R. (11/8/28), cols. 582–92.

sweeping changes to be made by an English legislature reconstituted on a popular basis.

In 1829 a Catholic Emancipation bill was passed. It was similar to the 1825 bill except that it did not provide for payment of the Catholic clergy. This legislation initially pleased Cobbett to the extent that he measured out grudging praise to O'Connell and the Association. Cobbett was hopeful that this step would serve to weaken the Church of England.[52] He was briefly reconciled to O'Connell by the latter's speech in favor of manhood suffrage, frequent parliaments and the ballot at the East London Catholic Institute on February 25, 1829.[53] However, less than a month later, Cobbett made a lengthy attack upon O'Connell and the Catholic Association for not being vigorous enough in defense of Catholic interests. Before the month was out, he announced his opposition to the new legislation.[54] When Cobbett saw that the Irish were prepared to accept the bill without a strenuous campaign for further reforms, he began to indulge in ridicule and in peevish attacks upon Irish character.[55] Clearly, the wise refusal of the Catholic leaders in the United Kingdom to identify their cause with that of the English reformers had completely exasperated him.

It is, therefore, to the obscure columns of the *Political Register* and not to the well-known and often reprinted *History of the Protestant Reformation* that one must turn for the revelation of Cobbett's real attitude toward Catholic Emancipation. From this source we learn that Cobbett was primarily interested in Catholic relief as a weapon against the government and that he did not want the elimination of grievances but wholesale changes, which must, of course, be part and parcel of a radical reform. Even the *History of the*

---

[52] P.R. (2/14/29), col. 197 and col. 219; P.R. (2/21/29), col. 248.
[53] Reynolds, *op. cit.*, p. 132.
[54] P.R. (3/14/29), cols. 321–38; P.R. (3/21/29), col. 354.
[55] P.R. (8/29/29), cols. 257–74.

Protestant Reformation is significant in this respect. As Marx is supposed to have hated the bourgeoisie more than he loved the proletariat, Cobbett's book perhaps reveals more of his aversion to the whole political, economic and social system which dominated the United Kingdom than love of medieval Catholicism.

Cobbett's support for the relief of Catholics from repressive legislation was sincere enough as his early statements show. His intense feeling for the past, his love of tradition and quick sympathy toward victims of visible injustice would make him incline toward the Catholic cause. However, his hatred of the boroughmonger system, buttressed as it was by the established church, was his main concern and idealism was secondary. Stubbornly remaining a member of the Church of England and unconcerned with church politics centering around Cisalpines and Ultramontanes, Cobbett was, on balance, an asset to the Catholics. His writings, a mixture of humanity, common sense, exaggeration and vituperation, brought home many truths to his readers and helped create a more receptive climate for emancipation before fear of revolution in Ireland made it a reality.

So we see that when he painted his fanciful descriptions of English life in the Middle Ages or made pointed references to the disposition of church property after the Reformation, it was with the intention of illuminating current difficulties in society. History had no value for him except to contribute to the understanding and the solution of contemporary problems. This helps to explain why his *History of the Protestant Reformation* is one of Cobbett's least edifying books. Read in conjunction with the careful, scholarly account of Lingard, Cobbett's lack of moderation appears even sillier.[56] In his

---

[56] Cobbett had no doubt as to which book he felt would have the greatest influence. After praising Lingard's *History* as "far superior" to that of David Hume, he remarked that it would not produce a thousandth of the effect for all time as his own would in three years. P.R. (10/30/24), cols. 272 and 288. Unhappily, a Gresham's Law of journalism might

first volume Cobbett tried to show that the Reformation, instead of being a change for the better, "was engendered in beastly lust, brought forth in hypocrisy and perfidy, and cherished and fed by plunder, devastation, and by rivers of innocent English and Irish blood." He considered it unlikely that Christ would have allowed a false Church to exist for fifteen hundred years, or would have abandoned nine-tenths of His followers. The Reformation was started for plunder and resulted in the pauperizing of the people, a decline of hospitality, intellectual life and population, and the growth of new classes composed of rapacious landlords and married priests. In the second volume he concentrated upon contemporary issues and struck out again at the wealth of the Church of England, plus its spiritual torpor and lack of charity.[57] The issue was put more succinctly in a *Political Register*.

Englishmen Hear Me!
In Catholic Times.

There were *no paupers* in England.

The Catholics maintained the Poor, the Aged, the Widow, the Orphan, the Stranger, and the Infirm, out of the *Tithes* and other *Revenues of the Church*.

The Catholic Clergy built and repaired the Churches out of the *Tithes and Church Revenues*.

There were, in those happy days, no *Poor-Rates, no Church-Rates, and no Workhouses*.

Acts of Parliament of those days declare Beef, Pork, Mutton, and Veal, to be the common food of the *poorer* sort of people.

The Catholics built all our *Cathedrals*, founded and endowed

---

support Cobbett. The book not only sold well at the time, but in 1884 we find John Ruskin writing in a letter that Cobbett's book on the Reformation was "the only true one ever written as far as it reaches . . ." E. T. Cook and Alexander Wedderburn (eds.), *The Works of John Ruskin*, Vol. xxxvii, London, George Allen, 1909, p. 503.

[57] *History of the Protestant Reformation in England and Ireland*, Vol. I, passim. Vol. II, London, William Cobbett, 1829, passim. Vol. II consists primarily of a listing of church property confiscated at the time of the Reformation.

all the great *Schools* that are even now in England, and founded every great *Public Charity* that now exists in England.

In Catholic Times England had no Standing Armies; and yet she conquered France, and held Boulogne and Calais till she had Protestant Kings.

In Catholic Times there was no Tax on Beer, Malt, Hops, or Candles, and there was no *National Debt.*

Englishmen, think of these things, and I know you will act justly.[58]

It is no wonder that with this fanciful version of history in mind, Cobbett should find his own Church lacking.

Earlier in this chapter it was made clear that the large, amorphous group of worshipers known collectively as Non-conformists or Dissenters did not receive the blessings which Cobbett bestowed upon the Catholics. Although their numbers may have equaled those of the practicing Anglicans, in law they were still subject to severe penalties.[59] But for all practical considerations, these laws had been considerably relaxed since the fires of religious controversy, which had burned so brightly during the seventeenth century, had been dampened. The lack of persecution of Dissent was a reflection of this, as was the decline of dogmatism and concomitant growth of rationalism within the sects themselves. At the same time a new group, the Methodists, which had developed within the Church of England, became influential during the latter part of the eighteenth century. Later the Methodists separated from the established church and their ministers, emotional in their manner of preaching, had great influence among the lower classes. Cobbett did not care for the competition, and he disliked the Methodists and another newly-formed group, the Unitarians, more than the traditional dissenting sects.

58 P.R. (2/28/29), col. 257.
59 See Henriques, *op. cit.,* passim, for the disabilities affecting the Dissenters and a discussion of how they were removed.

Cobbett originally took exception to the enthusiasm of the Methodist preachers for non-political reasons, calling their exhortations "wild rant," and claiming that they wanted to destroy rural and athletic sports which he valued.[60] Later, his major source of antagonism lay elsewhere. It was the support granted by the Methodists to the government in its reactionary policies and their counseling of the poor to be resigned in the face of privation that stung him. For he was convinced that the Methodist preachers were servile tools of the ministry of the day, hoping for concessions in return for maintaining a correct political attitude. Cobbett did not want the worker "comforted" by patronizing charity or told that he should be content with the position in society in which it had pleased God to place him. Instead he wanted the worker (like the Catholics in both England and Ireland) to be aroused to anger and demand changes in his lot. Although Hannah More was an Evangelical member of the Church of England, the work of this "old bishop in petticoats," as Cobbett referred to her, set a pattern for the Methodists as well. Members of her school made perfunctory references to the responsibilities of the rich, but the tenor of their writings stresses mildness and cheerful submission as the type of conduct which it behooved the poor to adopt in all circumstances. Their optimism and comfortable aloofness toward other people's suffering, their refusal to apportion blame for the government's mistakes and to admit that anything substantial could be done to make the lot of the worker easier seemed to Cobbett loathsome hypocrisy. He preferred the neglect of the poor by the High Church Tories to the type of interest shown by the Evangelicals or the Methodists.[61] Although he claimed that the Methodist emphasis upon salvation by grace, "which every ruffian, who is terrified into a praying fit, easily imagines

60 P.R. (2/27/02), col. 175; P.R. (2/19 to 2/26/03), col. 287.
61 P.R. (5/25/11), cols. 1283–93.

that he has got," was silly and contrary to good morals,[62] he was primarily opposed to the sect on political and social grounds.

An essentially unsophisticated person would have little patience with problems of theology and might also consider that parliament was perfectly capable of regulating worship. Here we have another basis for Cobbett's dislike of dissenting groups, for while the Church of England was illiberal in its own secular outlook Cobbett had been brought up in it and regarded its competitors (except the Catholic Church) as parvenus. Apart from the Evangelicals the Church of England tended to ignore the poor but, as we have seen, the Methodists competed directly with the message of action which Cobbett tried to convey. Of course, Cobbett hated the Evangelicals and their great leader, Wilberforce, as violently as he hated the Methodists. Throughout most of his life he remained in general opposition to the dissenting groups and supported the repeal of the Test and Corporation Acts only because this action would weaken the established church and thus would be a step toward radical reform.[63] Unlike the Catholics, who stayed in the religion of their forefathers, the Dissenters were too conceited, in Cobbett's view, to remain constant to their religious heritage. When he extended this attitude toward the Church of England and remarked that its followers were in effect Dissenters themselves, he was anticipating in his own way Newman's famous comment about the same group, "We are all Arians." Yet, despite his irritable statements to the contrary, the Church of England seemed to possess sufficient historic and legal roots. The dissenting groups, however, he considered to be presumptuous, doctrinally unsound, but, most important, committed to a selfish policy of social ag-

---

[62] P.R. (6/12/13), col. 840. This inevitably brings to mind Chesterton's remark that inner light is the worst possible kind of lighting.

[63] P.R. (3/8/28), col. 304.

grandizement which required slavish adherence to the policies of the government.

Three other religious groups that Cobbett abused were the Unitarians, the Quakers, and the Jews. The Unitarians did not have a clearly defined position on social questions and consequently Cobbett did not entertain as impressive a hatred for them as he did for the Methodists. They were simply objectionable to him because they represented an extreme in the sects which evolved out of the impact of the eighteenth-century intellectual movements upon religion. This type of change was the product of intellectuality and "march of mind," and therefore was unappealing to Cobbett. The Trinity was a mystery which must be accepted on faith. To deny it by casting doubts upon the divinity of Christ would destroy the whole edifice of Christianity, and he could not admit an alternative religious system.[64] Concerning the Quakers his antagonism had other roots. During the time he lived in Philadelphia before moving to England Cobbett made several friends among the Quakers and had come to admire them so much that he subsequently named one of his sons after a Pennsylvania Quaker named James Paul. The kindness and generosity of his Quaker friends during his prison term in Newgate were frequently noted afterward. In 1813 he wrote, "Theirs is a religion that has an effect upon their actions in life. It produces cleanliness and neatness in their dress, it produces economy, sobriety, gentleness, kindness, honesty, and universal benevolence. I have never asked any of them what was their *creed*. I see the effects of their religion, and I judge of the tree by its fruits." [65] Obviously, this is just the type of religion which Cobbett might be expected to admire. Yet he eventually changed his opinion of the character of the Quakers, and accused them of dissimulation,

[64] P.R. (5/12/13), cols. 710–13.
[65] P.R. (6/5/13), cols. 814–15.

avarice, and living upon the rest of the community. It is noteworthy that while in America he lived among Quakers who were farmers and laborers, but in England he claimed that members of the sect did not work. What he actually objected to was the position which Quakers played in the financial and commercial life of the country. This was the basis of his dislike.[66] It should also be noted that his attacks begin after 1820 when so many of his other opinions hardened. Cobbett resented the support afforded to George IV by many Quakers in his attempt to divorce Queen Caroline.[67] The following is submitted as a not unfair example of Cobbett's logic. Admitting that a Quaker sea captain had refused him passage to England in 1819 after his American exile, Cobbett maintained, "Have I not a right to conclude that the *whole sect is bad,* upon that very ground, and no other? If a serpent sting me, and I lose my arm, am I not justified in destesting all serpents?" [68]

The role of Quaker and Jewish financiers in the British government's efforts to subdue Napoleon would have been sufficient to arouse Cobbett's prejudices. In the case of the Jews, however, he claimed to be able to perceive religious reasons to support his antagonism. The anti-Semitism which Cobbett manifested was so extreme, it resembled a parody. It was never qualified and was expressed in the grossest terms. At a time when his own faith was in a rather nebulous condition, he itemized the motives for his hatred, beginning with the assertion that the Jews mocked the religion of the Christians and ending with the accusation that they were traditional supporters of tyranny.[69] He approved of anti-Jewish persecution or discrimination in various parts of Europe, but looked back to the Middle Ages for examples which seemed even

66 P.R. (2/4/26), cols. 367–70.
67 P.R. (7/19/23), cols. 147–48.
68 P.R. (2/4/26), cols. 370–71.
69 P.R. (6/5/30), cols. 730–33.

more appropriate.[70] This stridency and unreason are exemplified by an incident which occurred in 1823 when Cobbett appeared in court with a Jewish turnpike keeper. Some of the unedifying proceedings were proudly reported in the *Register*. After sundry insults had been exchanged, Cobbett angrily complained to the judge about the "insolence" of his antagonist in calling Cobbett an atheist after he had referred to the turnpike keeper as a *"Jew thief."* [71] The attitude displayed here and his position toward Negro slaves, foreigners and those persons with whom he had mild disagreements and who later suffered misfortune should surely disqualify him from the role of inflexible champion of the underdog.

Personal but not intuitive in his approach to religion, Cobbett had a sincere but not deeply considered belief in God. Selections from his writings may not give this impression for there is much that is ill-tempered, capricious, or flippant. Only after the whole body of his works has been sifted is it possible to reach the conclusion that he retained a basic faith all of his life. It was proof against the skeptics of the Enlightenment and, of course, never had to be tested against the scientific developments that occurred after the mid-nineteenth century. Cobbett revealed his own opinion regarding the mysteries of faith by stating that "Men of sense do not attempt to discover that which it is *impossible* to discover. They leave things pretty much as they find them . . ." [72]

Questions of personal belief aside, it is apparent that Cobbett in his judgments of the value of a creed placed greater weight upon the temporal rather than the spiritual. This helps

---

[70] P.R. (1/5/28), cols. 21–23. ". . . the banishment of the *Christ-killers* from Russia, is really a proof to me that the Emperor of Russia, is not a tyrant." P.R. (10/25/23), cols. 215–18.

[71] P.R. (10/25/23), col. 213.

[72] *Rural Rides*, Vol. I (10/20/25), p. 285. The reader must remember that this was a time when even well-travelled, widely-read men, like Cobbett, could believe that horse hair could become living things and that frogs came in rain drops or rain drops turned to frogs upon striking the earth. *Ibid.*, pp. 284–85.

to account for his often expressed dislike of the Methodists, whom he regarded as a rival group with false ideas concerning society, while he almost ignored the Deists, who did not challenge him in this respect. Radical reform dictated his attitude here as well as with the cause of the factory workers or that of Queen Caroline. If the Church hierarchy had shown a disposition to work with him, grievances would have been forgotten, just as he was willing to forgive and forget in the case of the landlords. As far as the function of the Church was concerned, he regarded it as a department of state, dedicated to providing an ethical support, guarding morals and dispensing good works with a hearty cheer. This, in his eyes, was the way in which the medieval church behaved. Like the men of the Oxford Movement, he placed hopes in a revitalized Church of England, but how differently each saw the problem!

XII
Education

Just as the archaic condition of the English law in the early nineteenth century reminds us of the gulf which divides Cobbett's age from ours, education at the time suggests a past that was almost devoid of the modern insistence upon equality and system. While the increasingly important developments in industry were changing the pattern of English life, the need for innovations in attitudes toward education was slow in being met. As in other areas, necessity for adjustment was inadequately perceived and the response was hesitant and incomplete. From Oxford and Cambridge, governed by clerical oligarchies under statutes passed during the reigns of Charles I and Elizabeth I, respectively, to the once vital Grammar Schools, where absentee schoolmasters sometimes drew impressive stipends for teaching unwanted lessons to non-existent pupils, education was losing touch with the times. Even if there had been no industrial revolution, a change in existing attitudes would have been necessary. Changes in the methods of production complicated the situation by creating a need for an immense extension of education to portions of the population previously almost ignored.[1]

During the period of Cobbett's lifetime, efforts had to be made on an individual or a group basis as a national policy could not develop until fundamental changes had occurred in the political constitution of the kingdom. However, the problem was one which claimed the attention of numerous people, and there was no shortage of suggestions. The motives for extending education were diverse: a spirit of philanthropy, an awareness of the need for technically competent factory hands, and a vision of a brand new society to be obtained after human evil had been exorcised by universal education. It is not remarkable that there was a divergence of method as well as of motive among those interested in spreading education. Many of these methods appear strange, even bizarre, to us. Those who advanced them were of necessity pioneers, men of spirit and determination whose mistakes were, perhaps, inevitable in view of the novelty of their task. Furnished an ideological basis by the Enlightenment for a movement which the conditions of the times rendered essential, educational theory of the early 1800's was an amalgam of lofty sentiment, stubborn prejudice, and sheer practicality.[2]

Yet from all of this, Cobbett dissented. Indeed, on the surface, he shared some positions with the opponents of the spread of education: agricultural interests and the Church of England. These groups were worried about making the poor

---

[1] For a discussion of education in England at the time, see J. W. Adamson, *English Education, 1789–1902*, Cambridge, Cambridge University Press, 1930, pp. 1–121. Also, S. J. Curtis, *History of Education in Great Britain*, London, University Tutorial Press, Ltd., 1948, chs. III, IV, V, XIV.

[2] See Adamson, *op. cit.*, and Curtis, *op. cit.* Halévy, *England in 1815*, considers education in the context of English society of the period. See pp. 525 ff.

discontented with their lot and also about the vested interests of the Church. Cobbett's own opposition to educational reform was threefold and stemmed from his essentially reactionary social attitude. Stated simply, his position was that education on the lines desired by the reformers would not improve the morals of the working class but, instead, would give the worker ideas above his station and would place too much power into the hands of the government. This disagreement with the reformers was fundamental and obviously involved philosophy as well as method. For example, Cobbett was antagonistic to the belief that the ignorance of the common people led to vice which, in turn, caused poverty. In his view poverty was solely the result of the "System." The remedy, therefore, was not more education but the abolition of the "System" by means of radical reform. Speaking in parliament less than a year before he died, he claimed that the morals of the people had not improved with the general spread of education but that crime, drunkenness and bastardy had increased. Further, a smattering of education put into the head of the laborer the idea that he was not born to work.[3]

Swayed by his personal, paternalistic and highly stratified vision of English society in its Golden Age, Cobbett never believed that the spread of education, the educational reformers' beloved "march of mind" would relieve the overwhelming mass of the people from the necessity of toil. Since manual labor was to him a positive good,[4] he would not accept the views of those who looked ahead to a time when the need to labor long hours was eliminated. He was no equalitarian. In an unenthusiastic fashion, Cobbett did approve of the rise of a family in social position over several generations, provided that industry, care and skill were ex-

[3] Great Britain, 3 *Hansard's Parliamentary Debates,* vol. XXIV (1834), 131–33. Also, a frustrated student whose head had been filled with grandiose ideas might turn to crime. P.R. (12/7/33), cols. 581–95.

[4] ". . . he is best educated who knows how to work . . ." P.R. (11/2/22), cols. 316–17.

ercised. This he called "natural progress," to be achieved gradually, without any attempt to reach the top of society at a single bound. If the opportunity for such advancement did not arise, however, there was no great harm done to anybody. Cobbett could not participate in the dreams of those who persisted in advocating a complete reconstruction of society through education or some other panacea. Since he did not share with the reformers their fundamental assumptions on this issue, he quarrelled with them over the question of what type of education was most suitable.[5]

Although he was in entire opposition to the way in which the country was governed, he tended to look toward the past rather than forward to the brave new world which was being developed by science and industry. Also, while desiring a society in which everyone knew his place, he allowed scope for advancement to those who could demonstrate mental accomplishments. Cobbett acknowledged that a competent doctor or lawyer was the superior of the competent manual worker and should enjoy an elevated place in the life of the country. What he did object to was the pedant, the grown-up schoolboy who had been stuffed with Latin and Greek for years and who considered himself *ipso facto* the superior of those who were not similarly educated. Cobbett was adamant in maintaining the superiority of the efficient but unlettered laborer (for whom formal education would be useless) to those "word-mongers." In all this, we may detect a note of self-interest and resentment, for who knew better than Cobbett the extent of his own capabilities in relation to the classically-educated government ministers at the time.[6]

5 Cobbett's views on education are expressed most concisely in the letter addressed to James Paul Cobbett in *A Grammar of the English Language,* Letter #1 in *Cottage Economy,* and in *Advice to Young Men,* passim. He was deeply interested in the subject and wrote about it dozens of times in the *Political Register.*

6 See P.R. (6/17/09), col. 911; P.R. (2/23/11), col. 450.

Despite his notorious prejudice against foreigners in general, Cobbett had a greater affinity with Continental writers such as Rousseau and the Swiss advocate of a heuristic education, Pestalozzi, than he did with the Englishmen, Dr. Andrew Bell and Joseph Lancaster, who stressed the importance of the school.[7] Cobbett knew about the educational theories of Rousseau and accepted his idea of the spontaneous development of the child and education in the home. However, this agreement must not be exaggerated, for there is no evidence that Cobbett actually had more than a superficial knowledge of the writings of these men.[8] As one might expect, the point to which he took real exception with Samuel Whitbread [9] and the other advocates of universal public education was their implication that education was synonymous with book learning. To Cobbett this was an arrogant presumption. He responded with a defense of the unlettered farmer or artisan who had, nevertheless, mastered his trade and, therefore, had every right to be considered an educated man. He once said that ignorance could be defined as a man's not knowing "that which *he ought to know*," considering the person's station in life. Therefore, the person who understood his vocation was not ignorant, even if he did not have a knowledge of reading or writing. His belief that formal training in a schoolroom was undesirable for the majority of men actually intensified as he grew older and, of course, separated him from the great majority of those interested in improving the lives of the common people through education. Like Samuel Smiles,

7 Bell was a physician and clergyman who devised a system of education in which the older children educated the younger ones. Lancaster, a Quaker, popularized Bell's idea. Economical in cost, this scheme spread rapidly.

8 For Cobbett's views on education in general and references to Rousseau, see *Advice to Young Men*, paragraphs 286 through 330; P.R. (12/7/33), col. 596.

9 Whitbread was a philanthropic brewer and member of parliament who believed that education could turn the people from vice and thus eliminate the root cause of poverty.

he believed that character was created by home and work and not in school.[10]

Cobbett defined education as *"breeding up, bringing up, or rearing up;* and nothing more."* The outstanding character-istics of this principle were that education should be carried on in the home by example and not by precept and that character development and the training of the body were to be integral parts.[11] In the stress on physical and moral train-ing and in the rejection of any forced feeding of books there is an affinity with Rousseau. It appears again in Cobbett's insistence that education should be carried on in the home, where the parent may create the conditions by which a child may best educate himself. Here may be seen the third part of Cobbett's disagreement with most proposals for educational reform for he always had a great distrust of schools and regarded them as places for the indoctrination of children by the government. Schoolmasters he considered a band of spies.[12] Any plan of national education would create a new control in the hands of government.[13] All of this is consistent with Cobbett's general opposition to the growth of govern-ment power and in particular with his fight for a free news-paper press.

As far as actual teaching is concerned, after the child had been set an example of industry, sobriety, cleanliness, and thrift so that he might be able to earn his own living, he should then be introduced to books. As Cobbett told his son, he had never been bidden or even advised to look at a book, "But, while you have lived unpersecuted by such importunities, you have had the very great advantage of being bred up under a roof beneath which no cards, no dice, no gaming, no sense-less pastime [sic] of any description ever found a place." Thus,

[10] P.R. (8/29/07), cols. 329–32; P.R. (9/26/07), cols. 487–89.
[11] *Cottage Economy,* pp. 5–6.
[12] *Ibid.,* pp. 6–7; P.R. (12/7/33), cols. 581–95.
[13] P.R. (9/21/33), col. 729; also, P.R. (3/7/18), col. 298.

books naturally became the boy's companion and he learned to read through example just as he learned to hunt and shoot.[14] Yet not any type of book would do. Cobbett had an aversion to novels and felt that reading what he did not regard as useful, practical information was a frivolous waste of time. Poetry and romances he also frowned on, despite the fact that he was rather well-read in these fields himself and was a keen judge of literature. However, his favorites, the writings of Swift and Pope, and the frequently cited *Gil Blas* had been composed long ago. There is little evidence in his writing that he tried to keep up with developments in literature. One or two favorable references to the radical aristocrat, Lord Byron, and some scattered jeers at the Tory Scott appear, but little else. Those writers who had received either titles or pensions from the government were regarded as servile tools of the "System." Yet even here he preferred to attack the long-dead Johnson and Gibbon rather than the flagrantly vulnerable Southey. Cobbett had a particular hatred of Johnson, whom he frequently referred to as the "dictionary pensioner," possibly because they shared many superficial similarities of character and philosophy.[15]

History was regarded as the best form of literature to set before a child. Not "romantic stuff about kings and knighthood," but information concerning the condition of the people, their wages, dress and the price of food was to be the fare.[16] This serves to demonstrate another of Cobbett's beliefs—that truth could readily be ascertained by a study of facts. History is the book of experience in which all the political causes and effects that formed the country are to be found. An honest perusal would reveal the story of the people, to use the words of his contemporary, Ranke, "as it really happened," and

[14] *A Grammar of the English Language*, [5].

[15] See *A Grammar of the English Language*, passim, for Cobbett's criticisms of Johnson.

[16] *Advice to Young Men*, paragraphs 316 through 320.

would enable the reader to make judgments which were certain. There was nothing lacking either in Cobbett's faith in experience as a teacher or in his confidence in himself as a guide.[17]

This helps to explain why Cobbett would oppose on principle the founding of a national school system. As a member of the reformed parliament he opposed the initial grant by the government in support of education in the year 1833, which was a mere £20,000 (approximately one half the cost of the yearly upkeep of the king's stables).[18] His argument that universal taxation for the purpose of education is unfair to those who educate their own children is a reflection of long-held attitudes. Cobbett's motivation was not primarily economy in government. In addition, his hostility to religious influence made him antagonistic toward the voluntary system in primary education, although this was the method supported by the most influential part of the public and was the only politically feasible means at the time.

The British and Foreign School Society was founded on Lancastrian principles in 1814 and was advocated by the Dissenters. Its religious instruction was confined to Bible reading and undenominational teaching. A Church of England group had formed an organization, whose title is usually abbrevi..ted as the National Society, three years earlier. As originally constituted, the National Society taught religion based on the Catechism and the Book of Common Prayer. These two societies illustrate the problem which was to bedevil English popular education for a hundred years to come. As Robert Owen discovered to his loss, the temper of the times insisted that religion be the basis for any system of education. But what religion? The Church of England, despite its position

---

[17] He once suggested to his brother-in-law that he could improve his writing ability by reading a good deal. "You should go soberly through the history of England first of all." Letter dated (12/13/07), Cobbett MSS, No. 8, Nuffield College, Oxford, England.

[18] P.R. (10/12/33), cols. 91–93.

as the established church, was never strong enough to ensure that its policies would be universally accepted, and the Dissenters were doomed to remain just a powerful minority. Regardless of Cobbett's conservative beliefs regarding the structure of society, any suggestion that the poor should be taught by others to be humble and content with their place in life roused him to fury. It was precisely this that he felt the schools sponsored by these organizations were doing— educating working class children in servility and acceptance of poverty. Cobbett wanted to stir the people to effect an end to the "System" and he correctly saw these schools as an enemy. Besides, Cobbett regarded food and clothing as more important than the benefits of reading and writing. It was better to be well-fed, clothed and lodged and at the same time superstitious, than to be fed on potatoes and covered with rags but "learned." [19]

He was not happy either with efforts that were being made in the field of adult education. The 1820's were remarkable for the number of accomplishments recorded. The Mechanics Institutes, the Society for the Diffusion of Useful Knowledge, *The British Almanac,* and, of course, London University were all founded in this decade. The men who made them possible, of whom Henry Brougham, George Birkbeck, and Francis Place were among the most prominent, were, like Cobbett, dissatisfied with society as they saw it. Yet Cobbett displayed a distrust of their motives and greeted the new proposals with the same sort of ridicule which could be found in the reactionary press.[20] Part of this feeling was due to envy of their success, but there remains the fact that he thought the country needed a thorough change. Therefore, these measures were evil for they propped up the existing system. Despite his con-

[19] *Two Penny Trash* (5/1/31), pp. 243–44.
[20] P.R. (7/16/25), col. 151 and P.R. (1/14/26), cols. 130–33. He considered London University to be a finishing school for those ambitious to make a fortune in the stock market.

cern for the past, Cobbett had the mark of a true radical—he hated reformers more than reactionaries. Those who were making sincere and successful efforts to cure the illnesses of society received only scorn for their pains.

In Cobbett's eyes these movements to extend the range of education were simply schemes to divert the attention of the working classes away from the causes of their misery.[21] In the scores of volumes which he wrote there is no hint that the same process which was causing impoverishment for many was also creating a new class of prosperous workingmen. These men were not only interested in learning about the new techniques of manufacturing which were transforming their lives, but also in extending their knowledge generally. It was for them that the Mechanics Institutes and the Society for the Diffusion of Useful Knowledge were founded. Yet Cobbett could only see squalor and wretchedness wherever he looked. Worse, those who attended the lectures of the abominated "feelosofers" were simply regarded as potential tools of the existing system, anxious to gain a living without working.

It would be understandable that a self-educated writer with the skill which Cobbett exhibited would stress the importance of grammar in education. However, the zest which Cobbett showed for the subject transcended mere respect and, as usual with his writings, had political implications. He frequently allowed himself the pleasure of criticizing the style and punctuation of government dispatches and was particularly fond of analyzing the syntax of the king's annual speech from the throne. He also delighted in relating how he had memorized a grammar while on guard duty with the army in Canada. Nevertheless, Cobbett was no arid grammarian, as

21 P.R. (5/29/30), col. 710. Nor did Cobbett have any liking for the fine arts. Believing that art and liberty were incompatible, he spoke darkly of the degradation of the people through foreign music and painting. "The countries of painters and poets have not been the countries of freedom . . ." *History of the Regency and Reign of King George the Fourth,* paragraph 273.

his own famous *Grammar* abundantly demonstrates. He regarded the subject not as an end in itself but important for the communication of ideas in conformity to his expressed belief that really good writing "must be plain to plain men." [22] In Cobbett's eyes one could learn about the art of writing good English by applying himself directly to his own tongue. A knowledge of Latin and Greek, he pointed out, did not prevent a person from writing poor English, and with justice he noted that "Good Grammar, for instance, written in Welsh, or in the language of the Chippawa Savages, is more learned than bad Grammar written in Greek." [23]

In the same way, when one considers the practical bent of Cobbett's mind, it is not surprising that he hated what he called abstract learning. Everything which one read had to have some immediate practical application to render it worthwhile. It is characteristic that when he published a grammar of the French language, he itemized the reasons why one should learn French.[24] But the learned languages, Latin and Greek, which exercised such a fascination over the educated people of the time and were frequently quoted in parliament, were anathema to Cobbett and drew his most caustic invective. He regarded them as being worse than useless as a part of education and served only to keep the people under subjection by barring them from the professions. He trenchantly exposed the devotion of the classical studies of his day to barren technicalities of grammar instead of to literature. The snobbery of the universities, their place in the "Establishment," and the jejune character of their graduates were strongly criticized. In a phrase, the complacency of which surely exceeded anything that Macaulay ever wrote, Cobbett remarked that the Latin and Greek authors knew nothing of science, astronomy, or navigation, little about chemistry, "and, if they had seen

22 P.R. (6/30/21), col. 867.
23 *A Grammar of the English Language,* p. 68 and p. 108.
24 *A French Grammar,* London, Charles Clement, 1824. See Letter I.

one of Arkwright's machines, they would certainly have kneeled down before him, and worshipped him as a God." [25] Cobbett once stated that if Napoleon, "the greatest conqueror and the greatest law-giver that Europe ever saw," had had a classical education, he would have regarded the knowledge of words as more important than the knowledge of men and things. The following item is illustrative.

> The reader will recollect, that sometime ago, the editors of some of the London papers, treated us with an intercepted letter of Buonaparté, from which it was evident, that the poor little fellow was not only not a classical scholar, but that he was deficient even in that part of the art of grammar, which the "learned" call orthography, and which the "ignorant" call *spelling*. This letter was the subject of a good deal of merriment, which lasted for several days, and would, probably, have lasted much longer, had not the attention of the learned and witty been called off by the news of the battle of Austerlitz, which served, too, as a sort of practical illustration of the inutility of Latin and Greek in the performance of great actions in the world.[26]

It is not surprising that the former ploughboy did not hesitate to issue a formal challenge to the learned gentlemen of Oxford and Cambridge to debate the issue in the columns of the *Register*.[27]

It is easy to sympathize with Cobbett in this matter and also with his denunciation of the Oxford and Cambridge of his day.[28] Yet reform had already begun. Jackson and Eveleigh, at Christchurch and Oriel respectively, had done much to

---

25 P.R. (11/29/17), cols. 1067–82.
26 P.R. (11/14/07), cols. 750–51. Napoleon also drew Cobbett's praise for eliminating a knowledge of Latin and Greek from the degree requirements of French universities. See P.R. (3/7/12), col. 299.
27 P.R. (1/10/07), col. 36.
28 *Rural Rides*, Vol. I (11/18/21), p. 31. ". . . one half of the fellows who are what they call *educated* here [at Oxford], are unfit to be clerks in a grocer's or mercer's shop." Eton was referred to as ". . . that great seminary for Tax-eaters." P.R. (10/26/22), col. 196.

encourage learning at Oxford, and written examinations and the highly significant honors degree were established there in 1800. Cambridge, with its tradition of excellence in mathematics, was in some ways ahead of Oxford. A visitor to Oxford commented as early as 1812 that there had been an impressive improvement and it was now "much more *the thing* to read than to let it alone . . ." [29] Similarly, the public schools, which had reached their nadir along with the universities in the eighteenth century, were beginning to show signs of improvement and would soon press on to a position of intellectual leadership. Education in the schools and universities, which was not as bad generally as extreme examples would indicate, was reviving and, in addition, innovations in the educational pattern were beginning to appear. Cobbett was to oppose most of these new developments while continuing to condemn the traditional ways. No doubt he would have been antagonistic toward the ancient classics even if they had been taught in a more imaginative manner. Cobbett disliked learning about foreign customs while remaining ignorant of those of England and did not seem to feel that foreigners had anything to teach the English.[30] Like Veblen at the end of the century, Cobbett believed that a classical education was the mark of an individual who belonged to a leisured class. He would, no doubt, have enthusiastically accepted any critique of society based on conspicuous consumption.

Unlike Rousseau, Cobbett did not hesitate to apply his views on education to his own family. The best way to study this is to read *Advice to Young Men,* which was published separately in pamphlet form but finally printed as a book in 1829. It is a charming work—one of the best things Cobbett ever wrote—and in it he gives a clear picture of a somewhat naïve but intensely warm and satisfying family life.

29 W. L. Mathieson, *England in Transition, 1789–1832*, p. 121. See also Adamson, *op. cit.*, ch. III.

30 *Advice to Young Men*, paragraph 48.

There is little of the rancor here which mars many of his other writings. It is simple, candid and unaffected. When he describes his efforts to educate his children by example and through the clever instilling of motives to learn, the book is a splendid illustration of thought being translated into action. If a problem about the farm had to be tackled, the family would read up on it first and then promptly set to work using the knowledge just gained. The dichotomy between school and home that marks the life of most children did not exist in the Cobbett family. In a world in which the lives of people have become fragmented, this artless humanism is quite appealing. Cobbett's method of education is a delightful contrast to the grim austerities so prevalent in the schools of the time, and he had the satisfaction of seeing his sons grow up into sturdy, intelligent young men. Yet, in order to be successful, a scheme such as this requires a man of exceptional character. Perhaps Cobbett was too powerful a personality for his purpose, for it is rather clear that his sons tended to be pale copies of the original. Consciously or not, he dominated their lives, even after they reached manhood. A letter from his second son, John Morgan Cobbett, to the eldest son, William, written when they were both over thirty, suggests a stifling influence. John Morgan pleaded with William not to leave England despite unspecified "embarrassments," and expressed regret that early in life they were not put to some trade or handicraft, "something, however low, by which we might now be earning our own bread." [31] For the record, these two men and the third son, James Paul, were barristers. His fourth son, Richard, became a solicitor. As for Cobbett's three daughters (who all remained spinsters), the eldest, Ann, acted as his secretary and also was an author in her own right, but the other two lived out their long lives in obscurity. Cobbett was no supporter of feminism. *Advice to Young Men*

[31] Letter dated (11/8/30), Nuffield College, Oxford, England, Cobbett MSS, No. 243.

reveals that he regarded the woman's place as being in the home performing the time-honored household chores. The young girl was not to fill her head with thoughts of singing or piano lessons but to learn domestic tasks as the apprentice of her mother.[32]

Cobbett once said, "I am something of a scholar myself . . . books and literature have been my delight: I honour learning, find it where I will." [33] Perhaps no remark could better illustrate his paradoxical relation to education. Except by the narrowest definition, the first clause of this quotation is correct, yet the last is almost completely wrong. At times Cobbett demonstrated all the finer qualities of a self-educated person: a wide range of interests, great intellectual curiosity, a lack of respect for academic posturing and humbug, and a corresponding appreciation of real achievement. Yet, he also suffered from the faults common to one whose education has lacked the stiffening of a formal training: over-confidence in his own acquired knowledge and capacity, impatience with the discipline necessary for a real mastery of a subject, a complete lack of scholarly tolerance for conflicting opinions, and, of course, a tendency to over-simplify. This self-proclaimed practical man often saw the changes transforming society less clearly than many of his despised "feelosofers," for all their Latin phrases and Greek puns. Cobbett's concentration on radical changes made him reject piecemeal alterations and he was unaware that the gradual reform of society, including education, was rendering his ideas ever more obsolete.

32 P.R. (4/21/21), cols. 193–94. Cobbett was at last able to see a use for the novel—in lighting the oven for a batch of bread.

33 P.R. (3/7/29), col. 293.

XIII
Member of parliament

The last five years of Cobbett's life, 1830–1835, represent an eventful period in the history of England. Of towering significance was the most important piece of legislation passed by parliament since the aftermath of the Glorious Revolution: the Reform Bill of 1832. This act was followed by the first effective government measure to regulate factory labor, an attempt to modernize municipal government, the freeing of all slaves within the British Empire and the Poor Law Amendment Act of 1834. Immensely important as this legislation was, it did not entirely overshadow events which happened outside the walls of parliament. For at this time occurred the last great protest of the downtrodden agricultural workers, stirrings of trade unionism and, with the reduction of the power of the established church, the beginnings of the Oxford movement. This is also the period when the England with characteristics which we call "Victorian" finally won the day from the lusty world of Tom Jones. Through legislation and the gradual evolution of social attitudes, a change was worked so that by the middle of the century many adults were amazed at the disappearance of a way of life which they had known as children.

In a study of Cobbett, consideration of these years must begin with the great Reform Bill. Even more than most Englishmen, Cobbett was affected by its passage. For him it meant encouragement after many years of frustration. As an agitator, he played a conspicuous, but not very important, role during those hectic months before the Tory lords stood aside and allowed the bill to become law. Thanks to the resulting liberalization of the election system he acquired a long-sought-after seat in the parliament which was elected following the passage of the bill. Cobbett was then sixty-nine years of age and had a little over two years to live. It had been more than a quarter century since his first stirrings of ambition to sit in parliament before the Honiton election of 1806. But Cobbett was destined to be disappointed and his election in 1832 at Oldham proved an anticlimax. The remainder of his life saw him baffled and ill-at-ease, shorn of whatever influence he had once possessed. Since the campaign for the reform of parliament and the resulting legislation determined his last years, it is useful to note its lengthy history and observe Cobbett in relation to it.

One of the most significant facts which strikes the observer of parliamentary reform agitation during the last quarter of the eighteenth century is that it was the preoccupation of a minority. It cannot be said that this agitation lacked support altogether, for there seems to have been an abundance of committees and societies, and more or less radical proposals were advanced for the reform of parliament almost every year. Yet there was no concerted drive for reform, no *movement,* and what did exist were simply a number of uncoordinated gestures. Even if the differences of motivation, platform and class could have been reconciled by the advocates of reform (Whig aristocrats, Yorkshire squires, London demagogues and urban artisans) to the extent of allowing at least a confederacy, it would not have been able to dent that peculiar manifestation of privilege and corruption, the English parliament. One could easily draw up a substantial list of reasons why these groups collectively favored reform, but in applying them to each, the lack of mutuality of interest would be made evident. Thus reform was confused and fragmentary, a minority movement among the classes able to express themselves politically (which, after all, were the only classes to which the terms "minority" and "majority" would be relevant at this time), and perhaps even unpopular with the people as a whole.[1]

The reasons for the weakness of reform do not all involve the outbreak of the French Revolution and the subsequent war with that country. These were tremendously important events to be sure. They were not the less significant because they concentrated the energies of the squirearchy, whose members were sometimes irritated by the power of the boroughmongers, upon the great patriotic war against an ancient enemy which had assumed a horrible new demeanor. Still, Pitt's cautious proposal of 1785 to extend the franchise in the counties, disenfranchise thirty-six rotten boroughs and add their seats to the number of county seats had already failed. This was because it was necessary to reckon with the negative attitude of the king and the power of vested political interests. These schemes, of course, were proposals for parliamentary reform in the direction of greater popular

---

[1] See P. A. Brown, *The French Revolution in English History*, London, George Allen and Unwin, Ltd., 1923, chs. 1–3 for a description of some of the reform groups. Also, S. Maccoby, *English Radicalism, 1786–1832*, London, George Allen and Unwin, Ltd., 1955, chs. 1–3. E. Porritt, *The Unreformed House of Commons*, Vol. I, Cambridge, Cambridge University Press, 1903, passim.

representation, parliaments of shorter duration, equal electoral districts and similar demands. Progress in making the government more economical and less subject to the will of the king was being accomplished throughout this period. It was the proposals for substantive reform which met with the most stubborn opposition. In the face of this reality only a coordinated program with powerful friends in parliament could win the day, but this was not to come about until 1832.

As for the reformers themselves, persecution by the courts and that singular phenomenon, the Tory mob, made an end to the efforts of the middle class professional men and artisans during the early 1790's. The reform group in parliament retired from the contest after the decisive defeat of Grey's proposal for reform in 1797. Led by Fox, they almost seceded from parliament and left the field entirely in the hands of the Tories. The rank and file became frightened and kept silent, or just lost interest in a program that had no leaders. War hysteria was being whipped up and the country was almost solidly behind Pitt in his apparently single-minded concentration upon winning the war. Beginning in 1794 a series of repressive measures made talk of reform highly dangerous and even foolhardy. Habeas corpus was suspended, meetings and lectures were strictly curbed and the law of treason was redefined in such a way as to make criticism of the constitution a risky venture. It was through a self-appointed defense of this constitution that a young English ex-soldier, then living in Philadelphia, came to the favorable notice of the Tory ministry.[2]

For the first decade of the new century, there was little expressed interest in parliamentary reform. The accumulated events of the mid-1790's had been a nasty shock and although conditions had moderated, the leaders of the erstwhile reforming group in parliament, Fox and Grey, stayed at home for long periods of time sulking, like Achilles in his tent. Reform

[2] Brown, *op. cit.*, chs. 4–8; Maccoby, *op. cit.*, chs. 4–7.

appeared a dead issue, crushed not just by repression but also by the massive indifference of the people. None of the handful of radicals still holding aloft the banner of reform, trying to rally their forces, seemed to realize that substantial change in England had to await the victorious ending of the war. The "respectable" elements among the reformers almost disappeared. When the Honiton election of 1806 brought Cobbett gradually into the field, he became the agent for generating most of the little enthusiasm that existed.

A series of open letters from Cobbett to the electors of the Borough of Westminster, whose wide suffrage and politically sophisticated voters provided one of the few constituencies in which a fair campaign was possible, mark the beginning of his career as a radical political leader. The point of these letters was to impress the electors with the responsibility incumbent upon them and urge them to vote for the best man, resisting all attempts at bribery.[3] Many times in future years he was to exhort Westminster to vote in the manner which he desired and thus set an example to the rest of the country.

The idea of Westminster inspiring England by the example of its rectitude is a reminder that Cobbett, like many zealots, had an overoptimistic view of what one honest person could do in a corrupt legislature. "If I had been in parliament at the close of the war against Bonaparte, in the year 1814; or, in 1816; or, in 1819; or, in 1822; if I had been in parliament at either of these epochs, things could not have been as they are now. The *cash-measures* never could have been taken; the land and labour could not have been oppressed as they now are; the debt could not have been what it is now. . . ."[4] His subsequent failure after 1832 revealed how hollow these promises to impose his will on parliament were. One reason for this irritation with radicals in parliament was his inability to grasp the problems which faced them. Cobbett's faith in

3 P.R. (8/9/06), cols. 193 ff.
4 P.R. (1/10/24), col. 67.

his message was so strong that he believed that it would win wide popular acceptance if only it were presented properly. He was convinced that the failure to realize his objectives was always due to the venality or cowardice of those in parliament who were supposed to advance them. There was never any question in his mind regarding the suitability of the message itself. This made the choice of those who were to serve in parliament a responsible one indeed. It also accounted for the pains which he took to instruct the electors that voting was a duty they owed to the country, which must be fulfilled independently of any pressures that might be brought to bear.[5] ". . . Let us keep ourselves free from all thick-and-thin engagements and attachments; let each of us for himself make due inquiry, and act upon the decision of his own mind; let us not be persuaded or coaxed to do that which our own reason tells us is not right; let us form and preserve an attachment to *principles* and not to *men;* above all let us despise the watch-words of party. . . ." [6]

For the next twenty years the cause of reform of the manner of selecting representatives for the House of Commons and of the distribution of seats was in a decline. Even in the late 1820's, when a fresh tide of progress, which softened the penal code and liberalized trade might have been expected to produce ripples in other directions, there was no response. Nor did the removal of disabilities from the Dissenters and Roman Catholics provide an immediate impetus for a reform of parliament. Roman Catholic emancipation did, however, upset the alignment of groups in parliament. The rabid anti-Catholics thirsted for revenge against Prime Minister Wellington and divided the Tory party. This permitted a Whig government to take office in 1830. On the other hand, the working classes sought the cure for their misery within the economic system and the Whigs themselves were unenthusiastic

---

[5] P.R. (10/24/12), cols. 514–15.
[6] P.R. (5/6/09), cols. 673–74.

about anything which would benefit the Radicals.[7] In 1829 a major alteration of the political system seemed almost as far off as in 1815. Nevertheless, change was going to come, though from an unexpected quarter.

In July, 1830, the second French Revolution in just over forty years began. Unlike the first, this one had the effect of giving a modest stimulus to reform in England.[8] The July Revolution is significant in French history for shifting control of the government from the landowning aristocracy and Catholic clergy to the upper bourgeoisie. This development in one way foreshadowed events in England, as it was disappointing to many who took part in the revolution hoping for greater changes. The major consequences of the July Revolution outside of France occurred in the successful revolt of the Belgians against their Dutch overlords and in the thrill of excitement which the events in Paris sent through the listless ranks of the English radical reformers.

Cobbett himself was quick to respond and the revolution became the dominant subject for discussion in the *Register* for several months. He regarded it as a working class revolt in response to their rulers "robbing" them of their right to be represented in the legislature, not an aristocratic conspiracy for gain, as was the English revolution of 1688. In the *Register* and in a series of lectures later published as "Eleven Lectures on the French and Belgian Revolutions," he discussed this theme of a workers' uprising and also made vague references to Charles X as a puppet manipulated by the English boroughmongers.[9] The details of his argument are frequently

7 Halévy, *The Liberal Awakening*, pp. 281–82.

8 The impact of the French Revolution of 1830 upon English reform has probably been exaggerated in the past. See Norman Gash, "English Reform and French Revolution in the General Election of 1830" in Richard Pares and A. J. P. Taylor, *Essays Presented to Sir Lewis Namier*, London, Macmillan & Co., 1956, pp. 258–88.

9 P.R. (8/7/30), cols. 161–85. See also every issue for the following six weeks. *Cobbett's Register and Lectures.* "Eleven Lectures on the French and Belgian Revolutions," passim.

inaccurate, as, for example, when he ignored the factor of nationalism and blamed the Belgian revolt upon heavy taxation. Yet his own misunderstanding of the international situation is trivial alongside the mere fact that the revolution had taken place within a month after the death of George IV. This happy coincidence stimulated change. As Cobbett noted with some justice, "All Europe is in a state of commotion, every-where are the people on foot to obtain a just share in the government of their country; and is it to be believed that England is the only country in which the people are not to succeed!" [10]

When the newly-formed Whig government, led by Grey, introduced its bill for reform, Cobbett supported it. He realized that the bill proposed considerably less than what he had heretofore insisted was necessary; yet he also perceived that any attempt to amend the bill in a radical direction would ensure its defeat. On this question he disagreed with Henry Hunt, who opposed the bill as inadequate. Cobbett's decision to accept the Whig proposals was wise, although in enthusiastically describing to the workers benefits which might be expected from the elimination of the rotten boroughs, he greatly overstated the case for reform. Toward the Whigs as a whole, Cobbett continued to display considerable mistrust and he could not conceal his irritation and contempt for them. Lord Grey himself was praised, cajoled, criticized for his slowness, flattered or goaded, depending upon the progress of the bill. Still, in a rare display of tactical wisdom in the face of great provocation, Cobbett supported the government—this, despite the prosecution which it undertook against him at the time of the revolt of the agricultural workers. Although justifiably angered by false charges of instigating the riots and in danger of a jail sentence, the normally acerbic journalist restrained his feelings to a remarkable degree and was able

[10] P.R. (3/26/31), col. 820.

to separate a skillful defense of himself at the trial from the reform issue.[11] Highly noteworthy were his correct assessment of the factors which dictated that the bill remain inviolate and his determination to assist the ministry despite disappointment and actual persecution. To obtain the goal of parliamentary reform he curbed his loathing of the Whigs.

The campaign for the passage of the bill and his subsequent seating as a member of the House of Commons from Oldham were highlights in Cobbett's life but they did not produce any permanent changes in his political views. He had clearly recognized that the proposed legislation was only going to provide a moderate extension of the franchise, plus the elimination of the rotten boroughs, and endorsed it on that basis. Unfortunately, however, he seems to have convinced himself that what he had told the workers about the implications of the bill was true. After its passage, when there was no rooting out of the old system, he was quickly disillusioned with the new Whig government and he compared it unfavorably with the record of Wellington's ministry.[12] Cobbett had never trusted the Whig aristocrats but seems to have expected them to do better with their newly-won power. Even before the bill had passed the Lords, he became suspicious and revived his program of universal suffrage and annual parliaments. For a time he lost faith in rank. "The man to choose [for parliament] is, in the first place, a man that has no very great regard for riches. Industry, sobriety, moderation in his expenses, no fondness for luxurious living; these are qualities that electors ought to look after; and in addition to these, a good store of knowledge, some talent, and great resolution." [13] To this end he urged that the House of Lords be reformed so that it could join the common people in order

11 For an example of his treatment of the subject, see his moderate, circumspect analysis of the political situation in P.R. (3/26/31), cols. 789–824.

12 P.R. (12/13/34), cols. 648–50.

13 P.R. (6/2/32), cols. 540–41.

to prevent an aristocracy of "mere money" from arising.[14]

When he was finally sent to parliament, the man who had once claimed to be more fit for the office of Prime Minister than any other person in the kingdom [15] had nothing constructive of a political nature to offer. Much of his time was spent in carping criticism of the Speaker, the smallness of the Commons chamber and the late hours.[16] His recommendations to improve the conditions of the people and allay discontent were negative. All but one of the nine points which he enumerated in a plan of reform urged the repeal of some law and the other called for an act to induce farmers to restore the custom of having servants to board in their houses.[17] Only his colleague from Oldham, the radical manufacturer Fielden, provided consistent support; other members ridiculed him. After devoting thousands of columns of the *Political Register* to attacking his enemies for their inability to rule, Cobbett merely demonstrated his own lack of fitness to be a political leader. In the House of Commons he can be described as a general nuisance.

From 1833 to his death in May, 1835, he was antagonistic to more than the Whig poor law act. This episode shows him in a favorable light and has often been recorded. Proposals for Irish Church reform and the inquiry into municipal corporations, which was eventually to result in the passage of an act that would do for local elections what the 1832 legislation accomplished for the nation, were both opposed by Cobbett. His stated reasons for this resistance are merely silly—that "harsh" landlords in Ireland would replace "easy" ones and, in the case of the municipal corporations, the poor quality

14 P.R. (6/22/33), cols. 717 ff.
15 P.R. (12/22/27), col. 774.
16 Great Britain, 3 *Hansard's Parliamentary Debates*, Vol. XV (1833), 66 ff.; P.R. (3/2/33), cols. 514–15; P.R. (3/30/33), col. 781. The diarist, Charles Greville, refers to Cobbett quickly finding his own level and sinking into insignificance. Roger Fulford (ed.), *The Greville Memoirs*, London, B. T. Batsford, Ltd. 1963, p. 101.
17 P.R. (11/22/34), cols. 474–75.

of the lawyers who made up the commissions.[18] He also spoke against foreign trade, civic improvements in London and a grant by parliament to aid polar explorations.[19] Improvements in London alarmed him as they would encourage residence in the "Wen." Cobbett professed to see good in the arrival of the first cholera epidemic in 1832 because it would cause a dispersal of idlers from the capital. These remarks show the elderly Cobbett to be a confused and frustrated egotist. "I have always led the way at a great distance forward; I have forseen, foretold, every event, every effect; my *predictions* have, in due succession, become *history;* I have been the teacher of the nation . . ." [20]

Thus said Cobbett at age sixty-seven. The reader will realize that the man who wrote these words was to receive a terrible shock to his vanity. When Cobbett's dream came true and he was at last able to take a seat among the lawmakers (he helped himself to a position on the Treasury bench), what a rapid disillusionment! From the foremost popular journalist in the country and victor over some of the most able members of the government at his recent trial, he became an annoyance and a figure of fun. He was not even outstanding among the little band of radicals in Commons. In a long *Register* article which was written after eighteen months in the Reformed parliament, he accused the ministry of being "full of mischievous measures; full of hostility to the best rights and interests of the people; marked at once by extreme imbecility, and by arrogance extreme . . ." And this was not all. Old grievances were reopened; Grey was attacked personally; and the government was accused of "pursuing this jack-ó-lantern, which you call the 'Spirit of the age' . . ." because it made innovations in municipal government and the Church.[21] In

---

18 P.R. (8/3/33), cols. 262 ff.; P.R. (10/5/33), cols. 11–13.
19 Great Britain, 3 *Hansard's Parliamentary Debates,* Vol. XV (1833), 346–47; Vol. XVII (1833), 1030–31; Vol. XXI (1834), 1364–65.
20 P.R. (4/10/30), col. 452.
21 P.R. (9/13/34), cols. 644–63.

this way Cobbett acknowledged to his remaining followers that his wisdom was not going to be utilized by the new party in power. Certainly he was an old man by this time but it is difficult to believe that he could ever have filled any parliamentary role other than that of an obstructionist.

It has been said that of all the fund of instruction which Cobbett presented to the people, the political part was the least original.[22] This is true if "original" means a fresh point of view playing intelligently upon political problems; for Cobbett was certainly "original" in terms of a personal outlook. There was nothing of a strictly political nature that could match the vigor of his views on education or his advice to farmers. This is a major reason for his inability to attract a noticeable following. Despite the powerful organ of opinion which he had in the *Political Register,* Cobbett was never able to wield much influence or gain a following on a purely political issue. He failed to achieve originality, in part because he did not believe that the condition of England called for new ideas, but also because he was incapable of producing them. Inflexible even as a young man, he could not adapt in old age. His basic beliefs about the purpose of government remained consistent over the years. Yet in method he could be moderate or extreme and in 1830, when Cobbett chose to support the Whigs on the parliament act, Henry Hunt could unfairly accuse him of betraying the cause of reform.

Politics being just a means to an end for Cobbett, the subject did not captivate his imagination. Like Andrew Jackson, whom he admired so much, he held that the problems of government were not extraordinarily difficult. Character, not ability, was the first requirement which he asked for in a lawmaker. There may be some merit in this view but Cobbett's persistent oversimplification of problems played him false. Complex issues, subtle motivations, delicate shadings of

22 Brown, *op. cit.,* p. 196.

political opinions did not exist for him. He saw all aspects of government in straightforward terms and much of his irritability was due to a failure to understand the honest qualifications made by others. Too much was expected of the reformed parliament. The measures that the Whigs did take were doubly irritating to Cobbett, for they left untouched what he wanted changed and by amending society they put off necessary major alterations.

His actions during the early 1830's prove that in the closely related spheres of theoretical and applied politics, Cobbett was out of his element. That great historian, Sir Lewis Namier, in assessing the career of Mazzini, noted that "Liberty calls for sanity, a modicum of skepticism, and tolerance: a man must be prepared to believe that he may be mistaken, if he is to treat others as equals." Mazzini, a man of vision, had small regard for the opinions of others (particularly moderates), and never showed a real understanding of parliamentary government.[23] Like Mazzini, Cobbett was doctrinaire; captivated by his ideas, he was, on balance, a failure. Unlike Mazzini, he had few disciples. Even his sons, who tried to carry on his work although lacking their father's indisputable verve, could not follow in his footsteps. Usually considered to be more conservative than Cobbett, they were just the opposite. They had been born too late to appreciate the romantic notion of a lost Eden which held Cobbett captive and prevented him from coming to terms with the new economic conditions which were shaping English society. Although John Morgan Cobbett finished his own political career in the Conservative party, together with his brothers he was actually more in sympathy with change than was his father. It had been demonstrated all too clearly in the twentieth century that a true believer, however mistaken, may still attract a following if what he says seems to have relevance to existing conditions.

23 Sir Lewis Namier, *Vanished Supremacies, Essays on European History, 1812–1918*, New York, Harper and Row, 1963, p. 40.

The millions of words which Cobbett wrote, however, only struck fire spasmodically.

In an age when conditions were improving for even the lowliest, there was justification for the obituary notice in the *Times* which described Cobbett as simply an "episode" in English history. G. D. H. Cole has disputed this, seeing instead a man who, although rooted in the past, struck out at visible injustice, a protector of the masses of factory workers and a powerful contributor to worker-operated movements of a later date.[24] Cole's view was based on a belief that the Industrial Revolution was sudden in its inspiration and traumatic in its social effects. He considered Cobbett to be the voice of the countryman who had been uprooted from the land and thrust into a factory hell. Recent investigation rejects this by repudiating any drastic concept of the rapidity of industrial change. We may also look in vain for evidence that Cobbett had a great amount of influence upon future generations.

Most Chartists, the ineffable Feargus O'Connor excepted, had little in common with Cobbett. George Harney, for example, shared Cobbett's hatred of political economists and those who showed concern for Negro slaves while remaining aloof to the suffering of English workers. Yet Harney's radical optimism and Jacobin disregard of the past indicates a state of mind which was fundamentally at odds with Cobbett's.[25] Although A. W. N. Pugin and William Morris did bear a strong resemblance to Cobbett in certain of their ambitions, they and other dissenters from the crudeness of industrial England could not realistically be called his followers. Factory legislation had begun before his death and was in no way influenced by him. The trade union activity of mid-century would have been beyond his ken. He could have been depended upon to

[24] Cole, *op. cit.*, pp. 431–35.
[25] A. R. Schoyen, *The Chartist Challenge, a Portrait of George Julian Harney*, London, Heinemann, 1958, passim.

become irate about government-sponsored legislation of the
type which Edwin Chadwick was associated with.

It is true that in some of his writings, especially his advice
to farmers in *Cottage Economy* which concerned home in-
dustries and the care of a farm, Cobbett found a theme which
had continued to echo in England. The replacement of home-
produced bread, beer, furniture and clothing by factory manufactured goods was not an unmixed blessing for society. Not
just in terms of the quality of the product was loss seen, but
also in the decline of skill and independence of the individual
worker. Social critics were quick to point this out. Here may
be seen William Morris with his principle that art matters
only "if all can share it." Here also is Robert Blatchford,
another ex-soldier with little formal education who turned
popular journalist, whose resemblance to Cobbett is evident
in his desire to overthrow capitalism in favor of a nationalistic,
protectionist England in which party politics would play no
role. Perhaps contemporary critics who share with Raymond
Williams the notion that "culture is ordinary" have affinities
with Cobbett. Certainly, there seems to be a thread of gentle
radicalism, a non-violent dissatisfaction with the present that
looks to the past as much as the future, which runs through
modern English life. In this respect Cobbett "belongs."

Historians who have written about the period in which
Cobbett lived have not been able to agree upon a classification
for him. It is indeed difficult to summarize briefly such a
protean personality. Perhaps if a label is desired, "utopian
reactionary" is as close as one might come to identifying Cobbett in a word or two. Reactionary because his ideal was fixed
firmly in the past, utopian because it was visionary, basically
a product of his imagination. For all his gibes at the dreamers
of his day, Cobbett himself was thoroughly romantic. He was
certainly not a radical; nor was he conservative, if that much-
abused term means a devotion to the preservation of established
institutions. Cobbett's reaction to such establishments as the

Bank of England and the national debt, to use only two examples, was to seek to uproot them. He was traditional in his social and personal values: home and hearth, simple living, rural pastimes, class distinctions. In the twentieth century these concepts find a certain affinity with those of the authoritarian conservatives, perhaps mistakenly termed Fascist, who dominated pre-World War II Austria and still rule in Spain and Portugal. These people reject the modern world and stubbornly adhere to values which are elsewhere found to be increasingly irrelevant. Like Cobbett, the authoritarian conservative scorns ideology and proclaims faith in the time-honored principles by which he claims to live.

It was this tendency to see a Golden Age in the past which estranged Cobbett from the next few generations. The world of Macaulay and Samuel Smiles was not receptive to his nostalgia. His influence, tenuous at it was, waned along with the romantic movement in the arts. It was when the great era of Victorian prosperity and assurance itself ebbed and doubt and anxiety became the characteristics of the new century that Cobbett's writings became fashionable. Lovers of the agrarian life, Guild Socialists and Roman Catholics all have found a message in him and most recent writers treat him almost uncritically. A person who wrote as much as Cobbett and who seemed to be wildly inconsistent would necessarily leave behind a mine of ammunition for practically every interested party. This is why Cole's biography and Chesterton's appreciation could appear almost simultaneously, each with its own emphasis. This is also why Lord Astor could praise Cobbett in a speech a few years ago, yet ignore his radical career.

It is not hard to find praiseworthy qualities in Cobbett. His personal incorruptibility and tenacity compel respect. Despite frequent confusion, misunderstanding and even occasional evasion, many of his sentiments were genuine and admirable—his interest in the material welfare of the common people, for example. "I wish not to belong to a Nation, of which nineteen twentieths are *'poor.'* I think myself dishonoured by being one of a Nation of paupers. The people of England are I know well the most industrious and persevering in the world. They deserve to live better than the people of any other nation. Until of late years this has been their way of life. And never will I cease my efforts . . . to restore them to that state of merited preeminence." [26] Here we see Cobbett at his best, militantly concerned about the condition of the poor and outraged at the injustice inflicted upon them. He always possessed this feeling, though at times his motivations were less worthy. But good intentions are not sufficient to justify such an important place in English life, and if he was a failure in politics, a dunce regarding most economic matters, out of touch with a changing society, and of very limited influence in his lifetime, where does Cobbett's importance lie?

Perhaps the question can be answered in part by identifying his books which have been kept in print. *A History of the Protestant Reformation,* of which there are many editions, and *The Last Hundred Days of English Freedom* are valuable polemics; hence their republication by interested parties. Of Cobbett's works which have greater importance, four are available in fairly recent editions. *Cottage Economy* shows Cobbett at his most knowledgeable, writing about problems of the small farmer and offering good advice in his vigorous style. *A Grammar of the English Language* makes a dull subject interesting and even colorful with its frequent humorous allusions to contemporary society. These sallies at his enemies do not prevent the book from providing sound instruction in the rudiments of the language. *Advice to Young Men* counsels the reader on how to live simply and honestly. Cobbett was spared the labor of searching for good examples for his precepts by using himself as a guide. Finally, *Rural Rides,* the best known of all his writings, is still read because of the unrivaled picture

[26] P.R. (9/22/21), col. 648.

which it provides of the English countryside in the early nineteenth century. What seems to be permanent in Cobbett, then, is the part of his work which should be considered peripheral. The core of his writing, the *Political Register,* dealt more directly with the weighty issues that concerned him constantly. Today, the *Register* is largely dated and reveals far more of Cobbett than it does of his times. This is, perhaps, the inevitable fate of this type of journalism, but it is unfortunate for Cobbett's reputation. The best parts of the *Register* have been selected to form books such as *Rural Rides;* the rest is seldom read. Yet, although Cobbett made his reputation as a journalist, what he actually wrote is not as significant as the fact that he was able to embrace this career and win a lasting reputation.

Cobbett was correct in holding that the violence shown by industrial and agricultural workers was caused by hunger rather than a desire to overthrow the government. His advocacy of a free press rings true, although others did more to achieve it. Many of his comments on farm management, child rearing and education have lasting merit. Despite this, neither his contemporaries nor we may judge him to have been a success. On the most vital political, economic and social questions he was not simply wrong consistently but he was wrongheaded. Time after time he refused to reconsider his opinions despite evidence that this was necessary. Also, in addition to frequent inability to grasp essentials, he lacked the quality of heroism which compensated for similar failings in others in history, noticeably John Lilburne, but also Cobbett's own contemporary, Richard Carlile. Cobbett's significance in English history lies not in what he did but in the fact that he did it. The humble son of toil who mastered English grammar became perhaps the most prolific writer of quality in the history of the language. He carved out a career as a popular journalist in the teeth of opposition from very powerful quarters and, with magnificent panache, took his seat in parliament among the mighty. This achievement needs no apologia. Cobbett's career is his best defense. To invest him with qualities which he did not possess is foolish and perhaps even does him an injustice.

Near the end of his life Cobbett wrote a series of tracts which resemble missals. These "Legacy" books represented an attempt to summarize his mature views, which would have been elaborated upon had he lived. The dedication to Blomfield, Bishop of London, in Cobbett's *Legacy to Parsons* reveals how he saw himself after decades of struggle.

> Bishop,
> About six-and-twenty years ago, you drank tea at my house at *Botley*, when you were a curate of some place in Norfolk; or a teacher to the offspring of some hereditary legislator. How rugged has my course been since that time: how thickly has my path been strewed with thorns! How smooth, how flowery, how pleasant, your career! Yet, here we are; you with a mitre on your head, indeed, and a crossier in your holy hands; I, at the end of my rugged and thorny path in a situation to have a right, in the name of the millions of this nation, to inquire, not only into your conduct, but into the utility of the very office that you fill.[27]

Here is a man possessed of so much virtue that worldly success has forsaken him. For mankind as a whole has little regard for (and is even embarrassed by) such uncompromising rectitude. Confident in his moral rightness as well as in the abundance of his endowments, Cobbett never lost that self-esteem which allowed him to reject compromising offers and to withstand decades of misfortune. Within his severe limitations Cobbett was frequently an admirable man.

27 *Legacy to Parsons*, p. 1.

Bibliography

SECONDARY SOURCES

BOOKS

Adamson, J.W., *English Education, 1789–1902*, Cambridge, Cambridge University Press, 1930.

Allen, H.C., *Great Britain and the United States, A History of Anglo-American Relations, 1783–1952*, London, Odhams Press Limited, 1954.

Ashton, T.S., *The Industrial Revolution, 1760–1830*, London, Oxford University Press, 1957.

Aspinall, Arthur, *Lord Brougham and the Whig Party*, Manchester, Manchester University Press, 1927.

Barnes, Donald Grove, *A History of the English Corn Laws from 1660–1846*, New York, F.S. Crofts and Co., 1930.

Brown, P.A., *The French Revolution in English History*, London, George Allen and Unwin, Ltd., 1923.

Chesterton, G.K., *William Cobbett*, London, Hodder and Stoughton, Ltd., n.d.

Clark, Mary, *Peter Porcupine in America*, Gettysburg, Times and News Publishing Co., 1939.

Cole, G.D.H., *The Life of William Cobbett*, London, W. Collins Sons and Co., Ltd., 1924.

Cole, G.D.H. and Margaret (eds.), *The Opinions of William Cobbett*, London, The Cobbett Publishing Co., Ltd., 1944.

Cook, E.T. and Alexander Wedderburn (eds.), *The Works of John Ruskin*, Vol. XXXVII, London, George Allen, 1909.

Curtis, S.J., *History of Education in Great Britain*, London, University Tutorial Press, Ltd., 1948.

Darby, H.D. (ed.), *An Historical Geography of England Before A.D. 1800*, Cambridge, Cambridge University Press, 1936.

Fortescue, J.W., *A History of the British Army*, Vols. V through XI, London, Macmillan and Co., Ltd., 1921-1923.

Fulford, Roger (ed.), *The Greville Memoirs*, London, B.T. Batsford, Ltd., 1963.

George, M.D., *England in Transition: Life and Work in the Eighteenth Century*, London, George Routledge and Sons, Ltd., 1931.

Halévy, Elie, *England in 1815*, London, Ernest Benn, 1949.

Halévy, Elie, *The Liberal Awakening*, 1815-1830, New York, Peter Smith, 1949.

Hammond, J.L. and Barbara, *The Town Labourer, 1760-1832*, London, Longmans, Green and Co., 1919.

Hammond, J.L. and Barbara, *The Village Labourer, 1760-1832*, London, Longmans, Green and Co., 1919.

Hayek, F.A. (ed.), *Capitalism and the Historians*, Chicago, University of Chicago Press, 1954.

Henriques, Ursula, *Religious Toleration in England, 1787-1833*, London, Routledge and Kegan Paul, 1961.

The History of The Times. *"The Thunderer" in the Making, 1785-1851*, Vol. I, New York, The Macmillan Company, 1935.

Hobsbawm, E.J., *Labouring Men, Studies in the History of Labour*, London, Weidenfeld and Nicholson, 1965.

Hughes, A.M.D. (ed), *Cobbett Selections, with Hazlitt's Essay and Other Critical Estimates*, Oxford, Oxford University Press, 1923.

Maccoby, S., *English Radicalism, 1786-1832*, London, George Allen and Unwin, Ltd., 1955.

Maccoby, S. (ed.), *The English Radical Tradition, 1763-1914*, London, Nicholas Kaye, 1952.

Mathieson, W.L., *England in Transition, 1789-1832*, London, Longmans, Green and Co., 1920.

Namier, Sir Lewis, *Vanished Supremacies, Essays on European History, 1812-1918*, New York, Harper and Row, 1963.

Overton, J.H., *The English Church in the Nineteenth Century (1800-1833)*, London, Longmans, Green and Co., 1894.

Pares, Richard and A.J.P. Taylor, *Essays Presented to Sir Lewis Namier*, London, Macmillan and Co., 1956.

Pemberton, W. Baring, *William Cobbett*, Harmondsworth, Penguin Books, 1949.

Porritt, E., *The Unreformed House of Commons*, Vol. I, Cambridge, Cambridge University Press, 1903.

Prothero, R.E., *English Farming Past and Present*, London, Longmans, Green and Co., 1917.

Radzinowicz, Leon, *A History of English Criminal Law and Its Administration from 1750. The Movement for Reform, 1750–1833*, New York, The Macmillan Company, 1948.

Reitzel, William (ed.), *The Autobiography of William Cobbett, the Progress of a Plough-Boy to a Seat in Parliament*, London, Faber and Faber, Ltd., 1947.

Reynolds, James A., *The Catholic Emancipation Crisis in Ireland, 1823–1829*, New Haven, Yale University Press, 1954.

Rostow, W.W., *British Economy of the Nineteenth Century*, Oxford, Oxford University Press, 1948.

Routh, Harold V., "The Georgian Drama," A.W. Ward and A.R. Waller (eds.), *The Cambridge History of English Literature*, Vol. XI, New York, G.P. Putnam's Sons, 1914.

Schoyen, A.R., *The Chartist Challenge, a Portrait of George Julian Harney*, London, Heinemann, 1958.

Seebohm, M.E., *The Evolution of the English Farm*, London, George Allen and Unwin, Ltd., 1952.

Stern, Fritz (ed.), *The Varieties of History from Voltaire to the Present*, Cleveland, World Publishing Co., 1962.

Sykes, N., *Church and State in England in the XVIIIth Century*, Cambridge, Cambridge University Press, 1934.

Thompson, E.P., *The Making of the English Working Class*, London, Victor Gollancz, 1964.

Trevelyan, G.M., *English Social History*, New York, Longmans, Green and Co., New York, 1942.

Ward, B., *The Dawn of the Catholic Revival in England, 1781–1803*, 2 vols., London, Longmans, Green and Co., 1909,

Watson, J. Steven, *The Reign of George III, 1760–1815*, Oxford, Oxford University Press, 1960.

White, R.J. (ed.), *The Conservative Tradition*, London, Nicholas Kaye, 1950.

White, R.J., *Waterloo to Peterloo*, London, William Heinemann, Ltd., 1957.

Wickham, W.H., *The Struggle for the Freedom of the Press, 1819–1832*, London, George Allen and Unwin, Ltd., 1928.

Young, Arthur, *A Six Weeks Tour through the Southern Countries of England and Wales, etc.*, London, W. Strahan, 1772.

Young, G.M., *Early Victorian England, 1830–1865*, Vol. I, London, Oxford University Press, 1935.

ARTICLES

Ashton, T.S., "The Standard of Life of the Workers in England, 1790–1830," *The Journal of Economic History*, Supplement, Vol. IX (1949).

Cone, Carl B., "Richard Price and Pitt's Sinking Fund of 1786," *The Economic History Review*, Series 2, Vol. 4 (November, 1951).

Foord, Archibald S., "The Waning of the Influence of the Crown," *The English Historical Review*, Vol. LXII (1947).

Heaton, Herbert, "The Industrial Revolution," *Social Education*, Vol. II (March, 1938).

Kegel, Charles H., "William Cobbett and Malthusianism," *Journal of the History of Ideas*, Vol. 19 (June, 1958).

Pumphrey, Ralph E., "The Introduction of Industrialists into the British Peerage: A Study in Adaptation of a Social Institution," *The American Historical Review*, Vol. LXV (October, 1959).

Silberling, Norman J., "Financial and Monetary Policy of Great Britain During the Napoleonic Wars. I Financial Policy," *The Quarterly Journal of Economics*, Vol. 38 (February, 1924).

Silberling, Norman J., "Financial and Monetary Policy of Great Britain During the Napoleonic Wars. II Ricardo and the Bullion Report," *The Quarterly Journal of Economics*, Vol. 38 (May, 1924).

Spring, David and Travis L. Crosby, "George Webb Hall and the Agricultural Association," *The Journal of British Studies*, Vol. II (November, 1962).

Williams, E.T., "The Cabinet in the Eighteenth Century," *History*, Vol. XXII (1957).

PERIODICAL

Black Dwarf (March 12, 1817).

PRIMARY SOURCES

BOOKS

A French Grammar, London, Charles Clement, 1824.

A Grammar of the English Language, New York, William Cobbett, 1818.

A Year's Residence in the United States of America, 3 vols., London, Chapman and Dodd, n.d.

Advice to Young Men and (incidentally) to Young Women, London, William Cobbett, 1829.

An Accurate Report of Mr. Cobbett's Lecture Speech on the Present Distresses of the Country and their Remedies, etc., Halifax, N. Whitley, 1830.

Cobbett's Legacy to Labourers, London, William Cobbett, 1834.

Cobbett's Legacy to Parsons, London, n.n., 1835.

Cobbett's Register and Lectures, "Eleven Lectures on the French and Belgian Revolutions, n.p., n.n., n.d.

Cottage Economy, London, C. Clement, 1822.

History of the Protestant Reformation in England and Ireland, London, Charles Clement, 1824. Vol. II, London, William Cobbett, 1829.

History of the Regency and Reign of King George the Fourth, London, William Cobbett, 1830.

Paper Against Gold and Glory Against Prosperity (2 vols.), London, J. M'Creery, 1815.

Rural Rides, Cole, G.D.H. and Margaret (eds.), 3 vols., London, Peter Davies, 1930.

The Emigrant's Guide, London, William Cobbett, 1829.

The Poor Man's Friend or Companion for the Working Classes, London, H. Stemman, 1826.

Three Lectures on the Political State of Ireland, Dublin, P. Byrne, 1834.

Thirteen Sermons, London, C. Clement, 1822.

PERIODICALS

The Porcupine, 1800–1801.

Cobbett's Political Register (also known as *Cobbett's Annual Register* and by other names), 1802–1835.

Cobbett's American Political Register, 1816.

Cobbett's Evening Post, 1820.

Norfolk Yeoman's Gazette, 1823.

Cobbett's Two Penny Trash, 1830–1832.

PUBLIC DOCUMENTS

Great Britain, *Hansard's Parliamentary Debates* (3rd Series), Vols. XV, XVIII, XIX, XX, XXI, XXIII (1833–1834).

MANUSCRIPTS

Nuffield College, Oxford, England, Cobbett MSS.

Index